George Orwell and the Radical Eccentrics

George Orwell and the Radical Eccentrics: Intermodernism in Literary London

Kristin Bluemel

GEORGE ORWELL AND THE RADICAL ECCENTRICS
© Kristin Bluemel, 2004.

First published in 2004 by
PALGRAVE MACMILLAN™
175 Fifth Avenue, New York, N.Y. 10010 and
Houndmills, Basingstoke, Hampshire, England RG21 6XS
Companies and representatives throughout the world

PALGRAVE MACMILLAN is the global academic imprint of the Palgrave Macmillan division of St. Martin's Press, LLC and of Palgrave Macmillan Ltd. Macmillan® is a registered trademark in the United States, United Kingdom and other countries. Palgrave is a registered trademark in the European Union and other countries.

ISBN 1–4039–6510–2 hardback

Library of Congress Cataloging-in-Publication Data
Bluemel, Kristin
    George Orwell and the radical eccentrics : intermodernism in literary London / Kristin Bluemel.
        p. cm.
    Includes bibliographical references and index.
    ISBN 1–4039–6510–2 (alk. paper)
    1. English literature—England—London—History and criticism. 2. Orwell, George, 1903–1950—Criticism and interpretation. 3. English literature—20th century—History and criticism. 4. Smith, Stevie, 1902–1971—Criticism and interpretation. 5. Anand, Mulk Raj, 1905—Criticism and interpretation. 6. Authors, English—Homes and haunts—England—London. 7. Holden, Inez, 1906—Criticism and interpretation. 8. London (England)—Intellectual life—20th century. 9. Eccentrics and eccentricities—England—London. 10. Modernism (Literature)—England—London. 11. Radicalism in literature. I. Title.

PR8478.B55 2004
823'.91209—dc22   2004045773

A catalogue record for this book is available from the British Library.

Design by Newgen Imaging Systems (P) Ltd., Chennai, India.

First edition: October 2004

10 9 8 7 6 5 4 3 2 1

Printed in the United States of America.

For George and Helen

Contents

Acknowledgments

The third chapter of this book was the most exciting to research and most pleasurable to write in part because it brought me in contact with several extraordinary women: the late Celia Goodman, Inez Holden's first cousin and literary executrix; Helen Fowler, Celia's close friend and, when Stevie Smith was alive, her close friend too; and Ariane Bankes, Celia's daughter and Holden's new literary executrix. Writers, editors, and intellectuals, I thank them all for sharing their friendship with me as well as time, memories, and expertise. I owe Ariane many, many thanks for entrusting me with Holden's diaries and scrapbooks, which I read in their entirety for the first time in June 2003. My deepest debt is to Celia, who first welcomed me into her home in the summer of 1998, and whose belief in her cousin's rare literary and personal gifts bolstered my own at an early stage of this project. Publication of this book would mean a lot more if Celia had lived to read it.

I would like to thank Monmouth University for many different kinds of support: for Grants-in-Aid-of-Creativity, which supported multiple research trips to London, Reading, and Cambridge; for travel grants, which allowed me to present drafts of chapters at conferences in Leeds, Houston, Fayetteville, New York City, Philadelphia, Chicago, Reno, and London, Ontario, among other places; and above all for generous awards of sabbatical and leave time that allowed me to complete the book. I'd also like to thank Monmouth University and Judith Stanley-Coleman for the award of the Judith H. Stanley Traveling Fellowship for Improvement of Teaching in the Humanities, which allowed me to return to London amid the celebrations of the Orwell centenary to prepare for a seminar on Orwell and His Times. Many thanks are due to my colleagues in the English Department at Monmouth who stoically took on the extra work that fell to them upon my extended absences from campus.

This little book has been long in the making and many scholars and editors have pushed it toward completion by reading drafts of chapters, listening to conference papers, pointing out muddles, suggesting improvements. My greatest thanks go to Phyllis Lassner for her generous, wise, and always good-humored advice. Thanks are also owed to readers or listeners Derek Attridge, Ariane Bankes, Joe Brooker, Debra Rae Cohen, Andy Croft, Patrick Deane, Stella Deen, Heide Estes, Prescott Evarts, Mary Grover, Christina Hauck, Jane Marcus, Elizabeth Maslen, Frank and Jenny Medhurst, Antony Shuttleworth, Stan Smith, Frances Spalding, and George Witte. I would also like to thank the anonymous reader for Palgrave whose report led to important changes in the book's structure and approach, and ultimately to its acceptance for publication. Thanks are due, too, to the patient and clever professionals at Palgrave Macmillan, especially my editor Farideh Koohi-Kamali and her assistant, Melissa Nosal, who have shepherded this study through all the stages of the publication process. I alone am to blame for any errors of judgment or fact that remain.

Looking back on the years this book was in progress, I am especially thankful for the help of family, friends, and professionals who made it possible for me to keep reading and thinking through the scary months and difficult years that followed my daughter, Helen's, complicated birth in December 1998. This includes my parents, Van and Paulette Bluemel, my sister, Lee Bluemel, and my in-laws, George and Eva Witte, dozens of doctors, therapists, teachers, social workers, and advocates, and two terrific Hoboken babysitters: Marie Healy and Lori Talerico. In these happier times I'd like to thank Crystal Zelman and Donna Catanese, my suburban support team, for their assistance. To my husband, George Witte, I owe my greatest thanks, and in the upcoming months, many hours of quiet time so he can finish his own literary project. He has bravely and cheerfully done everything that a feminist scholar-teacher-mother could wish for in a spouse, including mastering the supposedly feminine art of putting ponytails in the hair of four-year-old Helen when my research trip to London transformed him into a single parent for many weeks. It is to this pair, George and Helen, who have waited so patiently (well, one more patiently than the other) for me to leave the computer, that I dedicate this book.

Finally, I want to give kind thanks to Ariane Bankes for permission to quote from Inez Holden's unpublished diaries, to Bill Hamilton as the Literary Executor of the Estate of the Late Sonia Brownell Orwell, to Secker and Warburg Ltd. for permission to reproduce copyrighted material by George Orwell, and to New Directions Publishing Corporation for permission to quote from "The Suburban Classes" and "Suburb" from *Collected Poems of Stevie Smith*. Several sections of these chapters have been published previously and I am grateful to Ashgate Publishing for permission to reprint sections of "*There's No Story There*: Inez Holden's Lost War Literature," which first appeared in *Challenging Modernism: New Readings of Literature and Culture, 1914–1945*, to the Associated University Presses for permission to reprint sections of "Not Waving or Drowning: Refusing Critical Options, Rewriting Literary History," which first appeared in *And in Our Time: Vision, Revision, and British Writing of the Thirties*, and to the *Iowa Journal of Cultural Studies* for permission to reprint sections of " 'Suburbs are not so bad I think': Stevie Smith's Problem of Place in Thirties and Forties London."

Introduction

In the Space between Modernisms
George Orwell and the Radical Eccentrics

George Orwell enthusiasts remember 1949 as the year *Nineteen Eighty-Four* was published. That year also marked the appearance of another book, Stevie Smith's *The Holiday*. Smith had tried for years to find a publisher for this novel, and the typescript shows how she turned what had been a "war novel" into a "post-war novel" by making some simple alterations. Like *Nineteen Eighty-Four*, *The Holiday* evokes the landscape of an exhausted, bombed-out London, but unlike Orwell's last, most famous book, Smith's last novel identifies this terrain with the 1940s and populates it with thinly disguised versions of her wartime friends and associates. Celia Phoze, the novel's narrating heroine and one of Smith's fictional alter egos, tells us that the present time of the novel is "a year or so after the war," a period that defies easy description because it functions as a space between the known sociopolitical realities of war and peace. Celia's uncertainty about how to describe the period in which she lives is akin to critics' uncertainty about how to place Smith's novel among the literary periods and categories typically used to describe writing of the prewar, war, and immediately postwar years. I call this kind of writing "intermodernism" and begin to describe its qualities, ambitions, and contexts in the following pages, using chapters on Orwell, Smith, Mulk Raj Anand, and Inez Holden—their work and records of their intertwining lives—as supporting case studies. This book begins with Celia's words in *The Holiday*, "It cannot be said that it is war, it cannot be said that it is peace, it can be said that it is post-war," because they suggest a discomfort with the most common categories of national history and politics that is akin to the discomfort literary critics experience when working with Smith's and Orwell's writing (13). How to define, analyze, legitimize, and publicize the body of English literature to which *The Holiday* and *Nineteen Eighty-Four* contribute, of which "it cannot be said that it is modernism, cannot be said that it is postmodernism"? How to champion study of a kind of writing grounded in the experiences of England's working-class and "working middle-class" cultures that does not fit the familiar frameworks deployed by scholars of Bloomsbury experimentalism or Auden's generation, of revolutionary or reactionary prose, of Eliot, Joyce, Woolf, or Beckett?

Reading works by Orwell, Smith, Anand, and Holden should lead to these big questions about literary criticism and history, but will also inspire more modest inquiries. What critical language can explain the connections between Orwell's early works of the 1930s and the international triumphs of his later works of the 1940s?[1] What categories can illuminate the connections between Orwell's reputedly unique and solitary accomplishment and the writings of his friends and colleagues? And if such connections across decades and between writers can be documented, how to adapt an existing critical vocabulary so this undervalued body of writing will attract more critical attention?[2]

Intermodernism is my answer to these questions. Orwell (or rather "Orwell") appears at the forefront of this book's title and enterprise because his extraordinary reputation, still thriving outside the frameworks of modernism or postmodernism, is the most obvious challenge to existing literary-critical language.[3] Love him or hate him (I do a bit of both), Orwell is a cultural figure of the greatest importance whose vigorous, polemical prose has always demanded attention. Orwell functions as this book's charismatic figurehead, symbolically organizing its argument about the possible advances and current limitations of scholarship on mid-twentieth-century English literature. But the real argument of the book is built out of analyses of the literature and interrelated personal and political histories of Smith, Anand, and Holden, all of whom Orwell befriended in the 1930s or early 1940s. Although few of Orwell's readers will recognize the names of Smith, Anand, and Holden, together the four writers make up a small group that I label the "radical eccentrics."[4] Challenging the myth of Orwell's solitary genius, my study explores the implications for literary history of Orwell's alliances with two marginalized English women and one Marxist, anti-imperialist Indian man as they all tried to launch and sustain their literary careers in 1930s and 1940s London.[5]

I might just as well have labeled this group of radical eccentrics "dissenters and mavericks," the title of Margery Sabin's book on English-language authors who wrote about India between 1765 and 2000. While Sabin's concerns might seem irrelevant to all but the second chapter of this study (on the intermodern English writings of Mulk Raj Anand), the introduction to her study provides a helpful primer on the difficulties of defending a literary project that values cultural and historical meanings as much as aesthetic ones.[6] "Dissent," like "eccentric" and especially "radical," is a term that draws attention to those cultural–historical values, but then demands qualification because its meaning is so fluid. For Sabin, such fluidity means pointing out at the beginning of her book that,

> [S]ince Indian independence, the distinction between orthodoxy and dissent has shifted from decade to decade, depending also on where one stands and on whether one is male or female. The trauma of Partition and the rise of religious fundamentalism, state authority, and feminist protest, together with the mixed loyalties of Indians and Pakistanis living in what is now being called the Indian Diaspora, make any single honor role of postcolonial dissenters impossible to devise. (3)

For me, it means pointing out that "radical" is a weighted term that slides closer or further away from what are perceived as centrist or moderate political views depending on whether one is sympathetic or hostile to pacifists, suffragettes, workers, Communists, colonials, or Jews. Writers of 1930s and 1940s London, modernists and intermodernists, witnessed with everyone else in England the birth of the Peace Pledge Union, a female electorate, the hunger marches, the growth of the Communist Party of Great Britain, the Popular Front, the Gandhi movement, and Oswald Mosley's British Union of Fascists. And in 1945 they could celebrate or bemoan the victory of Clement Attlee's Labour Party amid the ruins of London. These historical markers only begin to hint at the diversity of radical positionings and persons it would be possible to identify with the period.

The shifting criteria for identifying English dissenters or radicals during the years Orwell came to fame make it easier to describe what an eccentric radical is *not* (i.e., he or she is not a modernist, not a postmodernist) rather than describe exactly what a radical eccentric *is*. Sabin again provides a model. Confronting both the necessity and limitations of literary-critical labels, she first describes her project in negative terms: it is not "a role call of heroic dissenters in the history of British colonialism in India" nor is it "an inclusive survey of writings critical of the British-Indian relationship" (3). Conceding that her study has conspicuous omissions, Sabin invites others to "propose additional and better examples of dissenters and mavericks or to define the concept of dissent differently" (3). While *George Orwell and the Radical Eccentrics* is not a response to this invitation, the fact that two of its primary figures, Orwell and Anand, could be central to such a survey, and that the two others, Smith and Holden, populate their fictional Englands with Indians, Jews, and other outsiders, tells us something about the potential importance of the radical eccentrics to diverse kinds of studies on twentieth-century English writing. One of the lessons Sabin's book offers is that Orwell can lead scholars of modernism, the Thirties, or the Forties to new projects that will challenge who or what matters to English twentieth-century literature. Smith, and to a greater extent Anand and Holden, are three of the many English dissenters and mavericks of the 1930s and 1940s who wait, just beyond Orwell, for discovery.[7]

This book claims that certain non-modernist texts of the 1930s and 1940s can be read to best advantage as cultural products of a single intermodernist impulse or movement rather than as products of distinct periods, neatly but arbitrarily separated by the beginning and ending years of two decades.[8] Without the category of intermodernism it is almost impossible to convey the sense of non-modernist cultural activity that endured throughout the 1930s and into the 1940s to which Orwell, Smith, Anand, and Holden contributed. The critical discussions that have evolved around study of other twentieth-century literary movements, including those signaled by the phrases Bloomsbury, the Auden Generation, the Thirties, the Forties, interwar and war literature, are certainly still relevant for studies like this one, but the addition of intermodernism to these preexisting discussions promises to bring exciting new materials and approaches to scholarship on the period. As much as critics will bemoan introduction of yet another label into critical discourse, intermodernism points out a new way across the gap between discursive territories signified by familiar labels.[9]

We need look no further than George Orwell's literary career and critics' treatments of it to understand the advantages intermodernism offers scholars of twentieth-century English literature. A survey of criticism on Orwell shows that few scholars choose to describe his literary work in terms of the dominant cultural movements of his time. He is rarely "Orwell, of the Auden Generation" or "Orwell, the World War II writer." With a literary career extending roughly from 1933 to 1949, and with books and essays ranging from discussion of the Spanish Civil War to freedom of speech or anti-Semitism in wartime, Orwell is of course of the Thirties and equally of the Forties. But Orwell's critics seem to resist describing him in these terms because they encourage a view of the literary-historical Orwell as a divided man, "of" two separate decades, and such a view provides no solution to the problem of naming Orwell's place in English literary history.

Those scholars who are uncomfortable describing Orwell as part of the cultural movements signified by the labels the Thirties or the Forties often choose to understand his writings apart from any literary or cultural movements. (This is not to say that critics have neglected questions about Orwell's political alliances and affiliations. Obviously, quite the opposite is true.) Orwell generally emerges from such studies as a uniquely autonomous writer, the common-man genius, working for the most part outside the society and communities that so concerned him. Ironically, the very figure who is recognized as the most astute analyst and satirist of English political discourse of the 1930s and 1940s appears in critical or biographical literature to be elevated above the people who produced that very discourse. He is "saint" George Orwell, the "wintry conscience of a generation." To habitually represent Orwell as a solitary figure working outside cultural communities or groups underestimates his deep engagement with his various jobs, his political activities, and the friendships, rivalries, and professional ambitions that informed his work. One of this book's goals is to place Orwell within one of his circles of acquaintance and show how the members of this circle, once read in terms of each other, challenge the perspectives of traditional Orwell criticism.

I do not claim that all critical projects on Orwell and the radical eccentrics or all projects on 1930s and 1940s writers should be read within the framework of intermodernism. I do believe that seeking an intermodernist Orwell points us toward potentially innovative approaches to his work and the work of others who do not fit into existing categories. In contrast to modernist writers, for example, intermodern writers tend to have their origins in or maintain contacts with working- or lower-middle-class cultures. As young people, they do not fit into the Oxbridge networks or values that shaped the dominant English literary culture of their time because they have the "wrong" sex, class, or colonial status. As adults they remain on the margins of celebrated literary groups. Intermodern writers tend to hold down regular jobs (soldier, secretary, journalist, factory worker, teacher) to supplement their income from writing. Perhaps as a result, they often write about work. When intermodernists experiment with style or form (as Smith does in *Over the Frontier* or *The Holiday*), their narratives are still within a recognizably realist tradition. They do not often demonstrate that archetypal modernist impulse toward mystic epiphany (Lawrence) or mythic allusion (Joyce or Eliot). This realist bias may be a symptom of the journalist skills many intermodernists developed while writing their more memorable novels, stories, or radio dramas. The intermodernists' social marginalization, financial dependence on jobs and freelance journalism, and debts to realism often resulted in writing that attends to politics, especially politics that may improve working conditions. Salvation or redemption in intermodern texts tends to be pursued through narrative strategies or symbolic influences that are intellectually and culturally available to ordinary, non-elite, working English men and women.

Intermodernism contributes to what F. R. Leavis famously called England's minority culture, but it also cheerfully partakes of and contributes to the mass culture Leavis distrusted.

Intermodernism, like modernism and postmodernism, is best thought of as a kind of writing, discourse, or orientation rather than a period that competes with others for particular years or texts or personalities. I offer intermodernism as a literary-critical compass, an analytical tool or useful guidepost, an attractive neologism that can help scholars design new maps for the uncharted spaces between and within modernisms.[10] Encouraging critics to think in terms of threes—"inter" always forging a connection or bridge between at least two other territories—intermodernism permits a more complex, sensitive understanding of many writers' relations to literary London and mid-twentieth-century English history.

My claim of much of the literature of the 1930s and 1940s for intermodernism is guided by three kinds of thinking. It is on the one hand a strategy of pragmatic, ends-based logic: criticism of modernism, no matter how revised, expanded, and renovated, has always had trouble accounting for the literature of writers associated with the 1930s and 1940s, even "highbrow" writers like Auden, Beckett, or Henry Green. While the "Auden Generation" has gained institutional credit for its distinct contribution to the Thirties, it is typical to find in general accounts of twentieth-century literature the admission that "Modernism and Thirties writing existed in uneasy coalition right through the decade" (Bradbury 211).[11] These same studies dutifully acknowledge the writing by men who worked outside of the networks of Oxbridge-educated writers of the 1930s, but then tend to dismiss that writing because it is not dominant. The writing of women of the 1930s—whether by university graduates, workers, or housewives, residents of London or provincial towns, single, married, or widowed, lesbian or straight, radical or conservative, gentile or Jewish— has, until recently, remained entirely extraneous to critical thought. And no one seems to worry at all about the ways in which the separation of the 1940s from "Modernism and Thirties writing" has exacerbated these problems of exclusion.

Instead of discounting nondominant 1930s and 1940s literature or striving to interpret it in ways that accommodate modernist or wartime criteria, this book urges scholars and teachers to value intermodernism in addition to, and at times, above, separate categories of modernism, the Thirties, the Forties, interwar, war, and postwar literature.[12] It seeks to legitimize the nearly invisible but delightfully various forms of interconnected 1930s and 1940s writings—the writing that is not associated with a "particular cadre" of men and institutionalized by a particular cadre of critics (Bradbury 208).

The second kind of thinking that motivates my construction of a category of intermodernism is respect for the theoretical advances of other revisionary critical movements and desire to extend the lessons of those advances to new materials. For decades, feminist and other dissident critics have questioned the traditional lineages of literary history and shapes of university curricula. The impetus to examine the "low" and the "high" (or in my case, what is between the two), to think in terms of text instead of masterpiece, of culture as well as poem, play, and fiction, to question the logic of period by taking "other" genres and sources into consideration—all of these scholarly movements have made research for and publication of this study possible, if not probable.[13] It is still an awkward kind of project to promote, occupying as it does the spaces in literary criticism and history on the borders of familiar categories and markets (the modernism, postmodernism, Joyce, Woolf, or even Orwell consumer base). But it is precisely the creation of awkwardness, the invitation of a prickly, irritated response, that can generate attention in otherwise preoccupied readers and perhaps inspire them to change their reading habits and critical assumptions.

In order to inspire change, awkwardness or irritation must lead to something pleasurable, and my concern with the pleasures (and displeasures) of reading is the third kind of thinking that has determined the shape of *George Orwell and the Radical Eccentrics*. Focused on writings by three "ambiguously nonhegemonic" Londoners, this study bets that readers will come to appreciate the special pleasures—the humor, the history, the ambition, or simply the colorful difference of Smith's, Anand's, and Holden's lives and works—once an intermodern lens brings them into focus. It also wagers that Orwell's extraordinary reputation will make readers more accepting of the underlying premises of this book: that Smith, Anand, and Holden matter for literary history, just as they mattered to Orwell, and that acclimatizing to a vocabulary of intermodernism can help teachers of English literature understand the achievement of the many writers active in 1930s and 1940s literary circles just as it helps them make sense of Orwell's career. This book shamelessly uses Orwell's reputation to attract readers, but then contradicts the standard biographical-critical picture by shifting the emphasis to consideration of Smith, Anand, and Holden, immodestly treating them as Orwell's peers, not his mere satellites.

I have chosen to focus on Smith, Anand, and Holden because their eccentric social positionings enrich our understanding of the history and possibilities of radical English literature in ways that the group's most powerful and famous radical, Orwell, cannot. I argue that their lives and writings are importantly eccentric and radical not because they are consistently socialist or Communist (they are not), but because they consistently resist inhibiting, often oppressive assumptions about art and ideology—about standard relations between literary form and sex, gender, race, class, and empire—that dominate English culture at every point of the political spectrum. The common meanings of radical as "socialist or revolutionary" and eccentric as "odd and unconventional" are certainly latent in the phrase "radical eccentrics," but these meanings are simultaneously too limited and too vague for my purposes. By describing the group as radical eccentrics (and inviting the inverted label of eccentric radicals), I want to bring to mind the spatial and dynamic meanings of each term, the sense of each writer's peripheral or eccentric position on the borders of multiple literary circles and cultural institutions and the possibility such positioning provides for various unpopular, uncompromising, resistant or radical literary commitments, styles, and movements. The label of radical eccentrics is intended to give these writers the kind of heightened visibility that emerges whenever people form groups and, by emphasizing the fascinating and often admirable differences of this group from the more popular personalities of literary London, help its members gain the kind of attention critics generally reserve for writers whose works more easily accommodate established aesthetic ideals.[14]

Such radical eccentricity (and eccentric radicalism) raises compelling questions: How can a non-activist suburbanite like Stevie Smith, conventionally portrayed as a childlike, self-involved poet more interested in tending to her beloved Aunt than involving herself in public activism, provide an alternative model of literary radicalism? Similarly, how can Inez Holden, adventuress and bohemian beauty turned socialist, enlarge our vision of non-Orwellian, anti-Fascist writing? And finally, how does our vision of the crisis-ridden decades of the 1930s and 1940s expand once we analyze these women's relationships with Anand, who in contrast to Smith and Holden, had always placed his Marxist, nationalist radicalism at the fore of his recognizably political fiction?

Orwell is famously radical in both his liberalism and conservatism, his prominence as a revolutionary English Socialist in the late 1930s to early 1940s and perhaps greater prominence as an anti-Communist voice for Cold Warriors in the late 1940s. Smith, Anand, and Holden, like Orwell at his best, affirm the more utopic impulses of the humanist project of Western democracies, but unlike Orwell their radicalism never leads them to expressions of defeatism, paranoia, or near-total despair. They stay "outside the whale," resisting as loudly as they can in their very different ways the gross injustices and horrors of their age. No one could reflect on their writings of 1940 and conclude, as Salman Rushdie does of Orwell, that the events of history or health had broken their intellects and spirits or that they had been reduced to constructing and justifying a literary escape-route from the pain of history and consciousness ("Outside" 96). Their careers

show political and aesthetic shifts of emphasis or in Holden's case, a dramatic change of artistic mission, but study of their writings does not suggest, as Rushdie's study of Orwell might, that writers of a radically eccentric literature can only influence English culture if they ultimately endorse the dominant values of that culture.[15]

Among the radical eccentrics, Smith is the one who is most likely to be identified with the politics of a dominant culture because she loved her conservative, lower-middle-class suburb of Palmers Green and wrote so admiringly of her "Lion Aunt," a staunch Tory.[16] Yet her fiction challenges some of that dominant culture's most cherished notions about family and gender roles, and is, in many ways, as unsettling and unaccommodating— as radical—as anything written by the others in the group. Smith's radicalism is different from Orwell's, Anand's, or even Holden's because its sources are the intimate details of Londoners' personal relations and domestic lives rather than their public debates about wealth, class, work, war, or empire. Signs of Smith's radical eccentricity can be found in her fictions' daring, nearly libelous representations of her conversations with and impressions of her friends. In *The Holiday*, for example, Smith records a personal history of intermodern Englishness through fictionalized descriptions of Orwell, Anand, Holden, and herself. Given the lack of archival records about two of these figures, Anand and Holden, Smith's novel provides invaluable, contemporary portraits of the writers who lie at the center of the chapters in this book.

Smith's attempt to define the curious reality of the "postwar" in the first chapters of *The Holiday* depends as much on the characters based on Inez Holden and Mulk Raj Anand as it does on the two characters who she based upon the (then) more famous George Orwell. Lopez, an Inez Holden figure, emerges first as the hostess of a wonderfully successful party that nurtures a "quick love-feeling" among its guests despite its regrettable offerings of "spam, ham, tongue, liver-sausage, salad-cream, cherries, strawberries (out of tins), whiskey and beer" (13). Lopez is the necessary antidote to the postwar. She is the healing, comic force that allows the other characters to survive their dreary lives in government bureaucracies, "working in Ministries in Relief, in Relations, on Committees, on Commissions, clearing up, sorting, settling" and "also writing and broadcasting" (13). In decided contrast to the secret sexual and spiritual renewal provided Winston Smith by Orwell's Julia (based some claim on Orwell's second wife Sonia Brownell), Lopez creates a social haven that allows her friends to "take hold of our happiness to make something of it for the moment" (13). The laughter she fosters is both part of and opposed to the sociopolitical reality of the postwar, which in Celia's words "works upon us, we are exasperated, we feel that we are doing nothing, we work long hours, but what is it, eh? so we feel guilty too" (13).

One of the laughing, guilty guests at Lopez's party is Raji, the character based on Mulk Raj Anand, who Celia describes as "the most intelligent Indian in London" (13). To his enduring credit, "Raji makes us laugh" (13). This laughter, like much of the laughter in *The Holiday*, is inspired by the absurdities of contemporary history, the stories generated by responses of marginal, eccentric characters to the powerful political currents that accompany the dismantling of empire. Whether or not Smith's invention of Celia and Lopez's postwar party conversation with Raji is based on real events, the following anecdote conveniently foregrounds this study's concern with the interweaving of laughter and the politics of nation, race, and empire as they were interpreted and acted upon by people living in the bombed-out, imperial center of London:

> [Raji] says he was with an English friend and two Indians in a restaurant. The Indians said: "Oh yes, we do not mind white people, of course, but every now and then there is beginning to run this feeling that we do not so much like them. Oh yes, now we are beginning to have to combat this disgusting and so un-free colour sense, but for the fastidious Indian there is for instance the smell of the white person. Yes, heigh-ho, that is how we are now getting."
> So we laugh too. (13–14)

So early in the novel, it is not at all clear who or what is comical to Raji or whether he and Celia and Lopez are laughing at the same things. Do they laugh together at the expense of the Indians in the restaurant, at the expense of Raji, or at the expense of people like Celia and Lopez who must finally hear from the Indians haunted by an "un-free colour sense" the unattractive truth about the whiteness of the master race? The hidden content and ambiguous aim of this political laughter guarantee its dissolution, as conversation at the party turns eagerly to gossip about lesbian loves in convent schools. In Celia's words, "The other talk, the history, the politics talk, is fine, too, but so often it falls down, because we are doing nothing, and so we wring our hands, the talk falls down, we are *activistes manqués*, it is Edwin and Morcar the Earls of the North" (14).

Basil Tate, a self-absorbed and gloomy friend who is at Lopez's party, does not suffer Celia's political and ontological doubts lightly. Always looking over or through Celia, he is interested in her male friends and relatives and the political tales they tell. He, along with Celia's mad and murderous cousin, Tom Fox, who broadcasts for the China Section, make up Smith's uncomplimentary fictionalized portrait of George Orwell. As Smith explained to Ian Angus in a 1967 letter, she thought Orwell believed that

> girls were a shade anarchic and did not know or care about rules at all, with the undertone, I fancy, that they did not "play the game" . . . [A]ll this comes

into *The Holiday*, in various lengthy conversations between the writer and two characters who divide between them many of George's opinions and characteristics as I saw them. I seem to remember I had the idea at the time that splitting George into two might lessen the danger of libel, not much of a danger, really. (*MA* 315)[17]

In one of those scenes of lengthy conversation, Smith represents Basil as loving only Tom, resentful of women because of their biological necessity. Anticipating Smith's comment to Angus, Celia tells us that Basil is "like a twelve year old boy, he thinks 'girls are no good' " (68). When Tom abandons Basil in favor of a book, leaving him with only Celia for an audience, Basil embarks upon a distinctly Orwellian monologue, hyperbolic, illogical, misogynistic—and hilarious. The humor is mainly Smith's. She captures in a few paragraphs the most absurd elements of an argument that conflates one of modernity's more frivolous inventions, scanty panties, with rampant capitalism and the collapse of the moral order:

> Basil said that eventually England would have to choose between money and kids, because under capitalism people would no have kids, it was too much to ask, and he began to inveigh against our ex-Ally which put me for once in a good humour with them. He said that America would be the ruin of the moral order, he said that the more gadgets women had and the more they thought about their faces and their figures, the less they wanted to have children, he said that he happened to see an article in an American woman's magazine about scanty panties, he said women who thought about scanty panties never had a comfortable fire burning in the fire-place, or a baby in the house, or a dog or cat or a parrot. . . .
> Or a canary, I said.
> Or canary, went on Basil, and he said that this was the end of the moral order. (69)

Celia's modest, absurd intervention does not recall Basil to his senses. He goes on going on, oblivious to the fact that he is making a fool of himself in the eyes of his unmarried, unstable, childless auditor.

In 1949 Orwell would have been too sick to care very much about his appearance in *The Holiday* as the selfish, mad, and barely heterosexual Basil/Tom. Inez Holden, on the other hand, was hurt by Smith's representation of her as the fictional Lopez. Frances Spalding, Smith's biographer, suggests that Smith and Holden drew apart after publication of *The Holiday* because the novel's narrator criticizes Lopez's writing (105). Only Anand could have found little in *The Holiday* to disappoint or irritate him. His fictional counterpart, Raji, is an endearing character and Smith pays him the highest compliment possible to a writer by recommending Raji's book on India (a fictionalized version of Anand's *Letters on India* (1942)) to her readers. She describes Raji's book as "so true about India, and so much the book that English people ought to read, and is so much the book that so many of them do not want to read" (97).

If Smith seems to be taking revenge on a couple of her friends in *The Holiday*, it is wise to remember that she never apologized to life or the living for her art. We can imagine her sympathy for Celia who tells us, "In my diary that night I wrote: I guess I am damned, the wickedness in my heart is something radical" (64). Celia's conviction about her own state of radical wickedness—extreme, devastating, alienating, defining—provides a rough emotional, spiritual counterpart for my more intellectual notion of radical eccentricity in the writings of Smith, Anand, and Holden.[18] How does one profess a highly eccentric, even alienating belief system so that it means something, or better yet *does* something, to improve the unreal reality that Celia identifies with the postwar and I extend to all the years spent fearing and fighting Hitler?

In part it is the prosaic contexts of modernity, the stifling spaces of home front bureaucracies that exist in a nation that is not at war and not at peace, that inspire Celia's urge toward literary expression. She compares her work to that of soldiers and sailors, to Libya and Russia, and wonders, "Eh, what are we up to, compared with the victory they got us?" (33). Given the dreariness of England's social, political landscape "a year or so after the war," it is no wonder Celia suffers from feelings of uselessness. Smith, Anand, and Holden may have shared the doubts of Smith's gentle protagonist, but this book argues that their literary, ideological battles, begun in their writings of the 1930s and at their most intense in the writings of the 1940s, constitute a kind of bold and heroic engagement. Always questioning the integrity of their own eccentric positions, identities, and artistry, these writers dared to counter the accepted, but often oppressive, myths of intermodern London's better-known political, cultural groups.

Biographical Frameworks

In 1941, Orwell accepted a position as Empire Talks Assistant and then Talks Producer in the Indian Section of the BBC's Eastern Service. Although Orwell was increasingly unhappy with his role as radio propagandist, he was able to find space for his friends' voices within the highly regulated vehicles of BBC programming. The BBC is the only mainstream institution that supported all four members of the radical eccentrics. The material benefits they earned from BBC contracts were only slightly more important than the sense of institutional validation they gained from broadcasting work. In the context of total war, when writers struggled to find time to write and publishers who could publish, the BBC provided at least the illusion of essential war work and a vital, artistic outlet.[19] Orwell asked Smith to contribute to his broadcast poetry magazine, "Voice," and persuaded Anand to contribute numerous pieces on politics, literature, and language to his programs. Eventually, Anand assumed responsibility for setting up series and contacting authors and speakers for Orwell. One of the authors Anand contacted was Holden, who he interviewed in June 1942 as part of his series "Meet My Friend" (in the BBCWA) and who Orwell later invited to participate in the experimental series, "Story by Five Authors" (included in West 95–111). Holden wrote the third installment of "Story by Five Authors" (Orwell, L. A. G. Strong, Martin Armstrong and E. M. Forster writing the other parts), turning its rich, upper-class villain into what biographer Gordon Bowker calls "an Orwell doppelganger" (285). According to Bowker, Orwell was not amused by Holden's little joke. But Holden's representation of Orwell in her story-installment, like Smith's representation of Orwell in *The Holiday*, gives readers an unfamiliar and thus valuable vision of Orwell—"Orwell through the eyes of keenly perceptive but put-upon women" (Bowker 285).

The story of the relationships among Orwell, Smith, Anand, and Holden begins before Orwell started working at the BBC, however, and takes us far outside its corridors. Holden and Smith became friends in London during the mid-1930s (Spalding 103), Orwell met Anand in the Spanish Civil War or shortly thereafter, and Orwell met Holden in the 1940s at a dinner with H. G. Wells (Bowker 277).[20] In her diary entry of 30 May 1941, Holden describes the beginning of her relationship with Orwell, which quickly but only briefly, became an affair:

> The writer G. K. [her symbol for Orwell] has been here several times[.] I met him one evening at supper, then afterwards when I was bycycling about [*sic*], . . . he came with his wife to have a drink, and then suddenly he appeared here and took me out to lunch at the Zoo and we spent this charming day and had lunch there and I went back and had tea at his flat, and then just as he was dressed up in his Home Guard uniform and ready to go off to his Parade he more or less "pounced" . . . I was surprised by this, by the intensity and urgency.

In the next diary entry of 9 June, she describes doing some of Orwell's theater reviews for him, going to plays, forming opinions, giving him summaries. In her words, "[T]his gives him more free time to get on with some of his more important work, he says he will give me half the money." Holden's diary shows how she turned her theater expeditions undertaken to earn a bit of much-needed cash into opportunities to observe trends in English popular culture. She notes, "If there is one thing that is old fashioned it is the English theater, it does not march with the revolution, I should say it doesn't."

Holden was as generous with her friendships as she was careless with her income. It is almost certain that she introduced Smith to Orwell shortly after she met him. Holden brought her friends to the Café Royal, where many of the more influential leftist writers such as Cyril Connolly, Kingsley Martin, and Stephen Spender could be found. Holden, Smith, and Anand always remained somewhat removed from the centers of publishing power that shaped relations among the Café Royal set, and their more intimate gatherings for dinner at the Orwells' flat, described in Holden's diary and fondly recalled by Anand (Spalding 150), must have given them a sense of welcome in an alternative literary community that had its own representative of cultural influence in the form of Orwell, the BBC Producer.

To Holden and Anand, at least, it must have been equally important to create a space where a commitment to nondoctrinaire socialism was presumed. The importance of this political solidarity is evident in Holden's diary entry of 29 November 1941. There she muses, "It is strange the class consciousness of England, when through conversation two or three socialists find each other it is like the early christians who were persecuted in Rome recognizing each other by some sign [sic]." Spalding records Anand's impression that his friendship with Smith made her more receptive to Orwell's politics in the early 1940s, although Smith never joined the others in outright affirmation of socialism (159).

The feelings of exclusion and persecution Holden records in her wartime diary mirror the emotions she associated with her traumatic early childhood. Holden's first cousin and literary executrix, Celia Goodman, recalls that Holden's home life was marred by violent battles between her parents, neither of whom cared enough about her to attend to her basic material and emotional needs. Although her grandfather was a Master of Fox Hounds and her mother reputed to be the second best rider in England, as a child Holden went barefoot in all seasons. She was sent to a school for the children of poor tradespeople, and was only allowed to continue there when her rich uncle on her mother's side paid the overdue fees. When she was fifteen, she went to Paris and then London, living on her wits and her exceptionally good looks (Goodman 29–30). Goodman's daughter, Ariane Bankes, finds in Holden's childhood trauma the sources of her adult eccentricity: "Inez was utterly original, utterly sui generis. . . . She simply did not subscribe to the conventions of society, and her crossing of boundaries is entirely explicable in terms of her early rejection by her family and her subsequent rejection of all that her family stood for—class values and all."[21]

Holden's first novels were published when she was in her twenties; *Born Old, Died Young* has an adventuress heroine named Virginia Jenkinson, whose cavalier approach to existence suggests something of the attitude Holden herself must have had at the time. Its hero, Arnold Thesiger, is an unlikely match for Virginia, who describes him to one resident of Dr. Stresa's Rejuvenation Home as "tiresome, jealous, mean, prematurely old" (192). At Arnold's birth, the nurse assures his worried mother, Edwardian beauty and wife to the aging Sir Aubrey Thesiger, that all newborns are wrinkled and creased. She chirps patronizingly, "The older they get the younger they grow" (21). But Arnold, unattractive emblem of a postwar generation, never takes on babyish contours. Instead, "his face furrowed more severely, his eyes sank deeper into his head and glinted more sadly, and his whole expression became knowingly weary" (21). The cause of this deformation, in the words of one Mrs. Mont Blanc, is "something Psy-cho-logical" (193). With this comment, Holden delivers her absurd, irreverent commentary upon the anxiety expressed by many middle-class men of her generation. Like the pathetic Arnold, blessed with the benefits of money, social position, comfort, and safety, they yearned for a chance at the epitaph that adorns brother Roland Thesiger's tomb and with which Holden begins her book: "Killed in action, 1914" (9).[22]

Skilled at the satiric portrayal of wealthy, upper-class families like her own, Holden herself was never assured of income and can accurately be described as working poor. Bankes explains that despite Holden's lack of formal education, "she was intelligent and witty enough to be an intellectual, and to move in intellectual-bohemian circles. As it also happens, she sympathised more with the working class than any other class—but she didn't belong to any class, by choice. She was an outsider."[23] Holden's diaries prove that she was nearly always in debt or broke, yet as her cousins testify, she was notoriously generous; for example, after the Orwells were bombed out of their home on 28 June 1944, Holden gave them the use of her flat at 106 George Street near the fashionable Portman Square. Especially as a young woman, Holden loved parties and gossip, and she always maintained a sense of drama and style uniquely her own.[24] Goodman writes that Holden

> simply found life endlessly amusing and interesting and was able to make it seem equally so to others. She was a keen and fascinated observer of human nature at all levels, but she was never malicious and she had a depth of compassion that prevented her from judging harshly any but the most odious characteristics. (35)

Holden's extraordinary wit and ear for dialogue made her a strong writer and delightful friend. Anthony Powell used Holden as the model for his flamboyant character Roberta Payne in *What's Become of Waring?* (Taylor 284).

Decades later he described her as "a torrential talker, an accomplished mimic, her gossip of a high fantastical category; excellent company when not obsessed by some 'story' being run by the papers, of which she was a compulsive reader" (Powell, *Messengers* 24). Bankes, a more intimate observer, admits "It is of course very difficult to convey the personality of someone as unique as Inez, but her maverick qualities were what set her apart, and made her the remarkable figure that she was."[25]

Eccentric, unconventional, endlessly amusing: these qualities undoubtedly won Holden the esteem of Smith, who was also a notorious mimic, loved to gossip, and needed companions who could sharpen her own keen wit. Before Lopez had appeared in *The Holiday*, Smith used her friend as a model for another Lopez character in her short story, "The Story of a Story" (1946). In the story, Lopez is described as "a very clever quick girl, she had a brilliant quick eye for people, conversations, and situations" (*MA* 52). More importantly, she likes the story that the protagonist, Helen (another Smith alter ego) has written about their mutual friends Roland and Bella. Lopez rings up all their friends with the news that "Helen has written a most amusing story about Roland and Bella. It is very amusing, exactly right, you know" (52).[26] *The Holiday* grants its Lopez character a more central role and provides one of the most colorful published representations of Holden available anywhere. Celia tells us that she

> keeps close to [Lopez] for company. Here is this admirable girl, I think, who has this admirable courage and this admirable high heart, for she is not a sad girl, she is not walking round in fury and despair. She writes and entertains the Government and the Section people, and the editors, and all the time it is nothing but a wonderful adventure for her to have, it is in the spirit of the Scarlet Pimpernel, or Sideways Through Patagonia, it is like that. (55–56)

By the time Holden's novel *Night Shift* was published in 1941, she was clearly challenging her reputation as a bohemian adventuress and party girl with the politicized label of socialist writer. *Night Shift* is a fictional account of her wartime work at an aircraft factory in North London. The novel is documentary in style and is told by an anonymous third-person narrator who is sympathetic to the working-class characters. Attention is also given to an exotic, pampered, bourgeois character named Feather, who seems more of a Holden-figure than the novel's narrator. H. G. Wells, in whose mews house Holden lived before she published *Night Shift*, praised Holden's novel in a private note that Holden transcribed in her diary on 18 December 1942: "Your book is first rate[.] Bravo Feather[.] I admit you can write[.] H.G." Wells modified this note for publicity purposes. His words "First rate" join J. B. Priestley's description of *Night Shift* as "The most truthful and most exciting account of war-time industrial Britain," in promotional materials for Holden's novel.

Although Anand shared Holden's interest in the lives of working people, his background was very different from hers. He grew up on the North-West frontier of India where his father, a clerk in the British Indian Army, was part of the imperial force commanded to violently subdue Pathan tribesmen. Anand observed at an early age the injustices and hypocrisy of British-style democratic imperialism. As a student at Khalsa College, Amritsar, he was beaten by police for breaking curfew the day after troops opened fire on an unarmed crowd in Jallianwala Bagh (Spalding 157). When he arrived in England as a doctoral candidate, he continued his active oppositional stance toward England's imperial policies by joining the Indian League, the student branch of the Congress Party in England, and reportedly, the Communist Party (Spalding 157).[27] He is the only radical eccentric examined in this study who sought social change through membership in political groups as well as through literary publication.

An acquaintance of T. S. Eliot and a visitor at the Hogarth Press, Anand was inspired to start his first novel when he overheard Edward Sackville-West remark that "There can be no tragic writing about the poor! They are only fit for comedy, as in Dickens! The canine can't go into literature" (Anand, "Sources of Protest" 23).[28] Anand's *Untouchable* (1935), published in England with a foreword by E. M. Forster, contradicts Sackville-West's assumption by adopting as its protagonist the eighteen-year-old Bakha, "strong and able-bodied," who lives in an outcastes' colony and works as a sweeper in the public latrines (9). Combining modernist technique with socialist political commitment, Anand makes Bakha's one-day odyssey to consciousness of the injustices of the Hindu caste system the subject of potential heroic transcendence. In the last pages of the novel, Bakha witnesses the speeches of Gandhi and the poet Iqbal Nath Sarshar (the historical figure who was Anand's mentor), hearing for the first time discussion of the philosophical and mechanical basis for destroying caste as a means to achieving a free, independent India. In the words of Anand's fictional Iqbal, "When the sweepers change their profession, they will no longer remain Untouchables. And they can do that soon, for the first thing we will do when we accept the machine, will be to introduce the machine which clears dung without anyone having to handle it—the flush system" (155). The fact that this conclusion does not dissolve into joke is testament to Anand's ability to make us identify with his ignorant hero who cannot understand the poet's big words or the intellectuals' debate that surrounds them even as he believes they hold the key to his deliverance from suffering.

In his next novel, *Coolie* (1936), Anand mounts a similar kind of protest about the conditions endured by the impish orphan Munoo, who is sent from his rustic home in the northern hills to labor as a virtual slave in the city home of a wealthy Indian family. After running away, Munoo finds jobs in an Indian-owned pickle and jam factory and an English-owned cotton factory. Despite the income from these jobs, which take him all over India, as an uneducated coolie Munoo cannot rise above the meanest existence and is essentially condemned to death by consumption. Although Anand worried that the "recital and the essay element" of his fiction threatened to overshadow his attempt to "achieve, as far as possible, an objective novel, a dramatic novel" that allowed the characters to "show their peculiar 'condition humaine,'" *Coolie*, like *Untouchable*, was widely and favorably reviewed in the English press (BBCWA, letter to Sir Malcolm Darling, 22 April 1942).

By the early 1940s, when Anand was a highly visible literary figure in London, Holden recorded the following impressions about him after a dinner gathering with Smith and the Orwells: "Mulk Raj Anand came by for a drink . . . He is an extremely charming fellow, it is surprising to find a foreigner also coloured belonging to a dominant race to feel well at ease and without any kind of neurosis as Mulk, he is very good company, affectionate, witty—" (19 November 1941). Holden goes on to note that Orwell is anxious to get Anand to broadcast and that only Anand's previous commitments to finish a novel and prepare lectures for the L.C.C. in the East End keep him from contributing. She writes that six months prior to this gathering Anand could not have considered BBC broadcasting "because so many of his friends were imprisoned by the British that the arm-chair broadcast from the Indian poet would have done a lot of harm" (19 November 1941).

Holden's recollection of Anand's troubled ideological position is confirmed by correspondence between Anand and Sir Malcolm Darling, a retired civil administrator and vice chancellor of the University of Punjab who was first hired to run the Indian Section in 1941. W. J. West, expert on Orwell's years at the BBC, explains that the British authorities hoped that Darling would be able to gather around him influential Indian authors of the same standing as the military insurgent Subhas Chandra Bose, who was broadcasting tirades against the British from Berlin to India with considerable effect (West 14). Darling eventually succeeded in his goal of collecting a group of Indian broadcasters and administrators for the newly formed BBC Indian Section, but Anand was not one of his recruits. Anand's letter declining Darling's job offer demonstrates how difficult it was for Indians of radical consciousness to know how to respond politically in the early years of the war. In this letter, Anand affirms his personal regard for Darling and his desire not to appear ungrateful for Darling's flattering offer, but then clearly outlines the contradictory position he would be placed in if he were to work for a British propaganda organization. Particularly since he had intimate connections with the oppressed Congress party, he felt he could not support the British war effort until his compatriots were freed by the British from prison (West 15). Anand admits that

> the one question that has been taxing my mind all these months is how to reconcile that [Congress] affiliation with my belief that fascism would destroy all I stand for. I am afraid the British Government has done nothing which may help to solve the dilemma which faces some of us: It has declared neither its war aims nor its peace aims—and India seems to be its one blind spot. This enforces on us a kind of vague neutrality, the strain of which can be very harrowing for the more timid individual, who is torn between conflicting loyalties. (West, *Broadcasts* 15)[29]

BBC correspondence from Orwell in December 1941 and January 1942 shows that he had not given up Darling's endeavor to get Anand on board at the BBC (West 176–77). Finally, in late January, Orwell secured Anand's cooperation. Anand's first BBC Booking Form is dated 30 January 1942 and lists two twelve-minute talks, one on H. G. Wells and the other on Bernard Shaw, in a series called "These Names Will Live." These talks were heard on Orwell's program, "Through Eastern Eyes" (BBCWA).

Smith's first contribution to Orwell's programs took place in that same year but got off to a rocky start. Somehow there was a miscommunication about when she was supposed to record her poems and she complained in a letter to Orwell, "I did not hear one word about that last broadcast until 20 minutes before it went on the air. Jolly good show, B.B.C!" (Crick 288). More defensive and acrimonious words followed, but the pair was obviously back on good footing one month later (see BBCWA, letter of 17 November 1942). Their relation was close enough that male literary gossip, fostered by Powell and Malcolm Muggeridge, associated Smith with Orwell's tale about "[having] a woman in a park" (Crick 288–89). Smith encouraged such surmise by obliquely suggesting to her friends Norah Smallwood and Ronald Orr-Ewing that she was having an affair with Orwell (Spalding 153–54). Others who knew Smith well, however, discounted such tales as out of character for both parties (Crick 289).

Smith, like Holden, was averse to marriage. She seemed to steer clear of such commitment because of an awareness of the unequal demands conventional unions placed on women, especially women who wanted to be accomplished writers. Her fiction, poems, and correspondence demonstrate her need to be free from husbands and babies, despite the cost of devastating loneliness. According to her lifelong friend, Helen Fowler, Smith believed that poets should be treasured and pampered much like children.

Her reputation for being jealous of children is probably grounded in misunderstanding over this issue. Smith did not resent individual children but rather the social customs that promoted satisfaction of their needs but not the needs of poets. Smith enjoyed being with Fowler's children and was held in great affection by them, especially by her goddaughter. Reflecting on her friendship with Smith, Fowler notes, "I accepted her quirks and eccentricities, enjoyed her wit, respected her considerable learning (something people tend to forget) and counted her among the friends I have loved." With such acceptance, the friendship endured.[30] This was not the case with many of Smith's other important female friendships, including her friendship with Holden. As other critics and biographers have noted, the autobiographical heroine of Smith's first novel, *Novel On Yellow Paper* (1936), seems to speak for Smith when she muses,

> My friendships, they are a very strong part of my life, they are as light as gossamer but also they are as strong as steel. And I cannot throw them off, nor altogether do with them or without them. . . . The rhythm of friendship is a very good rhythm. But now I am involved again in love, and I must marry, or I must not marry. And the rhythm of friendship is now so strong in my blood; I must go, I must come back . . . . (197–98)

Smith's narrator's ambivalence about commitment to any one lover or friend, her need to be able to "go" and "come back," is consistent with Smith's ambivalent relation to groups of people, especially people in political organizations. Holden provided an account of this relation in *It Was Different At the Time*, a fictionalized diary of wartime London life that was begun as a joint project with Orwell but was published without his contributions in 1943. In the diary, the character Felicity, "an average girl of chaos," is based on Smith (*It Was Different* 9). Felicity enters the narrative in the early diary entries of 1938 when Holden is assessing Londoners' responses to the Munich crisis. Felicity's problem differs from that of most people, however:

> She needed to belong to a group, but could never get a group to suit her. At the time of Munich she felt that she wanted to come out violently for some group—but which one? That was the difficulty. There she was, instinctively against certain sects of people, and these, like the objects of an unhappy passion, attracted her most. She attended political meetings. Apparently she did not go to these meetings because she liked them, but because she hated them. (20)

Smith herself hints at her problem with groups in *The Holiday* when she has Celia recount another character's belief that "the pleasantness of my [Celia's] life with my Aunt was just that neither of us like groups" (106).

The political groups that Smith would have been drawn to against her will included the leftist, pro-Soviet communists who populated English intellectual circles as well as Mosley's Fascists. Holden describes the repellent Mosley group in *It Was Different at the Time*, concluding that "Of all the myths, the racial myth must surely be the most obscure. I don't know if we are Aryans, but if we are we cannot help it, so I suppose we shall have to make the best of it. But whatever an Aryan is, no one would want to be one after listening to Sir Oswald" (24). In *The Holiday* we get a glimpse of Smith's representation of a very different type of group when Celia reports on a London meeting where Raji, whom she has known since her childhood in India, presents a paper on the English novelists who write about India. This scene works as high comedy at the expense of the "Anglo-Indian[s] of previous importance" who make up the majority of the audience (95). Smith writes: "Of course, first of all our Raji had to be introduced by the lady that was in the Chair. So this lady spoke at great length about all the people she had known and loved in India, and about the children she had reared, and their lovely Ayah, their dog and their washerwoman" (95). The satire continues after Raji's speech when other Anglo-Indians stand up to confirm their claim to the meanings of Raji's country and literature. The meeting draws to a close shortly after "A young violent English person" protests that "no easy feeling of equality between intellectual Indians and English people was possible in India so long as this evil thing (the British Raj) was still in existence" (96).

This scene is based on Smith's evening as Anand's companion at a lecture he gave to the Royal India Society. According to Anand, Smith's satire about the audience is "spot on," including her portrait of the "young violent English person" who was, in reality, George Orwell (Spalding 158). While the fictional narrator's affection for Raji parallels the esteem Smith's biographers believe she felt for Anand, both Smith and her fictional counterpart were divided in their loyalty to Orwell. It is worth remembering that Smith's tiff with Orwell over her first "Voice" talk was followed years later by *The Holiday*'s wicked depiction of Orwell as the misogynistic Basil/Tom. Documents suggest that the source of Smith's irritation with Orwell was his sexism, a conclusion, if accurate, that helps support my claim that Smith can serve as an important alternative model of admirable social, artistic, and (unorganized) political radical eccentricity, even in the context of the activities of her more activist leftist friends. Smith's sensitivity to exclusion or marginalization based on sex, coupled with her resistance to groups of any kind, complicates any easy definitions about the nature of intermodern radical eccentricity that might emerge from study of the fictions or broadcasts delivered by the other writers discussed here.

It is difficult, if not impossible, to separate these writers' personal relations and off-center political commitments from their anti-fascist and even patriotic stances. As radical or dissenting artists, they were acutely aware of the importance of the ideal of democratic free speech and the difficulties, in Churchill's England, of getting one's small, opposing voice heard. None were naive about the future of democratic speech under Hitler and all were outspoken in their condemnations of Nazism and Fascism. After the Soviet Union became an English ally, they were unwavering in their support of the British war effort, no matter how critical they were of the British government's imperialist policies or the more sexist, capitalist, classist elements of British cultural institutions. Ironically, the same off-center politics, the marginal vision that formed the foundation of their anti-Fascism, was the source of their problems with the BBC, upon which they all relied during the paper shortages that drastically limited wartime publishing opportunities.

The primary problem for Smith and Holden was simply attracting and keeping BBC assignments. Unlike Anand, whose status as one of the pre-eminent young Indian intellectuals in England gave him a surer path to publication of his novels and nonfiction, the women writers were desperate to gain the audience, prestige, and financial support of radio. The BBC files on Smith and Holden and Holden's diary show that during the war years they were repeatedly encouraged or even requested to compose pieces for Overseas programs or occasionally, the Home Service, only to be told afterward that their work couldn't be used. Smith, for example, proposed to Orwell a specific Christmas program for 1941 that included selections by herself, Holden, other eminent contemporary writers, Dickens, and assorted children's singing games and sea-shanties (Spalding 152). As she predicted, her program was declined in favor of a medley of innocuous Christmas carols (Spalding 152–53).

Holden's problems broadcasting her work are much more pronounced. In the same diary entry that mentions her theater reviewing for Orwell, she notes: "I am short of money and do not know quite what to do about a job, the B.B.C. never does come off. I think people who get jobs must be terrific tough go-getters." Two months later, in August 1941, she wrote the following:

> Again the B.B.C. drama has cropped up. It is now recurring, the same sort of problem as an un-requited un-ending passion. I went for the appointments board. I set out with new stockings, a well-brushed dress, a hat and shoes . . . brightly polished . . . The appointments board seemed to have been rather a success. The three middle aged men sat at an immense table, the grey haired staff administrator rather like a bank manager, the red-haired recruiting office and a non descript civil servant. There was a lot of getting up to their feet bowing and shaking hands. It went well. But all the same I got a note after six days which regretted that they were not choosing me to join the staff pool. So the possible war job, near at hand with good salary and work which I could have done went away in thin smoke.

Holden then comforts herself with the thought, "as it is not as fundamental as a love affair I could not mind much."

Correspondence from Holden's files in the BBC Written Archives show that Holden's troubles with the BBC continued even after she began getting pieces accepted and produced. Typical is an exchange in the fall of 1940 between Holden and Ormond Wilson of the BBC Overseas Department about her talk on an Out-Patients' Department Casualty Station in Camden Town. After Holden had her proposal accepted and had written up the talk, she received a dismissive letter from Wilson explaining, "We have had your material in one form or another several times by now, and it really comes to this—that only a completely fresh angle on the Blitzkrieg can now be used." Wilson concludes his letter by asking if she has "any fresh suggestions to make" noting that "we should like you to give a talk" (BBCWA, 5 November 1940). Since rejection was tempered with compliments, it is no wonder that Holden tried again, only to experience the same frustrating declines just at the point she expected to be paid. One finds oneself feeling very sympathetic to her complaint to Wilson on 7 January 1941 that each time she's written or given a talk for his program she's told it is "exactly what you are needing etc. etc. but on fifty percent of the occasions, for some reason, only half of the talks get produced—and paid for" (BBCWA). This letter begins with an apology about her delayed response to Wilson's last letter of 14 November because, "I did not know how to reply as it was rather difficult to discover whether you did or did not really want me to give a talk" (BBCWA).

Of course neither Smith nor Holden knew about the extent of the censorship that occasionally kept writers' work off the air. Although the BBC had always been politically neutral, radio was brought under the control of the Ministry of Information (MOI) during World War II and was censored more heavily than any other media (West, *Broadcasts* 13, 21). As a result, literally every word that was broadcast on the BBC was supposed to be censored for policy and security (West 21). Pieces that were thought to conform closely to government policy were only censored by BBC officials. The more "sensitive" pieces were sent on to the MOI. The stamps of various censorship departments are evident on the first pages of Smith's, Holden's, and Anand's wartime radio scripts as are Orwell's handwritten notes that direct the scripts to higher authorities. It is fascinating to compare the reasons BBC administrators gave to writers for rejection of their scripts with the interoffice correspondence that occasionally documents the intervening nay-saying force of the censors.

One of the most interesting examples of such limitations on free speech involves Holden's piece "Work and Bed—You Might As Well Be Dead," which she wrote for the "Women and the Call-Up Campaign." Drawing on materials that are similar to those contained in her private diary and her 1944 novel, *There's No Story There*, which is about conscripted workers in a Royal Ordnance factory, this short radio piece highlights the needless boredom and discomfort suffered by workers due to governmental mismanagement of their leisure time. The title of the piece is the motif that workers repeated to each other, variously expressing feelings of resignation, amusement, or depression. Holden seems to record objectively the workers' activities and emotions in the first three paragraphs of the piece, but then takes a more activist position and recommends that the government forget about improving factory lives with "pep talks" by outsiders and encourage instead such things as University Extension lectures and workers clubs. This script came to the attention of officials at various ministries, including an enraged Sir Frederick Leggett of the Ministry of Labour. Leggett objected that the talk had been submitted too late for the Ministry to take action on it and that it was "a deliberate attempt on the part of the BBC to depress young women going into industry" (recorded by G. R. Barnes, 27 May 1942). G. R. Barnes of the Home Talks Department responded to Leggett's criticism by telephone. His record of his spirited defense of the BBC handling of Holden's piece preserves this particular example of governmental tampering in artistic and BBC production. Barnes's record reads,

> I gave [Leggett] the BBC's point of view in the matter saying that all our evidence showed that workers did not want to hear sunshine of how well Government Departments were doing, but wished to have their questions answered and that that was the BBC's intention provided those answers were accurate and did not embarrass the work of the Government Department concerned. (27 May 1942)

After Barnes's talk with Leggett, Holden was persuaded to make "necessary alterations" to the script. It was sent on to Leggett the next day (BBCWA). Her diary entry of 30 May 1942 provides a glimpse of her private reaction to the "terrific affair," demonstrating both her desire to keep the authorities happy and her unwillingness to broadcast the story once it had been altered to "read in a way that was directly opposed to what I believed to be true about factories and what I had written elsewhere."

Orwell's first direct confrontation with censorship occurred over Anand's contribution on the Spanish Civil War that was part of Orwell's series on "The History of Fascism." West notes that all the speakers in this series were Indians and that Anand's piece was the only one to arouse controversy. A worried BBC censor sent Anand's piece to specialists of the MOI where it was promptly banned (West, *Broadcasts* 44). Orwell supported Anand to the extent he felt possible by requesting partial payment for writing done but never broadcast. Silenced in December 1942, Anand's piece is still effectively lost to scholars who read through files of the BBC in the hope of uncovering clues about censorship of political writing in wartime media.

Research on the literary productions of Orwell, Smith, Anand, and Holden provides understanding of the ways their radically eccentric writings contributed to cultural life in Britain. Research on the writers' radio talks that government officials either rewrote or silenced yields equally important information about the frustrations and contradictions of practicing anti-Fascist politics on behalf of that same culture. Smith's preoccupation with the seemingly trivial, feminine concerns of domestic and suburban life, Anand's outspoken criticism of British policy in India and his advocacy of Indian independence, Holden's disapproval of government complicity with institutionalized discrimination against working-class women and men teach us about the ideological contradictions and aesthetic limitations that accompanied Britain's wartime aim of representing democratic ideals in an England at total war against Nazi Germany and the other Axis nations.

Outside of BBC contract records, there is no way to know how much Orwell directly influenced the thinking and writing of Smith, Anand, or Holden. Biography and memoir tell part of the story of his impact, but it is one of the assumptions of this book that such a story is too partial to do anyone much good. Rather than tracing patterns of influence between more and less popular writers, this book aims to tell a story about the relations of a particular history and place on the writings of a group of writers and friends whose positioning within literary culture gave them a unique perspective on their nation and its people—citizens, immigrants, and visitors—during the crisis years when England lost its Empire.

Chapter 1

"Hurrah to Be a Goy!": Stevie Smith and Suburban Satire

Novel on Yellow Paper boasts the same, quirky, comical charms of the poetry that later made Stevie Smith famous. It is also distinguished, with Smith's second novel *Over the Frontier* and her wartime stories and sketches, by a commitment to integrating probing, often unflattering portrayals of English gentiles' attitudes toward Jews within a distinctly intermodern imagining of heroic English resistance to Hitler and Fascism. Like Orwell's essays that address the problem of anti-Semitism in Britain, Smith's fiction makes discomforting inquires into the ordinary English citizen's complicity with Hitler's treatment of Jews, of what Pompey Casmilus describes in *Novel on Yellow Paper* as "the sort of vicious cruelty that isn't battlecruelty, but doing people to death in lavatories" (104).[1] Also like Orwell's writing, her literary treatments of Jews earned her a reputation for anti-Semitism.[2]

Smith's biographers take the accusations of anti-Semitism seriously and their accounts prepare the way for the attempt to understand the meaning of Smith's provocative, seemingly malicious representations of English Jews for our understanding of intermodern literary culture. This chapter attempts to advance such cultural understanding by making a surprising association; it suggests that Smith's anti-Semitic fictional portraits can be understood as one facet of that radical eccentricity which at other points in her narratives manifests itself as celebratory, affectionate representations of English suburbs. I argue that both Jews and suburbs were integral to Smith's self-conscious effort to imagine an English character that could stand up to the multiple threats to national identity posed by economic depression, Hitler's domination of Europe, the losses of war, including the bombing of London, and the postwar loss of superpower status to America.

"Hurrah to Be a Goy!"

During the 1930s, despair and outrage over Hitler's threat to the still war-weary English did not translate into sympathy for much more vulnerable European or English Jewish populations. Knowledge of Hitler's concentration camps was common in England by the mid-1930s, yet English Jews increasingly became the scapegoats for domestic social discomforts and fears.[3] Writers who resisted the logic of anti-Semitism, including Smith's contemporaries Storm Jameson, Phyllis Bottome, and Betty Miller, were all too aware that European Jews were paying the price of the Western democracies' inability to contain Hitler (Montefiore 40). In contrast to these other novelists, Smith's relation to both Jews and fascism is much more complex and often less heroic. For this reason, Smith's novels are more uncomfortable and in some ways more valuable (because more typical) registers of prewar English culture than other, more overtly progressive, anti-fascist novels.[4] Smith's representations of the violence of complacency, her incrimination of suburban patriots like herself in Hitler's European war through analysis of domestic prejudices, could earn her three novels the respect due to war literature of first importance. Although none of Smith's fictions could be described as conventional war literature, her second novel *Over the Frontier* is filled with uniforms and soldiers and spies and is more likely to be described as war writing than Smith's other narratives. Yet Smith's first and most popular novel, *Novel on Yellow Paper*, her third postwar novel, *The Holiday*, and selected short stories and sketches, are as important as *Over the Frontier* to the argument of this chapter because they extend Smith's interrogation of English citizens' complicity with Hitler's treatment of Jews to the geographical and cultural forms of English suburban life.

Phyllis Lassner has set a precedent for focusing on Smith's fictional treatment of Jews as a means of understanding the relations her books establish between Nazi Germany and wartime England.[5] This chapter extends the implications of Lassner's insights, connecting Smith's fictional "crusade for a confrontation with the anti-Semitism latent in a [British] culture that had claimed itself Germany's rival as the 'highest civilization'" to Smith's status as a comic, experimental writer who provides an alternative to the Auden Generation's vision of intermodern Englishness (Lassner 182).

Like many of the most famous narrative works of the 1930s, Smith's fiction confronts ideological conflicts about class and especially race and ethnicity in an effort to imagine an Englishness strong enough to withstand the Fascist threat. Unlike these texts, it also confronts ideological conflicts about gender roles and women's sexuality. The explicitly personal rather than public contents, and experimental, humorous forms of Smith's novels further distance her work from the traditional vision of Thirties prose literature, of what Malcolm Bradbury has described as the "realist novel of the surreal dark twentieth century" (152).[6] The experiment and humor is scandalously evident in the protagonist's anti-Semitic comments in the first pages of *Novel*, suggesting that for Smith these things—style, humor, and racial politics—are interconnected, formative, and primary. It is left to readers to figure out what can be learned about intermodern literature and culture from her daring narrative experiments.

The anti-Semitism in the first pages of *Novel* forms an unlikely beginning for a novel that I'm treating as a radical antidote to the standard critical story about the character of wartime British writing. Just as readers get a feel for the flippant, airy, witty voice of the heroine, Pompey, they read the following:

> Last week I was at a party at Leonie's. Suddenly I looked around. I thought: I am the only goy. There was a newspaper man there and a musician and some plain business men. But the Jews. Well all to say about the Jews has been said, so I'll leave it. But then I had a moment of elation at that party. I got shot right up. Hurrah to be a goy! A clever goy is cleverer than a clever Jew . . . .
>
> Do all goys among Jews get that way? Yes, perhaps. And the feeling you must pipe down and apologize for being so superior and clever: I can't help it really my dear chap, you see I'm a goy. It just comes with the birth. It's a world of unequal chances, not the way B. Franklin saw things. (10–11)

How could the person who would come to write poems like "Not Waving or Drowning," with their insights into the plights of misunderstood, abandoned outsiders, have begun her career in 1936 with this apparent celebration of racial or ethnic superiority?[7] Is it as bad as it seems? The overtly political materials of Smith's novels compel reexamination of the hostile treatments of Jews in those novels, and, outside of Lassner's study, the almost total silence in literary criticism about this aspect of Smith's work.[8]

If it were not for Pompey's astonishing cry "Hurrah to be a goy!" it would be more difficult to make the argument that *Novel* contributes in significant ways to the intermodern project of reimagining Englishness in full knowledge of Hitler's threat. Smith's narrative instructs us to look for signs of acute cultural transformation in the thoughts and emotions of a London secretary whose life is built out of the routines of suburban life. Pompey's encounters with her London friends and suburban neighbors bring her to speak about anything from sex education to ladies' magazines to love affairs to Hitler. Smith makes this hodgepodge of subjects meaningful to intermodern literature in part through foregrounding Pompey's seemingly gratuitous anti-Semitism.

Pompey is a party girl whose every public comment is designed to amuse someone in her audience, usually at someone else's expense. Her weapon and her armor is her sharp satire, which she shines to comic brilliance by treating all people as potential material for her public performances. The result is that no one is safe from the barbs of her sometimes cruel wit. And it is this lack of distinction between deserving and undeserving subjects that makes the beginning of *Novel* upsetting. Why does Pompey pick on the Jews, the increasingly desperate underdogs of the 1930s? It seems cheap and low and downright destructive to use a persecuted group as the butt of jokes, the source of her comedy. Why doesn't Pompey pick on Hitler instead?

The most generous answer to these questions is that Smith self-consciously foregrounds her heroine's typical, "genteel" English form of anti-Semitism in order to examine the enormity of that prejudice. If we snapped the book shut after reading the opening paragraphs that I cite above, we would never discover that *Novel* does in fact pick on Hitler in viciously comic and highly instructive ways. Comparison of the initial passage that makes fun of Jews to later passages that make fun of Hitler demonstrates how the *potential* for progressive social critique emerges when we travel between those two comic moments. The aim of this chapter is to explore the narrative conditions promoting that progressive critique, as well as the cultural consequences of its inevitable, if intermittent, failure.

One of the first things that Pompey mentions in the "Hurrah to be a goy!" passage is that she is at a party when she suddenly discovers that she is the only goy. From this we learn that many of Pompey's friends are Jewish and that she must have been surrounding herself with Jews for years. Since she uses the Yiddish word "goy" to describe her difference from her Anglo-Jewish friends, we also learn that Pompey identifies herself as a superior outsider with a term that typically is used mainly by Jews to describe gentiles in a slightly derogatory way. The fact that Pompey even knows this word exists testifies to her status as something of an insider within this group of intellectual English Jews.[9] The racial or ethnic difference that Pompey seems to be discovering for the first time cannot exist as a stable, absolute difference if an outsider knows herself as such through the eyes and words of the insider. Like Smith, Pompey is located in an eccentric position relative to the cultural groups with which she identifies and she tries to know herself as English by constantly looking both ways. When Pompey looks toward the center of her group of Jewish friends, she feels alienated enough to discover a separate group, English goys, that we are encouraged to imagine as an identifiable crowd of which Pompey is an original, though to this date, undeclared, member.

Pompey's dual status as insider/outsider, made possible by a social position that can be imagined in terms of the eccentric circles illustrating geometry textbooks, is complicated even further once her comments at the party are considered within the larger context of 1930s England, in which Jews were not the insiders but the outsiders.[10] Pompey's statement, "A clever goy is cleverer than a clever Jew," cannot be read as patently, self-consciously absurd, a mere jab in the ribs to get a laugh, if it is situated in relation to Hitler's rhetoric about Aryan dominance and Jewish decadence. Nor can "A clever goy is cleverer than a clever Jew," be read simply or only as an anti-Semitic statement since it challenges the conditions and assumptions that support anti-Semitic discourse by making the goy, rather than the Jew, the subject of a discussion of difference. By 1936, the year *Novel* was published, private and public speech was saturated with a hysterical discussion of the "Jewish problem." Shifting the topic of discussion to goys, Pompey intervenes in a neurotic national discourse about Jewishness with words that mock goys like herself who feel superior to their Jewish friends. She accomplishes this mockery of herself and other goys by overtly describing unexamined, exaggerated feelings of being "so superior and clever." And integral to that proclamation of superiority and cleverness is an acknowledgment that people who feel this way know it is wrong, that it is something for which "you must pipe down and apologize."

My understanding of Smith's unusual focus on goyish, rather than Jewish, difference at the beginning of *Novel* supports Lassner's argument that in Smith's fiction "it is the Jew who tests all the characters' contradictory attitudes towards war" (182). Smith's sardonic focus on non-Jewish characters interacting with Jews has the potential to throw gentile readers' careless assumptions of normalcy, coherence, and dominance into question. And it is this crisis of identity that points to the progressive promise as well as the threat of prejudice that Smith's fiction extends. The threat is evident in Smith's voicing of anti-Semitic ideas and attitudes, no matter how complicated or qualified by the tones and motives of satire. The promise is the possibility that self-reflective characters like Pompey will prompt readers who recognize a part of themselves in her to realize the cruelty of their assumptions. Perhaps these readers will begin to scrutinize the danger their difference, understood as a difference of assumed racial superiority, poses to society rather than practicing the more socially accepted habit of scrutinizing a supposedly dangerous, inferior Jew. *Novel's* scandalous beginning paragraphs suggest that the first step toward fulfilling that promise is for non-Jewish Britons to join Pompey in recognizing themselves as goys. The possibility of that recognition supports the main argument of Lassner's article: that Smith's writing "forcefully expresses her feeling that Britain's ambivalence towards the Jews is part of the hypocrisy and complacency that gives license to Hitler's world conquest" (181).

We see the implications of this idea worked out in very different ways in *Over the Frontier*. In the middle of the book, when Pompey still resides at the fantastic but seemingly real Schloss Tilssen, Colonel Peck and Tom Satterthwaite pose the question that ultimately motivates her into uniform and across the frontier: "And the Jews?" This question comes as a provocation, a kind of test, of Pompey's apparently public declaration,

> I am on the side of my friends, for if they win they are the people I should choose to live with. [. . .] And often a principle may seem wrong, a national policy is antipathetic to the sensitive conscience of the individual. But it is the sensitive conscience that must abrogate, and in time of war I fight with my friends, with the people I like, with the people I can live with. (157)

This position statement is forced from Pompey by the question, "And on whose side are you?" (157). She has herself asked this of the seemingly absentminded secret agent, Colonel Peck, only to find it doubling back upon herself when he chooses not to answer.

Before Pompey can become a soldier on what we assume is Colonel Peck's side, Smith makes her deny the Jews. Tom and the Colonel create within her a confrontation between her principled self and "the racial hatred that is running in [her] in a sudden swift current, in a swift tide of hatred" (158). Repeating to herself the words, "Ah the Jews, the Jews" and "No I will not be drawn" (157), Pompey at first resists the silent offer of Tom and the Colonel to join them. But all it takes is one prod from Tom, "Come on Pompey" . . . "And the Jews?" (158), for our heroine to give assent to the "devilish hateful jibe, 'Would any but they have survived their persecutions?' "

> "None but the Jews would have survived their persecutions." [. . .] But I have had some very dear Jewish friends. Oh final treachery of the smug goy. Do not all our persecutions of Israel follow upon this smiling sentence? (158)

There are no quotation marks around the last three sentences, so we assume that Pompey keeps this admission of her final treachery, the treachery of the smug goy, to herself. She has not given in yet to Tom's attempts to make her admit publicly her failure to join the Jews' side of mercy and justice. She tells us "the virtue has gone out of me" and "these two soldiers with whom indeed I have little very little in common" are right; she would not throw in her lot to fight with the Jews, "however in theory and mercy justifiable their cause" (158).

> "I will fight with my friends my true friends my real friends the people with whom I am happy."
> "And these are not the Jews?"
> "No." (159)

Tom calls this refusal "a sort of loyalty," but Pompey knows better and calls it a "half perceived truth, that friendship is a more final truth than policy" (159). For Lassner, this is the moment when Pompey "Still choosing friends, . . . sacrifices the antipathetic Other to the very history in which she colludes as writer and as actor" ("Milk" 143).

For the reader familiar with the opening pages of *Novel*, Pompey's decision to turn her back on the Jews in *Over the Frontier* extends the confusion over the meaning of her anti-Semitism to her second novel. How are we to interpret Pompey's creed of battle, "I will fight with my friends" (not the Jews), given that only thirteen pages before we encounter these words, Pompey tells us of her long talk with Tom about home, "of London and of the many people there that he knows and that I know, of Herman and Rosa Blum, my musical friends of many parties, of Gustav, of Larry the Pansy, of Henry" (145). These musical friends are Pompey's Jewish friends, "some very dear Jewish friends" (158). What then to make of her half perceived truth that puts friendship before policy, but leaves Jewish friends outside of friendship? Why is it Pompey's denial of the side of the Jews (and the possibility of Jews on many sides), rather than, say, her denial of the Irish (157), that turns the book away from Schloss Tilssen, London, Bottle Green, and everything we have recognized as knowable reality in Pompey's fictional universe? "Anti-Semitism" is too simple an answer since it does not account for Pompey's recognition of her "final treachery," her descent into a uniform she instinctively hates, her departure from virtue and her acceptance of darkness, violence, ambition, and captivity.

Part of the answer to this troubling question, "Why the Jews?" can be found in the form of *Over the Frontier* rather than the content of Pompey's thought. After Pompey affirms goyish friendship over policy, the narrative breaks; there is a material break of white space between paragraphs, an imagined time break between tea time and evening, and a striking aesthetic-stylistic break between realism and surrealism. While everything after Pompey's denial of the Jews can be read "realistically," as an extension of the logic and plot of the first half of the novel and of Smith's previous novel, realism is inadequate to the symbolic pictures that make up *Over the Frontier*'s second half. The last one hundred or so pages of *Over the Frontier free the use of power*

are more poignant, moving, and meaningful if they are seen as an extension of Pompey's mental battles, of her "dream-reality." This dream-reality is more nightmare than fantasy, and it symbolizes the battles of her country and generation to resist the enticements of power and tyranny, to resist the pulse of the age that directs individuals and nations to seek pleasure in giving pain and managing death. Other critics have traced the patterns in Smith's writing of the most prominent symbols or pictures of the novel's surreal conclusion, but none have insisted that the novel be read as a coherent tragedy whose grim conclusion is predicted by its intermediate denial of the Jews.

When a People has Dictators

In *Novel*, Pompey's shift from mockery of Jews to mockery of Hitler is one of the things that makes it possible to justify reading or teaching the novel as a part of the literature of war when there are so many other narratives—novels of witness, Holocaust narratives, memoirs of survival in combat—that more obviously announce their importance. *Novel* and *Over the Frontier* demand our attention because their experiment and comedy make us ask different kinds of questions about the politics of intermodern literature and history. Insofar as those questions are associated with a woman's voice, experiences, and contexts, they offer a vision that is part of an experience or truth of war that until recently had been hidden by mainstream history and literary criticism.

It is no coincidence that this hidden women's or domestic context is integral to one of *Novel's* passages that mocks Hitler. Just after Pompey describes the cruelty of Germany as "doing people to death in lavatories," she goes on to exclaim:

> Oh how deeply neurotic the German people is, and how weak, and how they are giving themselves up to this sort of cruelty and viciousness, how Hitler cleared up the vice that was so in Berlin, in every postal district some new vice, how Hitler cleared that up all . . . .
>
> Now when a people has dictators, that is a symptom that they are running mad. They should then be watched. I think they should be watched very closely. And later they should be prevented. Now think it is not a nation but an individual, now see, this is like he had a disease.
>
> Why see, what is the matter with that poor Mr. Brown that has been looking so funny, he certainly looks queer, he looks a sick man? Oh yes, where is that Mr. Brown that we don't see now, it is a long time, that was sick? Oh yes he was sick. Oh yes he got dictators, it turned out afterwards. That's what he

got . . . . Ya, that's what he got, he been put away mister this long time now. Put away, locked up and prevented. (104–05)

The political effects of Smith's humor in this passage depend, in part, on her use of prosaic, domestic materials for her metaphors. She imagines Hitler's fascist leadership as a disease that an oh-so-harmless-sounding Mr. Brown might contract in suburban England. As a result, her description of gentile fascist inclinations to disease neatly, if inadvertently, reverses the century-long tradition of treating Jewishness as a disease.[11] It also produces humor and maybe even laughter out of its incongruous terms, mocking the tyrannical Hitler in a Charlie Chaplinesque way. This humor of incongruity is complemented by Pompey's idiosyncratic narrative style—Smith's alterations to standard English sentence and narrative structures and her use of the rhythms and slang of American speech. These observations about Smith's style of humor lead to a more abstract political point. The comparison of Hitler to Mr. Brown works in two directions; Hitler is Mr. Brown, and Mr. Brown is Hitler, and so too can Germany be England and England Germany. Accepting the possibility of an identity between England and Germany returns us to the larger argument of this chapter, that Smith's value as an intermodern writer of war literature is her scrutiny of the English complicity in the Nazi's racist attack upon the Jews.[12] This may seem like an obvious conclusion to arrive at upon reading the above passage, but few readers make it because it is disguised by Smith's comic style of writing.

One possible solution to the comedic puzzles of Smith's fiction is located in the alternative titled printed underneath the words *Novel on Yellow Paper*: "Work It Out for Yourself." Smith's most enthusiastic readers discover that they enjoy doing exactly that: working the novel out for themselves. They take advantage of her refusal to claim her assigned and assumed role as authority and assume responsibility for the meanings of her book. The demands upon readers of *Over the Frontier* to work it out for themselves are even greater and the critical record shows to what extent readers have struggled to make sense out of it.[13] Like *Novel*, one of its seemingly gratuitous puzzles emerges on the first pages. Why does a book about soldiering and spying begin with Pompey's description of her visit to an elegant London picture-gallery and her response to a painting there by Georg Grosz called "Haute École"? Pompey's enthusiastic, detailed monologue about Grosz's horse and rider begins with the words, "Now this one I will tell you about" (10), which seem to treat the painting more like a lively subject of suburban gossip than a visual product of material art:

Now this one I will tell you about. So. There is this very classical animal, this horse, that has a vivid plastique tail and his front leg is raised up to do the high step. His colour is a light and beautiful brown colour that hardly serves to cover the canvas, so ethereal and noble is this animal and his nostrils are spread wide. Very elegant indeed and high-born is this horse with his wide open eyes his wide-spread nostrils his sleek coat and his wide wide eyes that have that look in them that is a warning to the people that know about horses like me. (10)

The nobility of this "laughing and ferocious horse," so full of "passion and integrity," (17) contrasts with the decadence of his rider, who Pompey compares to "the slim full faced pouting degenerate people that you have in the drawings of Beardsley" (11). Pompey celebrates the horse's "malicious and indignant" nature and imagines with relish the ability of this sleek, prancing beast to cause the downfall of his supercilious rider who, should he tumble, would die with "nothing between his plump pink hairless head and the hard hard floor" (11). When we first encounter Pompey's references to Grosz's "Haute École," it is not quite clear to us, and presumably not quite clear to Pompey, why she loves this painting and feels she must possess it. Perhaps she sees herself as participant in a joke played by Grosz upon his human subject, a joke that emerges from the contrast between the native nobility Pompey ascribes to the horse and the rider's arrogant, false, and potentially fatal assumption of superiority.

A joke, a picture-story, a piece of gossip, a secret story promising intimate knowledge: once characterized in these ways, Pompey's meditation upon Grosz's picture, and particularly this meditation's odd status as the framework for a novel "set to anger and disturbance," begins to make sense (29). As Pompey moves further and further away from London, Bottle Green, and the staunch suburban worldview represented by her Lion Aunt, her interpretation of the painting provides a sort of key to the moral meanings of her changing allegiances and values. As I demonstrate below, it also provides an answer to the question of why the novel abandons the comical realism of its earliest pages when Pompey abandons the Jews, finding its end in a style and genre of surreal tragedy.

For the Pompey of Bottle Green and Schloss Tilssen, the classical, noble horse with his quiet animal brain represents an ideal that she and the other humans in the novel should strive to attain. A lion on an ancient Greek vase owned by her London friend Harriet evokes the following prayer or invocation, allowing us to measure at the novel's end how far she has strayed from the classical ideal that she projects onto certain animal images:

> Beautiful Lion Vase, sombre and ferocious lion, to set in upon himself, so quiet and aloof. And quiet horse of my earlier picture-gallery excursion, set in again in quietness upon a sombre ferocity. Ah, the animals are so quiet. There is no fuss up there, no fret and fume for guilt and delinquency, no mind sickness and a thought upon death. (46)

Pompey's tragedy is that she will never achieve such inhuman animal quiet. Though she will lose her habit of mind sickness once she exchanges Bottle Green, Harriet, and her lover Freddy for Schloss Tilssen, friend Josephine, and Tom, the cure becomes curse as she finds herself "turning towards darkness and death in darkness" (221). Despite her self-instruction to "remember to be sad, and remember and remember" (19), Pompey is all too eager to leave memories of home and unhappiness behind. Indications of this susceptibility to forgetfulness and departure emerge long before Pompey turns spy and soldier. She tells us early in the novel, "To say good-bye at one swoop to things hated and things loved (work it out for yourself) is a happiness and a turn of fate unlooked for by me" (80). The danger of this urgent need to be off and away becomes increasingly apparent as Pompey repeats her desire for absolute separation, a total abandonment of the past. The most dramatic instance of this impulse to escape follows Pompey's transformation into a rider in uniform. Betraying her gentile friends as she once had betrayed her Jewish friends, Pompey tells us:

> Already there is a great joy in my heart to think that all is for ever over and passed away that had so much and so tediously to do with chère Josephine and Haidée, and the nagging mannerisms, the overbearing, the so interfering *Schlossleben*.
> So now I am free of all that, and of all that lay behind it, and of all that far-distant London life that, for an absence and freedom from a grievance and a self-injurious very great bitterness, I must seem not only to endure but to approve. . . . For me no more, no more, no more ever again. (221)

It is almost impossible to come this far in the narrative and not see Pompey's journey "to that ominous Tilssen that is beyond Pillau and for me beyond thought" as a descent into Hades, or at least into a dream-reality of Pompey's unconscious (117). The repetition in the above passage forces us to take seriously Pompey's total denial of her past—she is free of *all* that, and of *all* that lay behind it—and the absolute denial of her past connections to her friends: "For me no more, no more, no more ever again." As others have noted, whatever else this desire for "no more, no more, no more ever again" may be, it is also a desire for death.

But this journey to the frontier is never *only* a metaphorical journey to Hades or death. When Pompey is in uniform, riding across "A very blasted plain," we see she has become under the influence of Tom Satterthwaite, Colonel Peck, and Mrs. Pouncer a double for Grosz's pink rider, who himself functions in Pompey's imagination as a double for Grosz. She represents herself the way she represents Grosz, as a person in flight from place and memory, looking for a future disconnected from the past, a person ashamed

of her knowledge of human cruelty and hopelessness. It is this total transformation of focus and identity, the exchange of the ideal represented by
Grosz's horse for the identity of the horse's degenerate rider, that has per-
plexed Pompey's devoted readers. Our affection for her, our desire that she
triumph over the unquiet of her age, that she resist the "powerful drug" of
cruelty that is "very much in the air now" (58), makes it difficult to pose to
Pompey the deceptively simple question she asks of Grosz's rider, "After all
what is he doing?" If we substitute feminine for masculine pronouns,
Pompey's answer to this question also answers the provocation of *Over the
Frontier's* unhappy ending.

> I think he is doing this, with great application and concentration this is what
> he is doing, he is forgetting to remember the shame and dishonour the power
> of the cruelty the high soaring flight of that earlier éclaircissement, . . . that
> rakehell of a beam of light that went showing up the very sad bones of that
> earlier situation [i.e., famished postwar Germany], this he is very actively for-
> getting and instead he will think of the easy generous light-running laughter
> of the English and Americans, and he is thinking of that American nation-
> ality that shall come dropping down dropping like a curtain to shut off from
> him *for ever* that sad sad situation that already perhaps he is a little ashamed
> to have seen once and for all time so top to bottom, so round and about and
> within, so in its flesh and bones and skeleton its sinews nerves and muscles,
> to the very last outposts of the black heart of despair of the situation. (17–18;
> my emphasis.)

How better to describe hell than in these last lines, "to have seen once and
for all time so top to bottom . . . ."? Despite Pompey's discovery of laughter
and something "funny" in the most threatening or macabre of situations,
she lives up to her namesake, the ancient god Mercury-Casmilus who could
come and go from Hades at will, by witnessing, escaping, and sharing
intimate knowledge of the body of despair (". . . flesh and bones and skele-
ton . . ."). She discovers hell in "sadness of a mismanaged love-situation" of
suburban London of the 1930s instead of the famine of Grosz's postwar
Germany of the 1920s, but the mundane circumstances of her discovery do
not diminish in the least her need for the final curtain that she imagines
Grosz has found in American and English laughter (18).[14]

Neither Pompey nor we could have predicted at the outset of *Over the
Frontier* that her curtain, her escape from sadness and suicide, will come in
the form of a mercenary's job. A "very willing captive" (167), Pompey in
uniform reflects "I guess I am not now purposed for death at all but for a
high-up commission and a staff hat" (223). Yet events over the frontier
show that Pompey is indeed "purposed for death," though not her own.
Reconciled to the notion of her own death, Pompey does not consider in

any depth the implications of her contribution to the deaths of many soldiers. And the despicable character of her victims, whether the monstrous Rat-face or Hitler-inspired enemies, cannot keep Pompey from the knowledge that a devilish hatred has grown within her under disguise of altruism. "How apt I was for this deceit, how splendid a material, that recognizing the deceit must take commission under it, forever following darkness" (256). The deceit Pompey refers to here is voiced by Professor Dryasdust, a man who wants to believe that Pompey is interested in politics, "in working for peace, in the fight against fascism" (256). Though Pompey denies the altruistic motives the Professor ascribes to her, later she defends herself against guilt, confessing to us that the challenge reflected in Rat-face's eyes—"*From whom do you hold your commission?*" (252)— originates in her own thought. Ordering away this inconvenient "ghost of nightmare" question, Pompey wonders on the next page if she has not, in fact, taken the devil by the hand by seeking an end "that only God can make?" (253).

Pompey as devil's worker, dealer in death, usurper of Godly privilege? I'm afraid so. These phrases describe her status at the end of *Over the Frontier*, at least if we read the novel's end in terms of the clues that appear in the first few pages in Pompey's meditation on Grosz's paintings. Deeply affected by Grosz's ability to capture "all of the ignobility and shameful pain of war suffering" (15), Pompey implicitly separates herself from "the English" who can choose, as victors in war, to acknowledge only the "funny-ha-ha Georg Grosz" of the chic London picture galleries. Curiously, Pompey cites English voices protesting Grosz's postwar vision (and thus protesting Pompey's affinity for this vision) in words that echo a memorable phrase from *Novel*: "it is sad but he should certainly be shut up and prevented" (*Over* 15–16). In *Novel*, the "he" who deserves locking up and preventing is Hitler. Here, the "he" refers to Grosz, an artist and one of Pompey's doubles. In other words, a phrase that in Smith's first novel comically signaled an admirable English resistance to war mongering here signals a foolish English blindness to art that resists war. Thus even the earliest funny pages of *Over the Frontier* point to its decidedly unfunny ending, its final vision of a distinctly intermodern English tragedy that can be described in exactly those words Pompey uses to describe Grosz's "A Post-War Museum": that "over it all and undertoning it all is shame and loss and flight into darkness" (*Over* 16).

Pompey's early musings on Grosz are closely followed by another meditation on art that has special relevance for those struggling with *Over the Frontier*'s ending. Allying her namesake, the devil Casmilus, with the great devils of English literature and allying herself with the great poets, Milton and Crashaw, Pompey identifies in these poets' works precisely the effect that *Over the Frontier* must achieve if it is to be judged a success:

> But reading these poets, and sensing the magnificent power of this swift-running, counterrunning, wrong ever wrong magic of their poetic vision, the sympathy of the reader too, if he has in him anything that is to make a response to the power of their verse, has to go running in this contrary current, that goes sweeping and licking up in a way that is contrary to truth and an abomination; but a sweet abomination and a very exceedingly delicious contrariness that is at the same time so dangerous. (31-32)

This passage, seemingly a peripheral or eccentric commentary on the "ever wrong magic" of Milton and Crashew's poetry, is itself "delicious" poetry disguised as prose. Pompey's admiration for Milton and Crashaw's sweet abominations is obvious and suggests why we should see the tragic form of *Over the Frontier* as a sign of its literary ambition, not its aesthetic incoherence. It is, quite literally, Smith's attempt to write an intermodern *Paradise Lost*.

Readers' dismay at *Over the Frontier*'s ending is proof of the success of Smith's endeavor. Pompey has brought us, barely resisting, into the darkness, unable to renounce her even as she has, time and again, renounced her friends. The seductions of Smith's sweeping, licking words have kept us, like Pompey, from seeing the following warning as a prophecy: "Oh no, Pompey, now careful. Don't let mighty Milton and this sweet Crashaw, and the others that are setting up to go after them, conducting these parties to the grim underworld, don't let them go to conducting your soul on this famous intourist party" (32). Reflecting back on these words from a position at the end of Smith's novel, we can see that Pompey chooses a passionate satanic path that she describes and admires in the very first pages of the novel. Like the readers of the seventeenth-century poets, we find ourselves delighting in a journey through hell. Smith's hell takes the shape of a blasted heath, an isolated tower, the town of Mentz, and its heroic, sweet devil is Pompey, "running too far, too far, too far altogether . . . to where it is getting dark, and very excessively dark and gloomy" (32).

The way I work it out, Pompey knows her commission is corrupt, immoral, dark, and illegal, betraying her just as it betrays us and as she betrays the Jews. She takes instruction from the decadent Generalissimo Clever Pie, whose presence at the tale's end creates a chilling formal symmetry once we recognize in his effeminate voice and manner another double for Grosz's Beardsley-esque rider. Of course by the end of the novel Pompey cannot hope to own Grosz's decadent painted man. She is owned: a mercenary, a prisoner, a military genius, set on a journey of no likely return. Having lost her ethical balance, her artist's freedom, she has become a careerist who may be "too set in and captive upon the will of these two men, upon [her] own pride" to resist the advantages that will come from renouncing, at last, her lover and mentor, Tom (266). She has her warning. Generalissimo Clever Pie asks her, "by the way, Pompey, you're not nuts on Satterthwaite, are you, not going to do a bolt, eh? That would be a pity?" Her flight into darkness, her escape into uniform, leaves her memories of Tom, Josephine, Harriet, Freddy, and London, but no emotional or real means to return to them, let alone save them. She is locked inside her room by the superiors who have praised her. While despising Jews, she has lost her England and her beloved suburb, the suburb that is her safe haven, her anchor, her past. The book is a domestic tragedy played out on a Miltonic landscape, one that attempts to give us in Pompey Casmilus a feminine, twentieth-century version of the seductive great devils of seventeenth-century English literature. As in *Novel*, Satan in this case is not Hitler, but the tyrannical, power-thirsty, decadent urges in us all that suburbs may disguise but cannot eliminate.

Readers should not be surprised that Pompey does not return in *The Holiday*. She has been committed by her author at the end of *Over the Frontier* to fearful dreams of modern history, the nightmare from which she cannot awaken, to war, to Mentz, to deals in death. Although she tells us that her godly namesake made himself unwelcome in Hades, tormenting the patient Pluto with his unannounced visits and sudden departures, she seems unable or unwilling to depart from her place in the dark world over the frontier and does not give us much reason to believe she will return to England. Critics (myself included) are loath to admit this. Again and again, we let Smith's comedy distract us from the early signs of Pompey's tragic fate.

When readers meet the tearful Celia in *The Holiday*, they identify her with the protagonist of Smith's earlier novels because Celia's thoughts are so similar to those of the Pompey of *Novel* and the first half of *Over the Frontier*. We are back in Bottle Green, back with the Lion of Hull, back in the London office and at the late-night parties. But Celia's suburban origins and loyalties should not eliminate the reality or surreality of Pompey's *Over the Frontier* escape. Although it is easier to dismiss *Over the Frontier* as a failed or psychotic novel than contend with or defend its puzzles, to do so is to sidestep the most important aesthetic, interpretive challenges—challenges that may begin with the simple question, what is Pompey saying about the Jews?—that are keys to understanding Smith's importance for intermodern culture.

My Not-So-Dear Friends

Smith's demand that we work out *Novel*'s puzzles for ourselves was not enough to excuse her heroine's anti-Semitic expressions in the eyes of those readers who were also Smith's Jewish friends. While these Jewish readers do not necessarily have privileged access to *Novel*'s interpretive puzzles, the autobiographical basis of Smith's fiction argues for consideration of personal history when judging the meaning of Pompey's anti-Semitism. Frances Spalding's biography is the best source for those interested in discovering which Jewish Londoners Smith befriended, the quality of Smith's relationships with these Jewish friends, and the meaning of those relationships for her writing. For example, Spalding recounts that the historical model for Leonie was Ionee Massada, who was introduced to Smith by Suzannah and Maurice Jacobson, a couple who Smith met in Aylesbury where Maurice was directing the Aylesbury Choral Society. The Jacobsons moved to London soon after Smith met them, were friends with many people who were active in London's musical organizations, and cheerfully invited Smith to their numerous parties. Smith modeled her characters Rosa and Herman after the Jacobsons. Both Massada and the Jacobsons were offended by *Novel*'s use of the words "Jew" and "Jewess" and were deeply hurt by Smith's unkind portraits of characters who they instantly recognized as versions of themselves. All three broke with Smith (Spalding 66–67).

Another Jewish couple to whom the Jacobsons introduced Smith, Selma d'Arco and her husband, were the historical models for *Novel*'s ballerina character Lottie and her American gynecologist husband Horace, who earned the following portraits:

> Lottie was mean and thrifty and Horace was too, and fat, and underneath greedy and cruel; but to Fifi [their Pomeranian] and Lottie he was their papa, their little big boy that was clever, and had a great big office where he made money, so that Fifi need never toil but could sit up like a lady on a fine cushion and drink out of a Jacobean goblet. (60)

Some familiar Jewish stereotypes are latent here—the rich, greedy Jewish papa, the superficial, too-maternal Jewish wife—but Lottie and Horace seem to earn Pompey's irony more for their absurd indulgence of Fifi and their improperly colloquial English than their Jewishness. In paragraphs that satirize their language and their treatment of their dog, the humor created at what Selma and her husband thought was their expense gathers its energy from emphasis on Lottie and Horace's foreignness. Pompey tells us that

> Lottie couldn't do English very well, and Reader have you noticed how foreigners, when they always are wanting to be very English, have to use not just the right word but something even more so, like *doggie*. And when they got back to Berlin-Charlottenburg-Nussbaumalle *Nummer etwas* they say: Oh *no* Hansi, the real English say *doggie*. (60)

The characteristic intimacy of Pompey's narration undermines whatever formality might inhere to the archaic address to the Reader, implicating each one of us in her prejudices about Jewish foreigners.[15] Smith's italicization of "doggie" furthers this transformation of diverse readers into intimately known Englishmen and women, by making Lottie's use of this most English of words seem like a phrase in need of translation, equivalent to *Nummer etwas* in its strangeness and pretension. Similarly, Fifi becomes an expression of Lottie and Horace's foreign code of values because he earns their love despite his broken or double-jointed front knees. Pompey tells us that "English people would say with those knees he would have been better dead" (60). Like Pompey's comments about being all shot up at Leonie's party upon discovering she's the only goy, her comment on the English response to Fifi's pathetic knees is only funny if we validate it in terms of what Spalding calls Smith's "shock tactics" (68).

Trying to understand Pompey's anti-Semitic barbs at the beginning of *Novel*, Spalding suggests that such shock tactics allow Smith to "undercut conventional expectations of the novel with her flippant, self-reflexive style" and to confront "the inadmissible: that Jews, despite her friendship with them, are somehow alien to Pompey" (68). Conceding that Smith might have shared some of Pompey's sense of alienation from her cosmopolitan Jewish friends, Spalding asserts, "No truly anti-Semitic writer would have made Pompey the focus for anti-Semitic sentiments as Stevie does. . . . Through Pompey, Stevie mocks those who pretend racism does not exist" (68). Spalding provides a generous and fair interpretation of the potential progressive meanings of Smith's representations of Jews with parallels to the position I describe above, but it is important to acknowledge the more destructive meanings and effects that may also emerge from these representations.[16]

In *Novel* Pompey exclaims over the joys of being a goy and a Londoner and adds,

> I have a lot of Jewish friends. It makes me feel januslike, doublefaced. Nobody knows but me what I think about that thing. But I get behaving as if they did know, and I had to pipe down and apologize, and not seem to be taking credit for the happy accident of Nordic birth. (11)

Pompey is so coy and facetious, her mockery bouncing back against herself as well as her many Jewish friends, that it would seem foolish to take at face value her statements about honoring the accident of Nordic birth. But Pompey seems to acknowledge the limited protection such self-implicating irony might provide in her statement about feeling "januslike, doublefaced." Certainly her Jewish friends suspected double-dealing. Smith wrote in an October 1936 letter to Rupert Hart-Davis, "I am getting rather isolated now because a great many of my not-so-dear friends will no longer speak to me—Rosa, Herman, all the Larry-party crowd, and Leonie more in sorrow than anger has withdrawn because she thinks I am an anti-Semite (if that is the word)" (*MA* 256).

The loss of friends was repeated in 1946, when Smith based her story "Enemy Action," on her observations of the troubled marriage of her friends Margery and Francis Hemming.[17] Francis Hemming not only threatened to drop Smith from his acquaintance if she published the story, but told her he intended to sue for libel. Smith's response was to write "The Story of a Story" about the reactions of a writer-protagonist, Helen, whose male friend, Roland, threatens to sue her for libel if she publishes a story based on her observations of him and his wife Bella. At the end of "The Story of a Story" Helen recounts a dream in which she is "standing up in court accused of treachery, blasphemy, theft and conduct prejudicial to discipline" (*MA* 57). The dream-Roland accuses her of "go[ing] into houses under cover of friendship and steal[ing] away the words that are spoken" (57). When Smith published "The Story of a Story" in 1946, the Hemmings, like the Jacobsons, felt betrayed and cut Smith out of their lives. This biographical anecdote tells us nothing about the degree to which Smith shared Pompey's anti-Semitism, but shows Smith's anticipation of her friends' horrified reactions to her artistic use of details from their private lives. Biographical research suggests that she did not lose her Jewish or gentile friends naively, but in full knowledge of the threats her publications would pose.

Perhaps the most poignant loss of friendship Smith suffered from her theft of her friends' words occurred with the publication of "Beside the Seaside" in 1949. Smith's biographers trace the parallels between the events in this story and Smith's August holiday with Betty Miller and her family in 1948. Miller, a successful writer, was also important for gathering at her home "a kind of Hampstead set" of novelists and editors that included Smith, Holden, Naomi Lewis, Cicely Mackworth, Kay Dick, and Marghanita Laski (Barbera and McBrien, *Stevie* 156). Barbera and McBrien record that Miller ended the friendship with Smith upon finding her family used so "unpleasantly" in "Beside the Seaside." The two biographers speculate that the cause of Miller's parting from Smith was Smith's representation of her Jewish character's anxieties about English anti-Semitism and the narrator's unsympathetic, even shocking, response to expressions of those fears.

Margaret, the wife and mother in the story, tells Helen, the Smith-like narrator, that her husband is "more locked up in being a Jew than it seems possible" (*MA* 19).

Oh dear, thought Helen. "Well," she said, "you are Jewish too, aren't you, and you do not feel locked up in it."

"No," said Margaret. "But, Helen, you cannot know quite what it is like; it is a feeling of profound uncertainty, especially if you have children. There is a strong growing anti-Jewish feeling in England, and when they get a little older, will they also be in a concentration camp here in England?" (*MA* 19)

Barbera and McBrien quote fully Helen's "shocking" reply to Margaret's fears, which begins with the words, "'One sometimes thinks that is what they [Jews] want,' said Helen flippantly, getting rather cross, 'they behave so extremely. Well, that is rather an extreme remark of yours, is it not, about the concentration camps, eh, *here?*'" (*MA* 19). They note, "Perhaps Betty Miller's anger came in part from her reaction to this passage" (*Stevie* 157). Spalding also finds in this section of the story possible cause for Miller's sense of betrayal, but she speculates that what upset Miller was the exposure of her husband, the public revelation that Miller had confided to a friend otherwise hidden conversations and details from her marriage.[18]

Whatever the precise story contents that caused Betty Miller to make the decision to exclude Smith from her life and home, the fictional Margaret is submissive in the face of Helen's intolerance. Helen's "Oh dear," shares with the reader rather than Margaret a sense of exasperation over an implicitly well-worn, presumably neurotic preoccupation. Helen's cross suggestion that English Jews want incarceration is absurd and flippant, but not funny. Unlike the materials from *Novel* that aroused readers' suspicions of anti-Semitism, the passage from "Beside the Seaside" is not satiric or ironic and leaves no room for doubt about the protagonist's feelings about Jews. Helen tells Margaret,

I do not hold with the theory that the Jewish people is an appeasing, accommodating people, knowing, as some say, on which side their bread is buttered, and prepared to make accommodations with conscience for their own advantage. No, I think that they are an obstinate and unreasonable people, short-sighted about their true interests, fanatical. They have not the virtues of a slave, you see, but also they have not the virtues of a wise person. (*MA* 19)

The theory about Jews that Helen rejects is insulting in its assumption of a biologically or culturally based quality of appeasement, an implicitly immoral or at least ignoble willingness to bend conscience to serve personal or group advantage. Yet Helen's alternative racial theory, that Jews are obstinate and unreasonable, blind, fanatical, slave-like, is equally offensive and irrational. This offensiveness is compounded by the potential distance between the story's publication date and the date in which it is set. It is not clear if Helen and Margaret are talking in the peacetime of the mid-1930s or the late 1940s. In either case, however, Helen's characterization of Margaret's fear that English Jews will be someday enclosed in concentration camps as "extreme" seems itself blind and naive. If the story is set in the peacetime of the mid-1930s, Margaret is perfectly justified in considering her family at risk in the face of Mosley's rallies and Hitler's intent to take over the Western world. If the story is set in the peacetime of the late 1940s, on the other hand, she is justified in considering her family at risk in the face of postwar rioting against Jews in Britain.[19]

Comparing Helen's characterization of Jews in "Beside the Seaside" to Pompey's representations of Jews in *Novel* lets us see more clearly Smith's dependence on notions of Jewish difference for her narratives' constructions of Englishness. In both narratives of 1949 and 1936, Jews are imagined as eccentric to the English and Englishness. While Margaret is not as foreign as Lottie, her worries make her guilty, in Helen's mind, of a false understanding of who and what the English are. Helen knows that real English people do not put up concentration camps and do not accuse other English people of wanting to put up concentration camps.[20] More interesting, the qualities that Helen selects to stereotype Jews (while seeming to set Margaret apart from her own family and from Helen's stereotype), are very different than the qualities Pompey highlights in her stereotypes of Jews in *Novel*. In contrast to Helen's characterization of Jews as "unreasonable," in Smith's first novel Pompey stereotypes Jews as having an admirable "practical intelligence" (103). This racial characterization is again different from the one that emerges from the pages of *Over the Frontier*.[21]

In Smith's second novel, there are no female Jewish characters and with the exception of Igor Torfeldt, the "blond Jew," the Jewish men of *Over the Frontier* are older, extremely rich, and resigned to their persecutions and their gold. More enigmatic because more symbolic than Pompey's friend, old Aaronson of Ool, is "Israel, lord of the hidden river," one of the directors meeting in the City with Pompey's employer, Sir Phoebus, and an imperialist colonizer. The significance of the financial dealings, dealings that presumably will shape England's approach toward war and conquest all over the world, differs for each man. Pompey parodies Sir Phoebus for his belief that gold means escape from boredom, Empire-Blue-Eyes for his belief that gold means satisfaction of his lust for pride and power (94), and Israel for a presumably well-tried belief that gold means "Unity, flexibility, secrecy, control" (86). To each Pompey instructs, "O.K. boy, keep it under your hat." Her frivolous advice hides her real anger at all these players with their privilege and power. Certainly Israel of the weary eyelids comes off no worse than Empire-Blue-Eyes, but Pompey's emphasis on the almost mythic status of Israel's search for "unity, flexibility, secrecy, control"

("Israel has lapped round that course already so many times, so many many times" (86)) anticipates her repetition of another myth about Jews: "None but the Jews would have survived their persecutions." Repeating while parodying the absurd stereotype of the Jewish financier, just as she both repeats and parodies the absurd stereotype that Igor inspires ("the very best type of young Jew—*like Our Lord*"), Pompey's irony shows little awareness of the special dangers deployment of Jewish stereotypes holds for a society hypersensitive to any signs of anti-Semitism (75). The best that can be said for her is the worst she knows about herself; that those who persecute and betray the Jews do so after saying, "Some of my best friends are Jews."[22] Bitterly, if not ironically, when Smith wrote these words in *Over the Frontier*, she could not echo Pompey and say, "Some of my best friends are Jews" since her Jewish friends had, by and large, rejected her.

In *Over the Frontier* Pompey's best friends are Harriet and Josephine, English gentiles, not English or foreign Jews. Her rock is Auntie Lion, to whom she both must and cannot return. Aunt is an embodiment of what Pompey represents as the best Victorian-style English virtues: "she is so reasonable, so balanced, so sound, and yet so kind and practical" (95). Late in the narrative, having said farewell to Aunt and Bottle Green, Pompey still muses about the English character, probing ever deeper into what we now would call her imagined community. She remembers the war stories of her gentle friend Ian, who told her that the British would have murdered their own grandmothers during a campaign in Archangel, Russia. Having described the English bayoneting of Russian soldiers, Pompey asserts that "Cruelty à l'Anglaise" is battle cruelty: "British do not maim or mutilate" (65).[23] An absurd statement given the evidence of history (presumably the "uneasy ghosts" Pompey alludes to), this claim is most usefully understood as part of Pompey's effort to defend her English nationalism in the face of her growing suspicions that it indirectly contributes to the tide of cruelty sweeping through Europe.

Over the Frontier, unlike Smith's other two novels, tries to describe English nationalism and English character in terms of empire building, military campaigns, and sturdy, no nonsense colonial administration rather than Aunt and her suburban home. Pompey dismisses sentimental and hypocritical rhetoric that tries to excuse England's self-interested motives for conquest, claiming for herself the higher ground of truth with the words, "I understand the motives of my country" (100). Translating a history of English imperialism into animal metaphor, Pompey states "England colonizes because England is a colonizing animal," an animal imagined more precisely as "Our so darling pet Lion of these British Isles" (98, 105). Proud of this Lion as she is proud of her Aunt, Pompey yet separates herself and the rest of England's poets from the feline body of the nation. The poet's job is "to trouble the Lion's dreams with the prods and pains he at times so richly deserves" (106). Yet once turned soldier, Pompey the once-prodding poet, is no longer able to enjoy the luxury of judging the Lion from the outside. She becomes the Lion, representing England and Englishness in a fight that pits the "dotty idealismus" of the enemy against the pragmatism of English mercenaries and their ragtag troops. Pompey boasts, "In England there is no national ideology, or not one that is formed, to be carried through, to be expressed in a word and impressed upon a people, as in Germany it is expressed and impressed" (255). Yet in the last two pages of the novel Pompey admits "I have been mistaken," no longer exempting herself or her country from responsibility for the brutal consequences of decisions made by men directing London board rooms and European battlefronts. She wonders, horrified, if

> we cannot achieve in our individualities this power are we any less guilty if we pursue it, or again, abandoning the sweet chase, identify ourselves with a national ethos, take pride in our country, in our country's plundering, or, if the mood takes us, in our country's victories upon other fields less barren, in science, art, jurisprudence, philosophy? Ours is the privilege, to us the laurels. (272)

Pompey's fall from grace is, like all such falls, a fall into knowledge. The innocence of national pride, of her delight in the sleek and darling English Lion, is revealed as a form of the base self-interest that is related to the emotions guiding the ruthless Generalissimo Clever-Pie. Considering her life from within her room at Mentz, Pompey locates the origins of her decadence and self-delusion in Bottle Green rather than her adventures over the frontier. After all, it is her memories of the torments of suburban love, not her anticipation of foreign war service, that set her book "to anger and disturbance" (29).

Though the end of *Over the Frontier* is somber, its most urgent, probing questions are always connected to its most comic moments. A perfect example of this is Pompey's story about those Bottle Green wives who seem to take such pride in their husbands' bullying:

> [It] is as if they would say, You may not think it but I am married to a tiger. No, I did not think it, for certainly I cannot penetrate this excellent disguise that this tiger has adopted, for certainly no better disguise for a tiger exists anywhere than the disguise of a Bottle Green husband. (215)

While Pompey is certainly mocking the women who can find tigers in their meek suburban spouses, her satire points out the relation between the underlying desire—the suburban matrons' embrace of ideals of aggressive, warrior masculinity—and the murderous pride of conquest and battle that Pompey comes to know once she goes over the frontier. The part of Pompey that is still a poet discovers at last that in the act of identifying differences between Bottle Green husbands and, say, conquering colonialists, in the act of dividing them from each other, the nation falls apart. "Oh corruption, of uncertain mortality, *how divide, without a national death*, the springs of our being?" (272; my emphasis). She locates national life, the springs of the English being, in the animal qualities of ferocity, integrity and aloofness that she finds in her Lion Aunt and projects onto Grosz's horse and Harriet's lion. These qualities are unknown to Freddy, the potential suburban tiger-husband and the washed out and abused tiger Flo that Pompey becomes at the end of *Novel*, but even tarnished and corrupted, they define an ideal in which the English discover themselves. Despite the risks she comes to see in this ideal, Pompey finally can't divide herself from it because she cannot bear to separate herself from her nation, from the classical notions of English and Englishness.

The "English" animal qualities Pompey so admires are rarely associated with Smith's Jewish characters. Jews are, in the end, outside her suburb, separated from Pompey's national ideal and debate. As opposed to the classical qualities of Harriet's lion vase, Aaronson, for example, still represents the sentimental romantic, doomed as much by modernity as he is by anti-Semitism, playing Chopin while a mob of chanting students gathers ominously in the streets outside his balcony. Likewise, the Jews of *Novel* are associated with music, decadence, nervousness. They do not create or occupy the pictures that fill Pompey's image-seeking, "leica-memory" (242). In Smith's novels they are as fluid as "pansy-Larry's" piano playing, at best survivors, at worst victims. They are never ferocious, never soldiers, thus never truly English. Smith denies them partnership with the English lions or tigers of the jungle, battlefront, and suburb. And they do not reemerge when Bottle Green does in Smith's intermodern stories, postwar sketches and postwar novel, *The Holiday*.

Intermodern Suburban Fantasies

By the time Smith found a publisher for *The Holiday*, the sleek English Lion of *Over the Frontier* had been worn down to a halting, meager beast. In the first pages of the novel, Celia mourns, "Some days, I said, are long and thin and there is nothing in them, and the peace goes badly, it goes very badly for us, and to-day there is a note to say that America . . . that Russia . . . England, I said, is stretched out and thin" (7). In *The Holiday*, the English are criticized by their allies, restricted to rations, awash with tears. Like the Jews of *Novel* and *Over the Frontier*, they are survivors at best, victims at worst. Though victorious, they are not really conquerors. Smith is all too aware of the bitter paradox that England's successful war effort cost it a superpower status. She makes the threat of further losses to English pride and power, most particularly the loss of India, a source of Celia's grief and increasing dependence on the strength of her Lion Aunt. Auntie Lion is a typical inhabitant of her suburb, a model of the ordinary middle-class citizen who Smith promotes as the backbone of the nation, an icon of Englishness. For better or worse, in *The Holiday* we can know this Englishness without knowing Jews.

The expanded national and political significance of Aunt's saving simplicity in *The Holiday* is anticipated by a few lines in *Over the Frontier* in which Pompey contemplates the failings of Europe's and England's leaders:

> And if the leaders of intellect will have truck with it [a fashionable cruelty], what hope for the crowd? Oh, just the hope that is in the crowd always, to save them by their stupidity from the gross injury the leaders will operate upon themselves to hand down to their children. (58)

The crowd's redeeming stupidity in *Over the Frontier* is analogous to Aunt's salvational virtues in *The Holiday*. In contrast to Celia, a neurotic intellectual writer who finds herself falling victim to modernity and its indignities, Aunt is "strong, happy, simple, shrewd, staunch, loving, upright, bossy" (*The Holiday* 28). She represents the crowd in which Pompey places her faith, the crowd that in *The Holiday* is composed of what Celia calls "the less wealthy sort of middle-class person, such as we have at home" (105). It is important to recognize that this home, this crowd, is celebrated for a distinct suburban geographical and implicitly Christian cultural identity. Smith, in contrast to little Englanders and the modernists, writes texts that locate national feeling in the homely fringes of London.

Although *The Holiday* focuses on a bunch of distraught and aimless cosmopolitan intellectuals—Celia, her cousin Caz, her colleague Tiny, their associates Clem, Basil, Lopez, and Tom—it does so in order to celebrate their strong, staunch opposites in the suburbs. In effect, the gentile intellectuals of Smith's last novel have taken on the role of the Jews in her first two, defining through their difference the virtues that we are to find most thoroughly, admirably English. Celia makes the connection between intellectual eccentrics and nonintellectual crowds explicit in the following passage, emphasizing the need for both if England is to survive:

> If it was not for Basil and Lopez and you and me, and perhaps Tiny, the middle-classes would be unbearable. But also without the middle-classes we should be unbearable. There must be that variety of virtue as of experience.

Basil is strong, simple, with a fine writer's mind and the reasonable faith of an intelligent revolutionary. These people see the middle classes as obstructionist box-dwellers, whose only thought is for themselves and for their families, as if that was not the common thought of the greater part of mankind. The free-blowing revolutionaries, the classless artists, these are the salt of the earth, for they have the power to see a thing while it is yet a long way off. But you cannot make a diet of salt, and it is through the use and practice of the middle-classes that the vision is made actual. (*The Holiday* 105)

Reading this passage autobiographically, with knowledge that Basil is a version of George Orwell, we see the radical difference of eccentricity promoted by Smith's texts from that of the most famous "intelligent revolutionary" of her day. Smith's description of Basil's contempt for the middle-classes as "obstructionist boxdwellers" perfectly evokes Orwell's scathing passages about George Bowling's neighbors in *Coming Up for Air*. Her alternative to such contempt, recognition of intellectuals' dependence on the ordinary (working) middle classes, expands our understanding of what Smith might call the "variety of virtue as of experience" that is the goal of this study to locate in the spaces between modernisms.

The radical eccentricity of Smith's vision of middle-class, box-dweller heroism is even more apparent if we turn from comparisons of Bottle Green and Bowling's West Bletchley to comparisons of Bottle Green and nonfictional descriptions of contemporary London suburbs. Written without Orwell's engaging venom or satirist's sense of protest, such accounts still validate Orwell's portrait of a permanently transformed English landscape. Put simply, "London and its outskirts became Greater London in the interwar period" (Bowdler 103). Known during the early decades of the twentieth century as the "outskirts" and "fringes" of the capital, London's suburbs quite literally achieved their regional identity as intermediate or in between spaces—between town and country, commerce and agriculture, concrete and nature, crowds and calm. Semi-detached houses, arterial roads, new underground stations, building societies, mortgages, vanishing woods, disappearing hedgerows, consumed villages, diverted streams—all of these geographical signs of tremendous social change accompanied the post–World War I mandate to build "Homes Fit for Heroes." Accompanying these changes was a corresponding shift in Jewish settlement. Just like other Londoners, Jews increasingly chose to move from the city to the suburbs. Yet the geographical signs and cultural consequences of this shift are not mentioned by the social scientists who tell the story of London's intermodern development. The Jews are invisible, even though the suburbs in which they chose to live—places like Golder's Green, Hampstead, and Hendon— are often mentioned in suburban case studies.

Suburbs had existed as identifiable regions in landscape and the public imaginary long before the 1919 Housing or Addison Act led to the first interwar development boom.[24] However, never had suburbs so troubled people's ideas of what it meant to be a Londoner or be English.[25] As John Carey documents, most intermodern intellectuals found the suburb so distressing that in their writings they came to equate suburban geography with a degraded humanity, treating both with contempt.[26] Many fantasized, in private if not public forums, that the suburbs and their inhabitants would disappear.[27] Given that some of these same intellectuals wished that the Jews would also disappear, it is worth asking if Jewish movement to the suburbs had anything to do with the widespread contempt for suburbia that Carey analyzes. Without readily available social science studies on Jewish movement to the suburbs, the question cannot be answered. The connection between intermodern English anti-Semitism and "anti-suburbanism" is only an intriguing possibility that by necessity hovers unexplored between the lines of this argument.

Smith never joins her contemporaries in wishing the suburbs or Jews away, although she is not immune from the widespread tendency of conflating suburban homes with the people living inside them. On the contrary, in *Novel*, her short stories, in a few poems, and in the sketches "Syler's Green" and "A London Suburb," the suburb becomes the most vital site for discovering the meaning of Englishness during the intermodern years.[28] This Englishness depends on stereotypes just as much as the Englishness Pompey creates out of her relation to Jews at the beginning of *Novel* and in the middle of *Frontier*. However, instead of knowing true Englishness through a process of dissociation, of recognizing and valuing Pompey's few "English" differences from Rosa and the Jewish Larry-party crowd, we discover it through a process of identification, of dismissing difference and valuing Pompey's few similarities to Aunt and the gentile suburban crowd. Smith's writing uses the intermodern "Jewish problem" and intermodern "suburban problem" to frame her construction of a new, nonrevolutionary, nonaristocratic, non-imperial ideal of Englishness, one that can defend against and ultimately overwhelm the politics, sympathies, and cruelties of Fascism or any other "-ism" that Auntie Lion might label "stuff and nonsense."

Three different cultural contexts illuminate the relations between suburban geographical fact and suburban literary fantasy and show the importance of these relations for the study of Smith's interrogations of English anti-Semitism and nationalism. First and most important is a geographical context defined by the architectural, social, and economic landscape of the London suburbs that were taking over the village and countryside, two regions traditionally regarded as the base of English national feeling. Second is the context of popular literature represented by two peculiar kinds of intermodern books, the ramble book and the series novel. Each of these popular subgenres represents a nostalgic effort to reclaim the lost world of pre-suburban, and implicitly more thoroughly gentile England at the very moment suburbs were perceived as England's most dynamic, developing regions. Third is the context provided by contemporary literary criticism that treats intermodern suburban spaces, both real and imaginary, but is typically biased toward texts written by intellectuals who tend to demonize the suburbs and their inhabitants. Taken together, these contexts provide a framework for understanding the cultural and political significance of Smith's affectionate, satirical representations in fiction, poetry, and sketches of her lifelong home, the (non-Jewish) suburb Palmers Green.

Homes Built for Heroes

The story of the interwar suburb starts during World War I, when the Ministry of Munitions became the first arm of the central government to involve itself in suburban residential building. Following the example of the London County Council, the Ministry formed estates that were designed for workers in munitions and areoplane factories (Bowdler 103). Such direct involvement on the part of the central government in suburban development was unusual. After the war, the government's involvement was represented by the 1919 Housing or Addison Act that came out of Lloyd George's Homes Fit for Heroes movement. In geographer Roger Bowdler's words, the Addison Act "encouraged the building of suburban housing and thereby enshrined—for the first time in official housing policy—the desirability of the suburb" (105). The London County Council estates, some of the largest estates in Europe, were the most dramatic instance of suburban housing created from this Act. The LCC oversaw the development of the huge Bellingham, Downham, and Beacontree estates, the latter eventually housing some 120,000 people (108). Government policy-makers and developers regarded such scale as necessary for cost reduction and as a response to the ever-expanding population of the capital. And that expansion was astonishing. John Stevenson records that "the south east of England absorbed almost two-thirds of the total population increase of the whole country during the interwar years and the London conurbation increased from 7 1/2 million people in 1921 to 8 1/2 million by 1939" (95). Stevenson sees in the mushrooming suburbs of London and in the new industrial estates of the mid-1930s signs of England's recovery from the Depression and support for his argument that the 1930s deserve to be remembered as much for the affluence they brought to a majority of the population as for unemployment and hunger marches they brought to the distressed areas (92).

PTO &
see Manner

Emphasizing the astonishing growth of the period that gave birth to the Beacontree estates or the acres of semi-detached houses on the fringes of London, Bowdler and Stevenson imply that the terrible housing needs of Londoners, and especially working-class Londoners, were met through good policy and enlightened development—that the heroes did for the most part find homes. A very different perspective emerges from Deirdre Beddoe's *Back to Home and Duty*. Rather than focusing on the completed suburban houses, her feminist history emphasizes the social impacts of incomplete or inadequate housing development. She too mentions that 1920s housing was seen as a reward for masculine military service, but notes that "housing was a woman's issue" and a fraught women's issue at that (90). According to Beddoe, "In 1918 the housing shortage stood at 600,000, five times its pre-war level" (90). Yet even such an appalling statistic about housing needs was not enough to inspire response by middle-class policy makers. It took rent strikes by urban women, among other things, to focus the middle-class public's eye on the shortage of moderately priced, adequately comfortable housing (Beddoe 90).

The housing problems of families and city planners brought tremendous opportunities for builders, estate agents, and building societies, all of whom were delighted that a significant percentage of the London renting population was turning itself into suburban homeowners (Bowdler 105). Orwell, the most famous of the intermodern rebel writers, expresses an entirely conventional horror upon witnessing this transformation. As readers may recall, in *The Clergyman's Daughter*, displaced villager and amnesiac heroine Dorothy Hare is saved from destitution by a distant cousin who finds her a job as a suburban schoolmistress. Dorothy goes to work for the awful Mrs. Creevy of Ringwood House Academy for Girls on Brough Road in Southbridge. Orwell describes Southbridge as "a repellent suburb ten or a dozen miles from London" (214). He continues viciously:

> Brough Road lay somewhere at the heart of it, amid labyrinths of meanly decent streets, all so indistinguishably alike, with their ranks of semi-detached houses, their privet and laurel hedges and plots of ailing shrubs at the cross-roads, that you could lose yourself there almost as easily as in a Brazilian forest. (214)

In other words, Southbridge is Orwell's heart of darkness.

By 1939, when *Coming Up for Air* appeared in the bookstands, Orwell still chose to represent the London suburb as a kind of hell on earth, the worst lie Western civilization had to offer its own natives. The first fifteen pages of the novel are a gleeful excoriation of the widely publicized amenities of the suburb. Orwell's hero, George or "Fatty" Bowling, comments:

> When you've time to look about you, and when you happen to be in the right mood, it's a thing that makes you laugh inside to walk down these

streets in the inner-outer suburbs and to think of the lives that go on there. Because, after all, what is a road like Ellesmere Road [that is, his road]? Just a prison with the cells all in a row. A line of semi-detached torture-chambers where the poor little five-to-ten-pound-a-weekers quake and shiver, every one of them with the boss twisting his tail and the wife riding him like the nightmare and the kids sucking his blood like leeches. (12)

The crux of the problem for both Georges—Bowling and Orwell—is political. The poor five-to-ten-pound-a-weekers think they own their houses and "have what's called 'a stake in the country.'" The insidious effect of this conviction is that the lower-middle-class inhabitants of Orwell's suburb are turned into the "devoted slaves" of the Cheerful Credit Building Society, Sir Hubert Crum, its baronet chieftain, and the capitalist ideology that legitimizes the predatory actions of both. In other words, by 1939 Orwell and his fictional spokesman do not just repeat Orwell's earlier criticism about the soul-stifling effects of the suburb's endlessly repeating structures, but are critical of the political effects such physical conformity represents. As Bowling notes, any one of the "poor downtrodden bastards sweating his guts out to pay twice the proper price for a brick doll's house . . . would die on the field of battle to save his country from Bolshevism" (15).

Although *Coming Up for Air* is certainly unusual in its suggestion that suburban development was part of a governmental policy to suppress Bolshevism, many people in the years between the wars voiced Orwell's complaint about the suburbs' tendency to sprawl—to eat up the English countryside and replace it with "Haphazard and restless ugliness" (Jackson 113). For a nation that had turned to images or fantasies about its countryside and villages to identify and understand itself, it is easy to understand how English people outside of London or even those inside the city center saw the gobbling up of grass and woodlands as an assault upon their heritage and national identity. Orwell is again representative of feelings popular among elites. In *Keep the Aspidistra Flying*, Gordon Comstock finds temporarily relief from the strains of his ongoing war on money by rambling in the countryside twenty miles outside London. Orwell's fictional woods fall before the novel's promised suburban pleasures. *Aspidistra's* ironic ending replaces bucolic scenes with nothing other than Gordon's unconvincing vision of redemption in a suburban life defined by marriage, babies, a villa, a radio, an aspidistra, and a place in the "strap-hanging army" (238).

Study of geography points to the material supports of Orwell's and other intermodern writers' suburban fictions. During the interwar years, Londoners had to reconcile themselves to advertised suburban satisfactions instead of bucolic renewal since development was making an irreversible claim on traditionally rural English countryside. In the fifty years between

1870 and 1930 the acreage of grassy lands in Middlesex fell by half, the numbers of cattle by three-fourths. Acre upon acre of agricultural land was developed; by the outbreak of World War II, hundreds of thousands of new houses covered countryside that had once defined and separated detached, autonomous villages like Hornchurch, Ruislip, and Morden as recently as the end of the previous war (Bowdler 114). Like Gordon Comstock, suburbanites learned to exchange the benefits of proximity to villages and woods seen as authentically English for the benefits of having an expanded, modern public transportation system linking them to the city's center. By the mid-1930s, 2.5 million people were traveling every day within greater London. In part as a consequence of such movement, "the commuter [came to challenge] the Cockney for the title of the Typical Londoner" (Bowdler 114).

Michael T. Saler's study of the London Underground in interwar London tells an engrossing story about the growth of the Underground under the direction of Frank Pick, the autocratic executive on the London Passenger Transport Board. Pick's passions and vision made possible the real and imagined ascendancy of the commuter in interwar London. Pick wanted to wed the social ideals of the nineteenth-century arts and crafts movement to modern art and postwar transportation technology in order to create a new community or corporate identity for London. He believed that the underground tracks would give the above ground metropolis a coherent shape, transforming what he and many critics saw as a sprawling, incoherent city into a bounded whole. Modern art was to provide the means by which Pick hoped to achieve this ideal. He commissioned artists like Charles Holden to fashion a unified style for the Underground, from the design of its waste bins to the architecture of its stations (27–28).

Pick's determination to achieve a whole or wholesome London is a prominent example of the kind of trouble the suburbs posed to the Londoner's imagination. Where was London amid the sprawl? How could it be recognized? Even named? Pick and Orwell, in their very different ways, represent highbrow approaches to the problems of regional identity posed by the suburb. The following examination of two lowbrow forms of writing, "ramble books" and series novels, shows how a mirror image of the troubled suburban fantasies of elites can be found in popular literature.

Rambles in the Outer Circle

In both ramble book and series fiction, nostalgia for the lost countryside and village motivates the book's plot, setting, and, one assumes, readership.

Such attractive nostalgia for lost geographical and social forms emerges out of the suburban destruction of greenery that these books implicitly lament. Paradoxically, such books would have found a part of their audience in the Gordon Comstocks of London, the members of the strap-hanging army who only found the daily journey bearable through the distraction of novels, even novels that omitted or even regretted their very existence (Bowdler 111).

The ramble book is exemplified by titles like *The Fringe of London: Being Some Ventures and Adventures in Topography* (1925) or *Where London Sleeps: Historical Journeying into the Suburbs* (1926).[29] All of these ramble books boast an avuncular first-person narrator who is bent on discovering the old or historical (the authentic) within the new suburban terrain. We need look no farther than the forced pseudo-eighteenth-century prose style of the extended subtitle of *The Fringe of London*—"on rambling round the outskirts of London, and of the unexpected turns, trials, and triumphs that lie in the path of the wayfarer"—to discover the depth of yearning for the past that undergirds these ramble books. The genteel, tedious nostalgia of the following passage from *Where London Sleeps* is also exemplary:

> Londoners live and sleep in places that in one's lifetime had been remote and inaccessible. The City, London's magnetic pole, attracts to itself for the working day a vast army of black-coated toilers numbering hundreds of thousands, who pour out again at dark, homewards . . . . (Bell vii)

By comparing suburbanites, and thus, we assume, his readers, to the undead of Dante's hell or Eliot's *Waste Land*, the author exposes the way suburbs challenged Londoners' regional identity. On the one hand suburbanites are outsiders who do not know London history and thus are not true Londoners. On the other hand, such outsiders can be taught to see London's "authentic" pre-suburban history and thus to recognize their true responsibilities and identities as Londoners.

A more entertaining example of such instructive confusion over regional identity is evident in Thomas Burke's *The Outer Circle: Rambles in Remote London* (1921). This ramble book distinguishes itself by mocking the ineptitude and ignorance of the urban narrator-rambler as much as that of the suburban subjects under review. In other words, its classical pastoral dynamic is more expertly diverting than that of the other ramble books, although it too reveals the ambiguous status of the suburb in the Londoner's imagination. Burke's narrator, a Londoner, begins by admitting a "shameful incident"; he got lost in London during Armistice Week. This unthinkable catastrophe happened as he was trying to escape by bus from the chaos of visiting revelers. When the bus deposits all riders in the dark of "Sherrick Green" he is aghast to learn from a shop keeper that he is not in "Middlesex or Hertfordshire" but his own native town:

> Ten minutes to Willesden. I was in London, then—at Sherrick Green, N.W. I stood on the deserted pavement and burned with shame. Sherrick Green, London; and I had never heard of it! A corner of my own city, where men ate and slept, and loved and hated; where tradesmen built bonny businesses; where babies were born; where children went to school and grew into men and women; and I knew not of it. Other remote suburbs I knew and loved. I had seen the lilac bushes exterminated from Crofton Park. I was about when the tramway was extended from Tooting to Hampton Court. I had watched the steady surge of houses from Lewisham to Sidcup . . . Yet Sherrick Green I had cut. (11–12)

Trivial as it may seem, this writing is doing interesting cultural work of transforming suburbanites into Londoners. While intellectuals might have preferred that Burke try to transform suburbanites into Bolsheviks, it is only fair to note that his narrative seems to be built out of and to support the same suburban fantasies as Orwell's more highbrow fiction. For both Orwell and Burke, redemption is located in the grand cycles of loving and begetting that transpire behind identical suburban doors. Of course, the narratives assume their readers can appreciate the absurdity of their mock-heroic visions, and are able to chuckle gently, or in Orwell's case, bitterly, at the notion of building a regional identity out of prams, radios, and commuter trains.

Books like *The Outer Circle*, which tried to minimize the claims of the suburbs on Londoners' regional identities, had to compete with unapologetic celebrations of suburbs in publicity pamphlets like *The Story of Golders Green and Its Development* (1923). Published by Messrs. Ernest Owers, Ltd., Auction and Estate Offices, *The Story of Golders Green* is not written to translate suburban into urban history, but to show without irony "the remarkable growth of the district in very recent years."[30] Packed with fold-out maps, tables on general district rates and poor rates and graphs of birth and death rates, population growth, and commuter statistics, its only humorous contents are its advertisements. All the earnest endeavor of local champions is still felt, years later, in the proud announcement that "J. Richards Ltd., The Dairy Specialists" has branches throughout Golders Green, Hampstead, and Hendon. More telling is the proclamation in big capital letters in the center of the ad that this is LONDON'S SAFEST MILK. This bold cry distills all the fascinating contradictions of the suburban space between: the bold assertion of purity, of a superiority implicitly derived from a historic connection to freely romping cows (London's SAFEST milk), and the underdog yearning to be seen as part of, while competing with, the larger entity, London, that defines and determines the fate of J. Richards, Ltd., and Golders Green more generally.

This slender book concludes with a chapter titled "Why Golders Green Succeeded," listing the things about which suburbs have always boasted: convenient access via public transportation to the city center, on the one hand, and open spaces made for easy development and access to "natural beauties" on the other. (He does not indicate whether there are any synagogues.) It is telling that the author measures the success of Golders Green through the drastic reduction of the community's unenclosed greens to the wee triangle of common ground in front of the tube station (34). A black and white photograph accompanies the description of this much-reduced green, and it is telling that the "green" memorialized in the suburb's name, cannot be distinguished from the gray of the Underground's paving stones.[31]

Readers who find materials for cynicism and regret rather than rejoicing in the "Story of Golders Green and Its Development" would be likely to enjoy the light, humourous series fictions of P. G. Wodehouse, of Angela Thirkell, E. F. Benson, or even Dorothy Sayers, all of which evoke in novel after novel or story after story a world far removed from the realities of interwar suburban anxiety or alienation. These writers would have depended on an urban audience, among them, let's imagine, a fair number of suburban commuters, for a percentage of their book sales. Yet none were brave enough to place their typically upper-class heroes or heroines in a recognizably suburban environment. Benson's Lucia is in the villages of Riseholme and Tilling when she is not in London; Thirkell's characters contend with the trials of gentle life in the County of Barsetshire (whose maps suggest a striking affinity between Thirkell's territory and Milne's Hundred Acre Wood); Wodehouse's Bertie Wooster drags us along on his vacuous, humourous wanderings about town; and Sayers's Lord Peter Whimsy and Harriet Vane solve their mysteries in the countryside, historic university towns, or London proper. Like the purchasers of the "Stockbroker Tudor" or "By-Pass Variegated" villas that Osbert Lancaster lampoons in *Pillar to Post* (1938), the characters in these series fictions offer the English imagination modernity dressed up in the nostalgic forms associated with traditional English life, what Priestley calls the First or Old England (Lancaster 62–63, 68–69; Priestley 300).

What a Woman Should Be

Like Osbert Lancaster, most intermodern intellectuals denounced the "false art and pretentious vulgarity of the Tudor fake" and resisted the nostalgic

appeals of popular fictional forms (Bowdler 121). Scholars are more likely
to know and remember the suburban satires by these same intellectuals: the
novels by Huxley, Orwell, Wells, Lawrence that Carey catalogs. Certainly
Evelyn Waugh's *Vile Bodies* (1930) deserves mention for containing the passage of suburban satire scholars are most likely to cite:

> Nina looked down and saw inclined at an odd angle a horizon of straggling
> red suburb; arterial roads dotted with little cars; factories, some of them
> working, others empty and decaying; a disused canal; some distant hills sown
> with bungalows; wireless masts and overhead power cables; men and women
> were indiscernible except as tiny spots; they were marrying and shopping and
> making money and having children. The scene lurched and tilted as the aero-
> plane struck a current of air.
>   "I think I'm going to be sick," said Nina. (284)

Carey calls this passage, which appears when Nina and Ginger are leaving
on their honeymoon, "Waugh's verdict on suburban England" (48).[32] He
assumes that right-minded readers will immediately recognize the need to
condemn Nina/Waugh as horrifyingly elitist. Carey doesn't bother to note,
as most critics dutifully do, the ambiguous origin of Nina's nausea (is it
vision of suburbs or tilt of plane?). Nor does he consider how to weigh
Nina's revulsion from the suburb against Waugh's satire of her and the other
vacuous Bright Young People, a satire that is far more devastating than his
satire of the suburbs.

Carey vividly, if not quite fairly, treats the most familiar and famous
modernist or intermodernist authors in the same way he treats Waugh,
selecting a nasty anti-suburban comment out of the context of any given
writer's lived politics or larger literary production in order to illustrate how
elites of all political stripes despised the suburban masses and, in their literary fantasies, created a terrain that is consistent with Hitler's *Mein
Kampf*.[33] Simon Dentith, guided by a similar interest in "high" culture's
relation to the suburb, examines representations of the suburbs in poetry of
the 1930s. He establishes a less depressing version of Carey's intermodern
suburban debate (or what he on second thought calls "the various kinds of
name-calling" that emerged around the "icons of a new degeneracy"—arterial roads, filling stations, cinemas, the wireless, semi-detached bungalows
(108–09)). Analyzing the generic difficulties exposed by poems like
MacNeice's "Birmingham" and sections of "Autumn Journal," he turns to
Smith's "Suburb" (*CP* 81–82), citing twenty-seven lines beginning with the
following:

> Round about the streets I slink
> Suburbs are not so bad I think

When their inhabitants can not be seen,
Even Palmers Green. (qtd. in Dentith 119)[34]

This poem prompts Dentith to ask an important ethical–political question about the relation between poetic speaker and suburban subject; "Does it make a difference here that the point of view of this poem is that of a pedestrian inhabitant of the suburb in question (albeit one who slinks about at night), rather than [MacNeice's] motoring correspondent?" (120). His answer? "Well, it doesn't and it does." It doesn't, in Dentith's view, because Smith employs the problematic "characteristic generic dispositions" of the period—"the reading off of inauthentic lives from inauthentic architecture and the trivial paraphernalia of petty-bourgeois lives" (120). Dentith is also troubled by Smith's "pervasive comic irony at the suburbs' expense," which may keep her from "treat[ing] the lives of the inhabitants of the suburbs with appropriate seriousness" (119). On the other hand, he realizes that Smith does not replicate in her poetry the kind of snootiness he finds in suburban poems by Betjeman, Auden, Day Lewis, and MacNeice. Attempting to define Smith's difference, Dentith concludes rather opaquely,

> The witty and self-mocking misanthropy is aware of no other *social* perspective by which to measure the inhabitants of Palmers Green, so that the ironies of the poem are self-consuming ones. Stevie Smith, in other words, transforms the thematics of thirties suburban poetry in ways that push the poem toward self-destruction or tonal illegibility. (120)

Oddly enough, this judgment is presented as the reason Smith *does* make a difference; it seems to be the positive evidence we're asked to take into consideration before responding to the dilemma of difference that Dentith outlines.

Yet how much comfort can readers really extract from the notion that Smith's poem and speaker achieve self-destruction or tonal illegibility? Isn't this a fancy way of saying, "I can't place this poem" or "This poem doesn't fit into the critical places I have opened up for it"? To see and hear the difference "Suburb" makes for our understanding of intermodernism, we have to accept that Smith, her speaker, even her rhymes and rhythms, are out of place, located somewhere in between known spaces and categories, somewhere between modernisms. Although Dentith dislikes the superficial, superior position of MacNeice's motoring correspondent, at least it helps him figure out how to place the poem, how to read and judge it. "Suburb" 's pervasive comic irony upsets our confidence in our poetic placing skills. It troubles our assumptions about the "appropriate" poetic tone of seriousness, challenging aesthetic and ideological standards that we've inherited from the "high" modernists. Readers who value Smith's "low" comic forms and effects (for example, the silly rhyme "think" and "slink") will find that "Suburb"'s humor produces opportunities for social connection just as much as its irony reproduces relations of social distance. In contrast to Dentith, I argue in what follows that Smith's suburban identifications, no matter how stressed by feelings of disdain or fear, lead us toward a valuable, "different" understanding of the suburbs' " place in 1930s and 1940s writing. Her representations of suburbs are valuable in part because her contemporaries found suburbs troubling, if not contemptible, just as her representations of Jews are valuable in part because many of her contemporaries found them troubling and contemptible.

The geography of the suburbs shaped Smith's life. It seems almost inevitable that James MacGibbon, her literary executor, begins his preface to Smith's *Collected Poems* by noting that "[Stevie] ran the small house, a place of fascinatingly ugly décor, not a stick of which, as far as could be observed, had ever been changed since [her] arrival [at age or four]" (8). Smith commuted for years from Palmers Green into London, working as a personal secretary to baronet publishers Sir Neville Person and Sir Frank Newnes. Her job brought her literary friends and associates, but her suburban home and alliances always kept her on the margins of the cosmopolitan literary culture she sought to enter.[35] Not exactly a suburban housewife nor yet urban intellectual, Smith struggled to orient herself in relation to multiple and seemingly incompatible identities and places. Publication of *Novel* in 1936 helped her find a way out of her exhausting emotional, geographical bind; it allowed Smith to exchange her culturally undervalued status of commuting clerk for the culturally valued status of Author and Novelist without forcing her to change her domestic loyalties or habits.

By the mid-1930s, Florence Margaret Smith had become Stevie Smith. Barbera and McBrien surmise that Smith's transformation meant that "in the manner of most writers she began to lead a double life. 'Peggy' she remained to a segment of her old Palmers Green world, but another self called 'Stevie' was ascendant" (41). It is easy to understand why Smith wanted to keep the ascendant writer-self a secret from the world of Palmers Green; her fiction and poetry often satirized the suburbs and suburbanites Peggy Smith seemed to admire. It is more difficult to understand her decision to stay in Palmers Green year after year, risking exposure and rejection.[36] She probably felt, among other things, that Palmers Green nurtured her art; it makes repeated appearances, in mildly disguised forms, in her intermodern poetry, fiction, and short prose.

Her poem "The Suburban Classes," from the 1937 volume *A Good Time Was Had by All*, is a funny, ironic verse about convincing the suburban classes to commit mass suicide. Its first four lines, spoken in the voice of a self-satisfied official or simply self-satisfied snob, are, "There is far too much of the suburban classes / Spiritually not geographically speaking. They are asses / Menacing the greatness of our beloved England, they lie / Propagating their kind in a eightroomed stye" (*CP* 26). Voicing an absurd extreme of the anti-suburban logic that was so common in highbrow publications, Smith's poem links elimination of suburbanites to the formation of a healthier nation. The mythical suburban vices of unquestioning obedience to authority, quest for fashion, voracious appetites for print and consumer goods, will all be used against them to create a sounder English body. The key is manipulating their nationalist emotions, convincing them that " 'Your King and your Country need you Dead' " (*CP* 26). The poem's humor keeps readers from totally identifying Smith's attitude toward her subject with the contempt of its speaker, although the poem's satire also distances Smith from the inhabitants of Palmers Green.[37]

Novel is more sophisticated suburban satire. Like George Bowling, Pompey Casmilus gleefully exposes the absurd trick or swindle of the suburban promise, but she finds it in the materials of women's lives. She focuses on the evil effects of advice columnists who persuade unmarried women they will only find happiness in marriage, home, and children. In other words, Smith exposes the fantasies that could transform blushing suburban brides into Orwell's Mrs. Bowling, riding her husband like the nightmare. Her vicious satire of young married women's search in suburban dwellings for the fairy tale bliss predicted for them by estates developers and women's magazines recalls the jaundiced view of family life conveyed by the fourth line of "The Suburban Classes": "Propagating their kind in an eight roomed stye." The contempt in both texts can be read as a sign of Smith's sense of superiority to those women Pompey calls "silly fatheads" or conversely, as an attempt to defend herself against their social success, their ability to embody in motherhood the loftiest cultural ideal held out for women.

Smith's fiction demonstrates that she remained sensitive to this cultural pressure and aware of the conflicts it could inspire in the lives of single women years after Pompey "lost" the marriage game in *Novel*. For example, Celia of the postwar novel *The Holiday* tells us that she loves her Aunt and her family life, "but I like also to go out and see how the other people get along, and especially I like to see how the married ladies get along" (27). These ladies at first are flattered by Celia's wondering praises about the amount of attention they direct toward their husbands—"How can you keep it up, Maria?"—but then Celia says,

> they begin to wish not to stress how martyr-like wonderful it is, and they begin to say how much one is missing if one does not have it; so I have had trouble with my married women friends. . . . But I can see that they have to

> do it if they are going to have a darling husband and a darling home of their
> own and darling children, they have to do it, there is no other way, and if you
> do not then you will live lonely and grow up to old solitude. Amen. (28)[38]

Celia, like Pompey, is not condemned to loneliness and isolation. She
shares a home with Auntie Lion, Smith's unlikely hero for an unheroic,
postwar age. More than ever, Aunt stands for a new ideal of Englishness,
one that is rooted in the habits and characteristics of the nation's suburb
dwellers, especially those of the lower-middle class.

Smith's heroines' bravado in the face of various threats, the threat of
marriage with its demands on the one hand and the threat of "old solitude"
on the other, resonates with Smith's reflections on her own youthful attitude
toward marriage. Smith told her friend Kay Dick in the interview that
became *Ivy and Stevie* that she did nearly marry because "At that period I
thought it was the right thing to do, one ought to—that it was the right thing
to do, one ought to—that it was the natural thing to do, hey ho—but I wasn't
very keen on it" (72).[39] Her repetition of the phrase, "it was the right thing
to do, one ought to," her implication that marriage once represented for her
a duty every good English woman would fulfill, conveys her sense of the terrible weight of the social codes that separated conventional from unconventional feminine behavior. In that same interview she confesses not contempt,
but admiration, for women who have children: "Why I admire children so
much is that I think all the time, 'Thank heaven they aren't mine'" (73). This
facetious comment expands upon a sentiment that Smith shared with Naomi
Mitchison upon learning that Mitchison had lost a baby. Noting that "This
child bearing puts a woman at almost as great a disadvantage as advantage,"
she expresses admiration for women who become mothers because the bravery demanded of them in the service of their progeny is of a kind "no timid
selfish person could willingly give" (274).

Barbera and McBrien read Smith's short story "The Herriots" as her
attempt to imagine her way in and out of suburban life with a husband and
child. The heroine of this story is named Peg and, like Peggy Smith, she lives
with an aunt and great aunt who bring her up to think that "men were to
fetch and to carry" (75). Her disillusionment comes when she discovers that
her mother in law, Mrs. Herriot, "unquestioningly put the wishes of the men
first. . . . She felt that she had married into an Indian or Turkish family" (75).
Mrs. Herriot's complaint to Peg's husband, Coke Herriot, about his wife
leads him to strike Peg. This violence, and the quarrels and tears that pre-
cede it, are the family's secret as they struggle with Coke's joblessness, Peg's
depression, the baby's cries, and Mrs. Herriot's intrusions. Relief from the
trials hidden within the suburban flats in the big houses of the prewar
period, in which "nobody could get away from anybody, there were always
nerve storms and people crying themselves to sleep," comes in the form of a

rich eccentric old woman who pays Peg to be her companion (76). When Coke's father retires and Coke assumes his position as traveling plumber, the suburb that has nurtured the nerve storms becomes the haven Peg and Coke always wanted it to be. The suburb, finally, is not exposed as a site of a special kind of hypocrisy, of false promises and secret family strife, but as a space that can offer a distinct kind of safety though it may nurture as well the characteristic (not specifically suburban) stresses of intermodern English life. Those who choose to see Peggy Smith in the fictional Peg may find in Peg's words to her beloved old lady signs of the emotional price Smith paid for choosing to remain with Aunt in Palmers Green: " 'If only we could get away,' said Peg, 'life would be so different. But I love Bottle Green so much, too; sometimes I think I could *not* go away, but always I say this: If we could get away. It is the sort of thing one says, nothing really' " (79–80).

Smith chose precisely those qualities of suburban life that she exposed in her fiction to praise in her sketches on Palmers Green written after the war. In 1947 she wrote for the BBC's "Third Programme" an essay called "Syler's Green," which is a fond recollection of suburban life designed for a nation of listeners grappling with the task of building out of the rubble of the Blitz a viable regional ideal and national identity. In Smith's essay, the suburb is not an upstart community, responsible for destroying countryside and English traditional life, but rather a solid, comforting artifact of English history. While admitting that her suburb has " 'gone down' " in a social sense, "the people are as bustling and happy as ever, and one thing they seem to me to have in quite extraordinary abundance, and that is babies" (96). In this comic but tender piece, the flourishing babies are not the source of despair, but one of the things upon which suburban residents are to be "*envied* and *congratulated.*" The other is their "rich community life" that prevents them from "existing in a bored box-like existence that is what people think of suburb life" (*MA* 97). The key to escape from stereotypical suburban monotony is the greenery of "Syler's Green," its roots in the old country, its preservation of some of the woods that she and her sister once named "Paradise." It is what Smith called in her 1949 essay "A London Suburb" a "true suburb, an outer suburb," one on the peripheries of London, its eccentric positioning a source of strength (103).

In this later sketch, the suburb functions in ways that the country or city center function in the intermodern ramble books or series novels that I've discussed: it is a sign of authentic, traditional English life, the basis for a robust regional identity, a source of inspiration for writers and a comforting nostalgia for readers. Smith, the satirist, sounds like a publicist in the following paragraph:

> The virtue of the suburb lies in this . . . it is wide open to the sky, it is linked to the city, it is linked to the country, the wind blows fresh, it is a cheap place for

families to live in and have children and gardens. . . . And behind the fishnet curtains in the windows of the houses is the family life—father's chair, uproar, dogs, babies and radio. (104)

It is notable that everything Smith lists in this last sentence as indicative of suburban virtue—father's chair, uproar, dogs, babies, and radio—were missing from her home. We can see Smith taking on the role in this radio piece that she granted to Aunt in *The Holiday*, making pronouncements for others that contradict her own social practices. Celia catches Aunt in such a maneuver at the breakfast table when Aunt is telling stories of her childhood, her sad, widowed father, and his wise wife, who "was a good wife to him, she was what a woman should be" (37). But as Celia tells us:

> [T]here was something of the Begum in her eagle managing eye and in the pronouncement "—what a woman should be." Ha, ha, I thought to myself, but there was no He-Begum in your life, no there was not, Alec Ormstrode loved you, but you would have none of him, no, you were not for him "what a woman should be." No, you are the Begum Female Spider who has devoured her suitors and who lives on and makes these crocodile-like pronouncements, and who is like a lion with a spanking tail who will have no nonsense. (38)

Celia's reflections upon her Aunt celebrate the quality of radical eccentricity that I am promoting for those seeking an alternative to Orwell's intermodern heroism. Described as an eccentric by critics of her period and increasingly admired as such by critics of our own, she deserves to be recognized as radical in her departure from the cultural norms for women and in her departure from the literary norms that were defined by the work of the men in the Auden Generation. Recognizing she was not "what a woman should be," Smith drew strength from her position in the outer circles of fashionable literary London, creating a self and literary voice out of the contradictions that emerged in her travels between suburb and city, between gentiles and Jews, between laughter and tears. Many years later, it seems that her special relevance for the history of intermodernism is her confrontation with the painful pieces of a traditional English nationalism, its imperialism, its militarism, and its anti-Semitism, and her creation out of this confrontation of a new ideal of Englishness based on ordinary suburban life.[40] Imperfect herself, she provides us with a near-perfect example of a vital intermodern literature that is radical without being revolutionary, eccentric without being trivial, invaluable in its comic, ill-bred departures from the "high" modernism that has until recently shut up and prevented serious discussion about many intermodern writers and texts.

Chapter 2

Mulk Raj Anand's Passage
through Bloomsbury

Shortly after E. M. Forster published *A Passage to India*, a very young, entirely unknown Indian named Mulk Raj Anand left scandal and school behind in Amritsar to pursue a doctorate in philosophy at the University of London. Anand has often told the story of his passage in the mid-1920s from the streets of the Punjab to the squares of Bloomsbury, but he has rarely commented in any detail on his career at the BBC, his friendships with George Orwell, Stevie Smith, and Inez Holden, or the relation of these things to his highly acclaimed novels of the period. Other scholars have mentioned Anand's contributions to the literary-political culture of 1930s London and Anand himself has playfully tried to recreate that experience in *Conversations in Bloomsbury* (1981), but the details of his life there remain vague.[1] In part this is a problem of record; critics have been too dependent on the older Anand for fuzzy or fanciful recreations of his much younger self.[2] This chapter focuses on writings by or about him written during or immediately after his twenty-year exile in England in order to examine his role as a radical eccentric and analyze his contributions to English intermodernism.

In the 1930s, when Anand enjoyed his greatest popularity in England, his novels in English about India earned him the reputation of being the best Indo-Anglian writer of his generation. They also earned him a reputation as the most revolutionary of India's English-language writers. The ambiguous legacy of this dual reputation—as fine novelist and outspoken revolutionary—parallel Anand's position in the much more intimate group of radical eccentrics. He was at once Dr. Anand, the group's only highly educated member who was esteemed for his warmth and generosity as well as his education and intelligence, and its only "joiner," the sole member of the foursome to attach himself to political groups and parties, including the Indian Progressive Writers' Association, the India League, the Indian Congress Party, and the British Labour Party.[3]

Signs of Anand's political commitment are everywhere evident in his art. Orwell's 1946 reflection on "Why I Write"—"to make political writing into an art"—resonates with Anand's 1946 description of the artist as "an inspiriting force behind all those men and women who face the tasks of reconstructing the future society out of the shambles of a near prehistoric present" (Orwell, *CEJL*, I 6; Anand *Apology* 134). Despite Orwell's and Anand's similar understanding of art's political function, Anand's novels are typically read in terms of Joyce's formal experiments or Forster's Indian settings and subjects. This practice has stuck because Anand was connected to several of Bloomsbury's and ("high") modernism's foremost practitioners. In addition to Forster, he knew Leonard and Virginia Woolf, T. S. Eliot, Edward Sackville-West, John Strachey, and Dorothy Richardson (Cowasjee, *So Many* 27). Yet Anand's Marxist commitment, tutoring by Gandhi, and experiences in Republican Spain point toward his stronger affiliation with the rebel artists who created the literature of the Red Decade. Although Anand himself has encouraged critics to read his 1930s novels through a framework provided by elite early modernism, his books' dedications, his letters, and all his autobiographical commentary of that time suggest that his intermodern writing is most indebted to his friendships and correspondence with Walter Allen, John Cornford, Cyril Connolly, Bonamy Dobree, Lawrence Durrell, William Empson, Ralph Fox, Eric Gill, Victor Gollancz, Aldous Huxley, C. Day Lewis, Jack Lindsay, Louis MacNeice, Henry Miller, Middleton Murray, Naomi Mitchison, V. S. Pritchett, Herbert Read, Montagu Slater, Stephen Spender, Dylan Thomas, Edward Thompson, H. G. Wells, and Orwell, Smith, and Holden.[4]

Modernist or Marxist, Anand's novels are unique to intermodern London for the following reasons: they are exclusively about India and Indians, are the first examples of Indo-Anglian fiction to adopt outcastes or social pariahs as their heroes, use English in a new way to communicate Indian idiom, and integrate into their narratives the political speeches of the period's most prominent Indian political figures, Gandhi and Nehru. More generally, Anand's fiction is seen by some critics as a cornerstone of the first generation of Indo-Anglian writers who came to represent independent and postcolonial India.

In his controversial introduction to *The Vintage Book of Indian Writing, 1947–1997* Salman Rushdie writes, "it was the generation of independence, 'midnight's parents', one might call them, who were the true architects of this new tradition" (xvii). Rushdie's comparison of writers in Anand's generation to "true architects," the real builders or creators of modern India's enduring English prose tradition, encourages us to see Anand's novels as doing something importantly new and innovative. More than thirty years before Rushdie made this judgment, Srinivasa Iyengar, one of Anand's most consistently supportive critics, made a similar argument in his 1962 *Indian Writing in English*.[5] Like Rushdie, Iyengar defends the hybrid genealogies of Indo-Anglian writers and places a similar emphasis on the newness of their enterprise. With less confidence but equal insight he makes a plea for critical open-mindedness since "an experimental literature would thus need an experimental critical approach for its proper evaluation" (Iyengar 20). The invention of "new modernisms" at the end of the twentieth century suggests that the theoretical and critical climate has changed enough to allow recognition of Anand's different kind of "modernist" experiment, as well as the necessity of a new, experimental critical approach to his work.[6]

Untouchable Experiments

Anand first gained the attention of reviewers in 1935 with the publication of *Untouchable*. The novel is about one day in the life of the eighteen-year-old Bakha, a sweeper who cleans public latrines in the morning, suffers the humiliating consequences of touching a caste Hindu mid-day, and by evening has begun to question the necessity of his social ostracism after hearing speeches by Gandhi and Congress Party activists. Anand has written that Bakha's misadventures are based on his memories of an outcaste sweeper boy with whom he played as a youth ("My Experiments" 7–8; "Sources of Protest" 26). As an adult with an awakened socialist consciousness, Anand saw the tragic life course destined for his one-time playmate and wanted to make that tragedy real for English readers who might then apply pressure at "home" for Indian independence. The frustrations that accompanied Anand's attempts to achieve his ideal of political art led him first to Gandhi and then to E. M. Forster. According to Anand, he had already written a draft of *Untouchable* when he encountered Gandhi's tale of Uka, the sweeper boy. Admiring the simplicity of Gandhi's story, he wrote to Gandhi and received in return an invitation to Gandhi's ashram at Ahmedabad in the spring of 1929. There Anand read aloud portions of *Untouchable* to Gandhi, who criticized the novel for turning Bakha into a Bloomsbury intellectual. After three months of heavy rewriting, Anand read the new novel to "the old man" who "more or less approved" ("Why I Write" 5–6). Back in England, *Untouchable* was rejected by nineteen publishers until Forster's decision to write a preface for it convinced the twentieth to accept the book ("Why I Write" 6).

Untouchable was followed in 1936 by *Coolie* and in 1937 by *Two Leaves and a Bud.* Together these novels earned Anand positive reviews in *The Spectator, Life and Letters To-Day, London Mercury,* and *New Statesman,* and leftist publications like the *Left Review* and *Congress Socialist.* Despite this critical acclaim, Anand's name is rarely mentioned in memoirs that evoke London's literary culture during the 1930s. To account for the silence about Anand's years in Bloomsbury this chapter analyzes the relationship between the revolutions created in and by Anand's fictional worlds of the 1930s and his reinvention and reinterpretation of those revolutions in his nonfictional narratives of the 1940s, most importantly his 1942 *Letters on India* and his 1946 memoir, *Apology for Heroism.* It argues that Anand's nonfiction writings of the 1940s provide more daring and concrete visions of his revolutionary socialist ideals than his earlier and more famous novels. Having achieved a literary form adequate to the content of his politics, Anand promptly lost the support of those English leftists who had been the strongest advocates of his earlier work. Sticking to his politics, Anand risked social alienation from his literary peers rather than suffer modification of his views on the necessity of India's immediate freedom from colonial status or his belief that Stalin's betrayal of Britain was no reason for Indians to give up on Stalin or Communism (Cowasjee, *So Many* 30). Ultimately he paid a high literary price for his commitment, losing not only a place in 1930s memoirs, but also a place in English literary history.[7] His contributions to English intermodernism most likely became the casualties of local, literary politics of anticolonial protest and colonial backlash.

My analysis of the gap between the reception in leftist circles of Anand's radical fiction and his radical nonfiction shows that his diminishing reputation had less to do with any failures of his literary imagination, and more to do with many English leftists' allegiance to England's imperial identity and specifically its right to rule India. Anand's ideas were simply too radical for these English leftists to accept. The construction of the Thirties as a "dishonest" decade is in part a consequence of the exclusion of uncompromising Indian nationalists or unrepentant Marxists like Anand from the textual record valued by dominant English intellectuals of his time and in part a consequence of the arbitrary designation of the 1930s, rather than 1940s, as the only radical decade of the early twentieth century.[8] Adoption of the category of intermodernism solves some of the problems resulting from the unfortunate, sticky label "dishonest decade" in part because it diminishes conceptual walls between somewhat arbitrarily defined periods: the Thirties, the Forties. Although I use the traditional period categories in my discussion of Anand's work, my larger argument is indebted to thinking across boundaries between genres and periods, of recognizing Anand's writings as part of one intermodern movement sustained, in various forms and with differing sociopolitical effects, throughout the 1930s and 1940s. Regarding Anand as an intermodernist rather than or in addition to a late Bloomsbury modernist, 1930s radical, or Indo-Anglian (post)colonialist, encourages critics to read and value his less famous texts, providing new rationale for including his name and writings in discussions of literary London during the years Orwell, Smith, and Holden were working there.

Many of Anand's nonfictional 1940s texts draw their rhetorical, ideological power from his contradictory experiences and identifications consequent upon his move to England. On the one hand, he was a highly educated, caste Indian, on the other he was committed to Marxism and international socialism. He advocated for Indian independence, but chose to do so in London, the center of imperial power. As productive as these conflicting allegiances may have been for the political development and imaginative freedom of Anand and his autobiographical heroes, his fictional low-caste heroes do not benefit in the same way. None of these heroes is able to envision a less oppressive, postimperial future for himself or India. Bakha returns to his family and work with little more than the first glimmerings of hope for a better future for untouchables. Munoo, the high-spirited, fourteen-year-old orphan boy from the hills who is the hero of *Coolie*, is propelled from one deplorable job to another in cities in every corner of India. The novel ends with his death from consumption while he is employed as a personal servant and rickshaw driver of a degenerate Anglo-Indian woman. Even *Two Leaves and a Bud*, which provides more concrete images of Anand's socialist belief in the possibilities of collective action, concludes with the defeat of a group of workers seeking better working conditions on a tea plantation and the murder of the novel's protagonist, Gangu, by a predatory Assistant Planter who is absolved by the English of any wrongdoing.[9]

Although Anand does not grant his first three heroes either wealth or happiness, they still represent remarkable feats of the imagination, coming as they do from the pen of someone with a drastically different caste and class background. Equally remarkable is Anand's failure to imagine female characters who are as convincing as his heroes. No matter what their caste or class, Anand's female characters are not realistic representations of women but symbols of Woman. They are drawn from a rich collection of cultural stereotypes—fantasies or nightmares of femininity reduced to its sexual meanings—but are never fully human characters, never equals to Anand's dynamic male protagonists. How could someone who was so adept at humanizing untouchables—of reaching across divisions of caste and class in the interests of a radical politics of equality—prove so inept at humanizing women in these fictions—of reaching across divisions of sex and gender to promote that same kind of politics? Analysis of Anand's problems with fictional women, his reliance on sexist female stereotypes to advance the heroic plots and politics of his novels, provides one of the keys to understanding the rise and fall of Anand's reputation in London literary circles. In the pages that follow, I argue that Anand's reputation in England depended on the conformity of his Indian female characters to Western stereotypes of women found in mainstream English literature of his day. I theorize that without these conforming representations, Anand's politics of rapid and total decolonization and socialization would have been too obvious and unsettling for all but the most stalwart leftists to accept.[10]

Inez Holden's diary entry of 15 December 1941 shows how some of the questions raised by my discussion of Anand's fictional women troubled Anand's understanding of his relations with real women:

> Anand walked homeward with me arm in arm down Oxford Street and Anand told me about his married life. He said he was married to a frustrated actress, an English girl. He said that she was a complete bourgeois but that he had improved her. It was a very complicated story which seemed to be now rather unhappy as far as their personal relationship was concerned. He told me also that she had accused him of acting in a Fascist way towards her, through trying to make her different, more free, more intellectual, more aware and so on. Anand said that he had written to several Indian friends asking them their opinion and if they thought his attitude towards his wife was Fascist. Several of them wrote back and said they thought it was.

While I do not agree with Anand's friends who thought his attitude toward his wife was "fascist," this anecdote does point toward possible connections biographers might one day discover between Anand's social relations and literary representations. No doubt Anand liked women and worked hard to end institutionalized cultural assaults on Indian women. Like many other people, he could love and defend women in some texts even as he advanced denigrating notions about women in those or other texts. It is always possible for progressive advocacy to be undertaken on behalf of nostalgic images or notions. My point here is that Anand's fiction prompts readers to think less of women as people and more of them as sexual objects (either positive or negatively valued) than is consistent with his egalitarian, humanist outlook.[11]

My charge, that Anand objectifies his female characters, is at odds with the majority of criticism that takes on the subject of Anand and women and is at odds with Anand's understanding of himself as a stalwart defender of the rights of women and advocate of their self-determination.[12] To understand the divide between what I see as complex, intentionally progressive, but intermittently sexist fictions and other critics defend as proto-feminist novels, I turn next to Anand's most "feminist" book of the 1930s and 1940s, an obscure nonfictional treatment of women and women's culture called *The Bride's Book of Beauty* that was published in 1947. Beginning at the end of Anand's intermodern career, I seek to establish a framework that prepares readers to see the complexities of Anand's position within Orwell's group of radical eccentrics, within English intermodernism, and twentieth-century English literary history more generally. Like intermodernism without Anand, it turns out that Anand without sexism is just too simple.

The Bride's Book of Beauty

In 1946, the year after Anand left Bloomsbury for Bombay, he and a coauthor, Krishna Hutheesing, finished writing *The Bride's Book of Beauty*, which, more than any other of Anand's intermodern writings, supports Anand's reputation as a feminist fellow traveller.[13] The book was published the next year when India celebrated the transfer of power and mourned national partition. It must have attracted an eclectic audience: perhaps a few brides and bridegrooms, but most likely educated Indian men and women seeking cultural and national affirmation through an English language record and interpretation of a traditional oral women's culture that had grown up around bridal rituals. At turns a conduct manual, feminist polemic, antireligious diatribe, folklore anthology, mythical-Marxist history, recipe book, and oral history, its chapters of prescriptions for "Beauty and the Mind," "Beauty and Health," "The Complexion," "The Mouth and the Teeth," "The Eyes," and so forth, are enlivened by traditional Indian proverbs, aphorisms, and verses, and are illustrated with reproductions of eighteenth- and nineteenth-century paintings and line drawings of Indian women in traditional ornament and garb. The book shows unusual understanding of what twenty-first century readers would call feminist history, condemning the oppression of contemporary Indian women in terms that challenge patriarchal institutions and ideologies of the dominant Indian Hindu and residual British colonial cultures. Its arguments for women's emancipation from the most horrific expressions of this oppression—child marriage, suttee, and cogenerational living—are advanced through original, even fanciful interpretations of Indian history and an unusual knowledge (that is, unusual for an intellectual man) of Indian women's culture.[14] All this is very good and should earn *The Bride's Book* new readers, feminists among them.

The preface of *The Bride's Book* explains its origins and objectives, along with its hybrid generic shape. The authors begin:

> This book has been a joy to write, for the hours we have sat through eliciting information from our friends about the potions and perfumes and necklaces and stones which decked them from the tips of their heads to their painted feet is fresh in our minds. We recall the jokes and pleasantries which greeted our first inquiries about the formulas of beauty, and the amazement which lit up the atmosphere when we pressed for details of closely guarded secrets.

Anand and Hutheesing's confession of their delight in the project seems as sincere as their offers of thanks to the many Indian women who dictated beauty formulas or recipes to them. In part due to the authors' story about their research, their acknowledged debt to female social experience, this text seems to better represent Anand's Marxist, utopian faith in the possibilities of cooperative action and education than his works published for English audiences. Aside from Hutheesing, the women who shared with Anand their knowledge of their sex-exclusive "customs and conventions" remain anonymous, but readers can sense their presence behind the thin veil of the printed word, an invisible, cheerful or squabbling female collective.

Anyone who picks up the book hoping to find romantic or titillating narratives about life as an Indian bride will be thoroughly disappointed. After the romance of the opening citations of India's "charming proverbs" about female beauty ("Moon-faced, elephant-hipped, serpent-necked, antelope-footed, swan-waisted, lotus-eyed" (15)), there's little to arouse sexual appetites in the individual chapters' rather dry descriptions of the beauty rituals. Anand and his coauthor reserve their passion for the book's political discussions, which confront the unsuspecting reader in the first pages of the book. Beginning at the beginning, with myths of origin, the authors observe that while the tales about the creation of woman by Brahma are pleasing, "The actual life of woman in India has been less metaphorical and more sordid" (16). The authors emphasize the disjunction between the ideals of femininity inherited from myth, symbolized by the bridal rituals they record, and the reality of living with a mother-in-law: "Obviously, woman in India has sometimes been exalted as a goddess, but mostly pampered as a doll or kept down and oppressed" (18).[15] Suggestive as this Ibseneque-statement may be of the need for demystification of Indian ideals of feminine beauty, Anand and his coauthor attempt instead to provide an idiosyncratic interpretation of a highly condensed, romance history of Indian women.

Anand and Hutheesing's story begins Edenically, with discussion of Dravidian civilization where there is no "joint family but 'gens' " based on "matrilinear descent under primitive communism" and quickly moves to characterization of nomadic " 'Aryans' who accepted 'the entire sum of that magnificent culture which the Dravidians had perfected' " (19). They expound on the social freedom and honor women enjoyed in this Aryan culture, attempting to glamorize ancient social conditions that they implicitly offer up as an ideal model for independent India. At a climactic moment in their peroration, when they need to capture in one vibrant, persuasive image the elevated possibilities for an implicitly transhistorical Indian Woman, they seize on the religious contexts in which "woman" is granted the status of goddess: "She is 'OM,' the mystic logos, the word or speech or sound, the spouse of the creator, in unison with whom, and through whom, the creator accomplishes his creation." She is, in short, "the embodiment of the poet's dream, the seer's fancy" (19). This is a very pretty vision of Aryan ideals, but it throws into question the depth of the authors' understanding of relations between symbolic woman and social women, between image, discourse, and experience. Slipping back into the rapturous, slightly ridiculous representations of women found in many of Anand's novels, the text at this moment of poetic excess affirms woman as the body of the poet's dream, not the poet, the fancy of the seer, not the seer herself. Caught up in their sentimental vision, the authors forget what they elsewhere promote, the idea that these ancient, Aryan women could, "on their own initiative or jointly with man perform the sacred rites, read the holy books and write them" (20).

This example of *The Bride's Book*'s divided female and feminine ideals throws into relief a peculiar relationship between the authors' style and politics. When the authors write poetically, they slip into canonical, patriarchal images and ideas. When they write prosaically, they work against patriarchal beliefs and institutions. In other words, fulfillment of the authors' good political intentions depends upon the triumph of historical over poetic styles. Feminist readers may find some comfort in *The Bride's Book*'s affinity with chronicle and cookbook; its nonliterary forms tend to check its discomforting poetic flights and minimize the threat that literature and the literary pose to the authors' project of extending the lessons of national rebellion to India's caste and sexual hierarchies.

The Bride's Book transmits feminist ideology to contemporary readers under the cover of its seemingly innocent project of preserving and sharing recipes. Framed by a fable about a communist, egalitarian civilization that gave birth to modern India, it tempts Indian women to boldly reclaim this vision as their rightful inheritance, encouraging them to work for greater political, social, and sexual autonomy. Working like sympathetic pseudo-anthropologists, the authors legitimize and preserve for public contemplation cultural rituals that are supposed to represent a unique, and thus independent, kind of woman's knowledge and power. The optimistically ideological character of *The Bride's Book*, represented by its generic status as fable rather than history, is apparent from the gaps in the authors' discussion of this women's knowledge. They do not ask their readers to consider the larger social–cultural context in which the knowledge of beauty rituals becomes meaningful. Aware of the link between patriarchal marriage, private property, and women's oppression, Anand and Hutheesing somehow glide over the complex relations between the beauty rituals they record and two institutions that are inseparable from them: marriage and art. They treat the rituals of bridal beauty as though they could be understood outside of the politics of family alliance and economics of inheritance. Similarly, they treat the aesthetic ideals informing these rituals as though they could be understood without reference to values that shape other kinds of Indian art, including the art that adorns the book's pages. Were they to consider relations between beauty rituals and the social and cultural contexts of which they are a part, *The Bride's Book*'s lovely, utopic belief that bridal rituals are signs of an unambiguous women's prestige would falter, as would its inspiring but utterly misleading suggestion that a few applications of oil or wax can set any Indian woman on the paradoxically ancient path to modern freedom.

Anand and Hutheesing cannot account for the complexity of Indian women's experiences of oppression or power in part because they are preoccupied with the damaging impacts and ideologies of religious leaders and institutions. Rather than looking at the ways ideologies from diverse spaces in Indian society coordinate to elevate masculinity at the expense of femininity, make female the other of male, the authors blame women's legal oppression and cultural devaluation almost exclusively on the machinations of greedy priests. To explain how the supposedly Elysian Aryan state of affairs dissolved, for example, they protest that "A more diabolical code of priest-made laws with regard to women cannot be imagined" (25). While the authors' examples of such priest-made laws do, indeed, sound diabolical, it is important to point out that there is more to the problem of women's degradation than evil priests. Even literature plays its part. For example, there are signs of a suspicious literary–cultural alliance in the very poetry that Anand and Hutheesing cite to prove the elevation of literature above women's "actual . . . sordid" lives.

Anand and his coauthor cite the husband's greeting from the marriage service of Dravidian peoples in order to prove that women were "accorded a high place in the ordinary social life of the community" and were regarded as "responsible partners" in marriage (20). The husband's greeting is beautiful poetry, but hardly the last or best proof of the authors' statement that Indian women were once "in no sense subservient to, or dependent on, the will of man" (20).

Come, O desired one, beautiful one with the tender heart, with the charming look, good towards thine husband, kind towards animals, destined to bring forth heroes . . . Live with thy husband and in old age mayst thou still rule thy household. Remain here now, never to depart; enjoy the full measure to thy years playing with sons and grandsons. (20)

Rather than testifying to a Dravidian culture of egalitarian sexual values, this husband's greeting illustrates the long history of modern India's patriarchal values, which allow women to function as objects of exchange between men because they are valued for their role as breeders of sons and grandsons. The authors are blind to the alliance between the masculine bias of a canonical literature they admire and the patriarchal marriage they seek to criticize. Writing *The Bride's Book* at the moment India achieved the political goal of independence from Britain that Anand had, for so long, supported through his writing, it seems he cannot resist the brave notion that Indian art and literature are rebel codes, unambiguously advancing the causes of sexual and national freedom.

The mythical spaces for women that Anand and Hutheesing find or create in India's ancient literature find their parallels in the authors' representations of contemporary European social and sexual relations. They paint a portrait of post-Reformation European woman as "equal of man, complete by herself, mistress of her own sex, and free to use it as she likes, to accept or refuse motherhood." Their Indian woman, in contrast, is "more and more a slave" (32). This comparison of European and Indian women does not admit the "actual . . . sordid" lives of many European women or diversely realized independent lives of many Indian women. As a consequence, *The Bride's Book* gives us bad history but pretty good feminist propaganda. While the book never comes close to the theoretical sophistication of Woolf's contemporary feminist texts about the origins and meanings of sexual difference and gender discrimination in English culture, it does offer readers who wanted nothing more than a recipe for good toilet soap reason to work for social change in gender relations and sexual values.

Few of these readers, English or Indian, would have sanctioned Anand and Hutheesing's belief that Indians should affirm an ideal of woman as "complete by herself, mistress of her own sex, and free to use it as she likes, to accept or refuse motherhood." Even those male and female members of the left-wing circles of intermodern London who embraced this ideal in their private lives, rarely produced fictional public characters who could safely and happily fulfill it.[16] For example, although Smith and Holden adopted lifestyles and values consistent with *The Bride's Book* ideal, the older they got and the more they wrote, the less they chose to represent their heroines' independence in sexual ways. By the late 1930s and early 1940s,

Smith's and Holden's writings suggest that sexual freedom for women means they are free to keep their sex to themselves. Neither writer addresses directly through any of her fictional or nonfictional writings the complex relations between female sexuality, literature, sexism, and political (for example, fascist, imperialist) oppression. They left this task to their well-intentioned, ill-equipped friends, Orwell and Anand.

Orwell and Anand represent in their fiction women who "give" themselves sexually to the heroes with whom the authors and readers are supposed to identify, yet these women are more "embodiments of the seer's fancy" than they are autonomous questers after their own sexual, existential, political, or poetic fulfillment. Even *Nineteen Eighty-Four*'s Julia, who initiates sexual contact with the decrepit Winston, is finally a textual other who is there to facilitate the protagonist's quest toward masculine self-determination.[17] Julia's corollary in Anand's intermodern novels is Maya, an evil landlord's beautiful daughter who falls in love with Lalu in *The Village* and who elopes with him in *The Sword and the Sickle*. Despite her elevated class background, she is not capable, as Lalu is, of intellectual or political growth. Her education takes place in almost exclusively sexual terms.[18] While Julia's and Maya's rebellions are not entirely meaningless, the women are more facilitators than agents of the novels' protests against the sexual effects of what Orwell would term totalitarianism and Anand would recognize as casteism and imperialism. For Orwell's and Anand's fictional worlds to achieve ideological coherence, female must still be different from and dependent on male. Significantly, neither writer could envision a fictional world where "Chloe liked Olivia," even if that means Chloe liked working or talking with Olivia rather than sleeping with her (Woolf, *Room* 82).

Patrocinio Schweikart's classic feminist essay, "Reading Ourselves: Towards a Feminist Theory of Reading," illustrates through analysis of the now canonical modernist texts Anand so admired, the costs of omitting Chloe and Olivia from sexual protest literature. Schweikart extends the analyses of second-wave feminist critics of androcentrism to argue,

> androcentric literature structures the reading experience differently depending on the gender of the reader. For the male reader, the text serves as the meeting ground of the personal and the universal. Whether or not the text approximates the particularities of his own experience, he is invited to validate the equation of maleness with humanity. The male reader feels his affinity with the universal, with the paradigmatic human being, precisely because he is male. (270)

To illustrate this process, Schweikart cites the epiphanic bird-girl scene from *Portrait of the Artist*, which invites readers to recognize their "alleged universality" of experience in "the riot in Stephen's blood"—a riot, like the reading, which emerges through confrontation with sexual difference, concretely, sexual difference from the girl (270). Female readers of the bird-girl scene can only experience it as an affirmation of their participation in a universal experience if, in Judith Fetterley's words, they "identify with a male point of view, accept as normal and legitimate a male system of values, one of whose central principles is misogyny" (qtd. in Schweikart 271). While feminist and gender theory has complicated the notions of a "male point of view" and "male system of values" in the twenty-five years since Fetterley first theorized the "Resisting Reader," the process of immascula-tion that she defined still describes the experience that awaits female and feminist readers of Anand's novels. Anand's readers, like Joyce's, will identify with his male protagonists in their intermodern quests for self-discovery and definition. Bakha and after him Munoo and Lalu may not seem at first like Indian Stephens, especially in their struggles with their own status as "other" against whom higher-caste Hindus "feel their differ-ence." But each young hero has his bird girl against whom the reader, male or female, English, Indian, or Anglo-Indian, is urged to realize the hero's positive difference, the underlying truth of his humanity.

Schweikart's project, to explain how "demonstrably sexist texts" like *Portrait of the Artist* or *Women in Love* "remain appealing even after they have been subjected to thorough feminist critique," is at least as important as Fetterley's criticism for discussion of Anand's fiction. Like Schweikart, I am interested in exposing the androcentric bias of texts that I also find deeply compelling. My defense of Anand's right to a firmer claim on our attention takes into consideration his limitations of imagination and polit-ical sympathy. I want to prove that Anand's intermodern texts provide an understanding of radical eccentricity as complex and exciting as anything we might read by Orwell, in part due to their combinations of androcen-tric bias and feminist utopian impulse.

Outside the Revolution: Women in Anand's Fiction

In contrast to *The Bride's Book of Beauty*, which can be seen as contributing bold and valuably different representations of female bodies, rituals, and sexual culture to Indo-Anglian literature, Anand's early novels represent women characters, no matter what their caste, class, race, or nationality, in stereotypical, conventionally androcentric ways.[19] Anand's novels elevate men and masculine qualities and denigrate women and feminine qualities in narratives that share the sexual values and ideology of contemporary mainstream English culture. I do not want to suggest that Anand should have conformed to some politically correct, feminist aesthetic or have anticipated postmodern or postfeminist critiques. Nor do I want to move Anand further toward the peripheries of literary histories of intermodern London. Rather, I want to persuade readers that they need to confront the important, and in some ways entirely English, political-ethical challenges and contradictions of Anand's fictions that emerge, more intensely than in his nonfiction, around questions of sex and gender.

The blindness of Anand's intermodern critics to the conventional and, for a professed humanist, contradictory value of masculine primacy affirmed by his novels suggests that the novels' female characters were not challenging readers' ways of seeing femininity as dependent on masculinity for its meanings. Anand's Indo-Anglian novels, like many popular English novels of the time, introduce female characters whose actions and relations support an old and paralyzing belief system in which men matter more than women, and when women matter, it's a question of their value to men.[20] In contrast, critics of various political stripes and from various decades of the twentieth century have recognized that Anand's male characters and their heroic plots challenge received belief systems and promote a radically different, egalitarian vision for Indian society. The discrepancy between critics' attentions to Anand's dynamic male and dependent female characters is important because it suggests that women are either excluded from or are secondary to Anand's challenge, his humanist vision. Women are simply not part of his revolution.

The contradiction between Anand's oft-professed humanism and his novels' sexist representations of women leads to a number of questions about the production and reception of his early novels. What made the weaknesses of his women characters invisible and implicitly acceptable to Anand's English readers, many of whom were leftist writers sympathetic to female suffrage and feminist thinking? Why do Anand's Anglo and Indian women have nearly identical meanings despite their very different relations to the hierarchies of caste and imperial rule? More important for the field of modernist or intermodernist studies, what does analysis of Anand's representations of women and femininity teach readers about the ideological limits of leftist intermodern novels?

My answer to these questions is that the contradictions signaled by Anand's conventionally gendered, female presences illuminate other, parallel contradictions in Anand's relations with his English readers and his adopted British homeland. Anand's fictional women provided the majority of his readers (nonfeminists, female as well as male) with an essential and essentialized referent that could smooth away threats of cross-cultural difference posed by his male protagonists. Although Anand could expect a sympathetic reception from 1930s leftists for his attack of class/caste elitism, for example, his novels threatened many members of London's intellectual circles with their tendency to lead readers from a criticism of India's caste and class systems to a criticism of British imperialism. The fact that Anand's novels do not require his readers in Britain or India to extend that same criticism to the patriarchal structures of British institutions implies that Anand was on some level asking his readers to accept sexism in order to uproot imperialism. It is likely that Anand's treatment of women and femininity provided a counterweight rooted in tradition that made his revolutionary anti-imperial argument palatable.

When I refer to the novels' "revolutionary argument," I mean their ability to challenge the norms of dominant, hierarchical English and Indian cultures in the interests of promoting more egalitarian social relations between Indians of different castes and between Indians and their English rulers.[21] The extent of the threat that Anand's fictions posed can be measured in a variety of ways. First, as Forster notes in his Preface to *Untouchable*, the contents of Anand's book will make "some readers, especially those who consider themselves all-white, . . . go purple with rage before they have finished a dozen pages" (v). Forster comes to this conclusion after recalling how one reference to the sweepers and commodes of Chandrapur in *Passage to India* inspired an English Colonel to pen in the margins of his book, "Burn when done" and "Has a dirty mind." More than ten years after the scandal of *Ulysses*'s publication, Forster still had to mount an attack on the moral equation of goodness and purity in order to defend Anand's novel about an untouchable cleaner of latrines.

Another way to measure the revolutionary potential of Anand's fiction of the 1930s is through the extreme reactions of the government of India, which banned *Untouchable*, *Coolie*, and *Two Leaves and a Bud* (Iyengar 261).[22] Any readers who knew of Anand's political journalism and activism also would have perceived his early novels as revolutionary. As a college student in India, Anand had participated in the 1921 Civil Disobedience campaigns against the British, which earned him a brief jail term. He was jailed again after joining a student strike against the British government's tacit support of the Sikh grandees. In 1926, shortly after his arrival in England, Anand was manhandled outside the Euston Square Station for refusing to blackleg against the General strikers. Witnessing the British government's treatment of English strikers taught him a powerful lesson: that "Britain was organized and run in the interests of a small minority which could suppress the majority as violently at home as it did in the Empire" (*Apology* 36). This experience convinced him that International Socialism was the only viable political means for addressing world problems (Cowasjee, *So Many* 12).

Anand became a dedicated Marxist in 1932 upon reading Marx's "Letters on India" (Cowasjee 12). The importance of Anand's in-depth engagement with Marx's writings is evident from *Apology for Humanism*, in which he writes: "A whole new world was opened to me. All the threads of my past reading, which had got tied up in knots, seemed suddenly to straighten out, and I began to see not only the history of India but the whole history of human society in some sort of inter-connection" (67–68). In keeping with his antagonism toward authoritarian rule, in 1936 he joined the International Brigade in the University Trenches in Spain, though he, along with other writers, was recalled by the Communist Party and put in a safer journalistic post, which he held for three months. His reports on the war came out of Madrid. In 1938 he made another trip to India, campaigning across the country for the Republican cause. He also worked for the Indian National Congress and the Kisan Sabha (Farmers' Union), and helped organize the Second All India Progressive Writers' Conference in Calcutta (Cowasjee, *So Many* 20–21). Back in London in 1942, Anand published his most explicitly anti-imperialist, overtly revolutionary book, the passionate, propagandistic *Letters on India,* which alienated even lifelong socialists. Leonard Woolf, who agreed to write the introduction to the book, distances himself from the views contained within it, describing it as "extreme," "very one-sided," filled with "a lot of nonsense" (Woolf vii).

Leonard Woolf's introduction to *Letters on India* gives us evidence of Anand's impact on one prominent Bloomsbury socialist; unfortunately, we have no similar kind of evidence of the impact he made on Bloomsbury's most prominent feminist writer, Virginia Woolf. Virginia Woolf certainly knew Anand. She hired him to do proofreading for the Hogarth Press around the same time that she was writing the lectures that were published as *A Room of One's Own*. She also would have known, several years later, that her one-time employee was publishing novels.[23] I'd like to think that if Virginia Woolf read *Coolie*, for example, she would have criticized Anand's representation of the text's Anglo-Indian women because they are blatant examples of sexually biased stereotypes. This is especially true for May Mainwaring, the last "owner" of Munoo, who is made to carry the burden of the British misdeeds and abuses cataloged by the book.

The immorality of Anglo-Indian male characters in *Coolie* is associated with a political power granted them by the institutions of British imperialism. In contrast, May's immorality is represented through her private sexual transgressions, behaviors that are as dangerous in the imperial center of London as they are in the imperial outskirts of Simla. She is a lecherous slut, an extortionist, a hypochondriac, an Epicurean, a snob, a reader of bad novels, a coquette, a social climber, a skin-whitener, a pervert: in short, "a picture of disintegration" (260). The cause of such decay? More than the corrupting influence of imperialism, May is condemned by her family's degenerate, immoral history at whose base lies the union between her English military grandfather and a "Musulman washerwoman" (250). Although Anand's book is dedicated to exposing the deathly consequences of structuring moral and social codes according to the idea that good equals the white and pure and bad equals the dark and dirty, May represents the worst of the English offenses precisely because of her "dark" origins and "dirty" behaviors. She defines the essentialized woman—one whose "dark" race proves the truth of her sex and whose sex confirms the taint of her race. Perhaps she did not inspire a protest from Bloomsbury socialists because their own prejudices against Anglo-Indians prevented them from expecting more from May Mainwaring.

Of Anand's later-day critics, only Cowasjee has examined in any depth *Coolie*'s fascination with Mrs. Mainwaring's sins and abuses. He complains that Anand spends five pages discussing the background of a relatively minor character "and seems to enjoy harping on her shady past, and somewhat shadier present" ("Coolie" 66). Cowasjee pauses briefly to note that no one can "understand why Anand, with his capacity for simplifying characters to their essentials, should at this late stage in the novel give so much time and attention to portraying a minor character" (66). In what follows, I attempt to provide such understanding, demonstrating why *Coolie* needed to "give so much time and attention" to this particular minor character at this particular point in its narrative. By reading Mrs. Mainwaring in terms of Anand's (presumably unconscious) pattern of reducing women to their sexuality, I hope to illuminate an unrecognized, but illuminating, aspect of Anand's passage through Bloomsbury.[24]

Mrs. Mainwaring is one of four "white" women we meet in *Coolie*; all these women are subject to vices of vanity, snobbery, and indulgence that are associated with and implicitly caused by an innate or essential sexual degradation. For example, we know there is something cheap and immoral about Nellie Thomas, the wife of the boorish Jimmie who manages the Sir George White Cotton Mills where Munoo works, upon reading Anand's first description of her: she is "a dried-up small woman with streaks of grey mixed with her shock of brown hair, her sharp face bright with enthusiasm, . . . with her legs spreading wide on the armchair, in defiance of all Munoo's conceptions of modesty" (226–27). To Munoo, she is simultaneously a thin, barren spinster-like woman and, with her legs spread on the chair, a grotesque sexual threat. To those who can read between the lines of her cockney accent she is simultaneously a weak victim of her husband's alcoholism, rage, and brutality, and eager shrew who may be deserving of such punishment given her parasitic position in India. There is little to encourage the reader to see how Nellie's racism, violence, and dependence are the consequences of contradictory lessons taught by an Anglo-Indian society.

In *Untouchable*, the wife of the Salvation Army's Colonel Hutchinson carries a peculiarly feminized representation of another kind of imperial abuse in India, the insidious blight of missionary privilege. Again, it is a woman's essential qualities of voice and body that point toward her social, political, and human worth or lack thereof. Anand provides a memorable and detailed physical description that tags Mary Hutchinson as another middle-aged, sexual grotesquerie, "a round-faced, big-bellied, dark-haired, undersized, middle-aged woman" whose origins as a Cambridge barmaid are revealed by the "low-necked printed cotton frock that matched her painted and powdered face and reached barely down to her knees" (131–32). Mary's sexual immorality is complemented by her status as whiskey-drinking, racist harpy. The extent to which we are supposed to despise her is evident from Bakha's reaction. He sees her as "a witch, with raised arms and crooked feet following him, harassing him" (132). She is more devilish even than the high-caste Hindus who insulted Bakha earlier in the day and she comes to carry the burden of our protest against the cruelties of the Indian social system.

But why make such a fuss about Anand's treatment of women like May Mainwaring and Mary Hutchinson? Isn't it appropriate, or at least under-standable, given that his novels of the 1930s were designed as protests against British imperialism? My answer to this question is that even those readers who can overlook sexist caricature in the interests of Indian independence should not ignore the way Anand's treatments of Anglo-Indian women are related to his treatments of Indian women. Dozens of Indian women roam the pages of his novels and they come in all ages and sizes; however, they still are shaken from only two imaginative molds: the good mother and the bad mother. In each case, moral and human worth is once again measured by sexual behaviors or sexualized appearances. Like Anand's treatment of Anglo-Indian women, his descriptions of the bodies of his Indian women characters will always indicate the content of their minds. This is just as true of his idealized character Sohini, sister to the noble Bakha, as it is of Sohini's nemesis, Gulabo, who is an Indian version of Mary Hutchinson. Gulabo "had pretensions to beauty and was notori-ous as an assertive old hussy who thought herself superior to every other outcaste . . . because a well-known Hindu gentleman in the town who had been her lover in her youth was still kind to her in her middle age" (24). In contrast, Sohini is described in rapturous terms. The narrator begins with mention of her "sylph-like form," "well-rounded hips," "arched narrow waist," and ends with the climactic description of her "full, round globular breasts, jerking slightly, for lack of a bodice, under her transparent muslin shirt" (22). The narrator's delight in Sohini's body seems to parallel that of the lecherous priest who molests her at the Temple later on in the novel. Yet no critics have commented on this parallel. Instead, they assume that Anand is demonstrating an affinity with Indian women by painting Sohini as a goddess. They might just as well theorize that he is painting her instead as an English pin-up calendar girl. For female and feminist readers, the experience of immasculation is the same.

Sohini, in her innocence, vulnerability, and beauty, falls into the slot of the good mother as she struggles to replace the idealized mother she and her brothers lost as children. Gulabo, mother to Bakha's friend Ram Charan, is a caricature of the bad mother. Instead of protecting and nurturing Sohini in her mother's absence, Gulabo protects her own family's status in the hierarchy of outcastes by abusing Sohini with the terms of bitch, slut, and prostitute. A similar abusive bad mother and saintly, sexual good mother can be found in *Coolie*. Bibiji, the wife of the Indian bank clerk who employs Munoo in his first job as family servant, is Gulabo in caste form. The narrator first introduces her to us through Munoo's eyes as his uncle drops him off for his first day of work. She has a "stern, flat-chested" form that we should expect will accompany her "sharp, long tongue" with its "inexhaustible resources of breath" (13). Bibiji fulfills her function as witch, and Munoo is driven out of her home into a series of adventures that could all be interpreted as attempts to find the good mother who will compensate, often in sexual ways, for the abuses of the bad.

There are several good mothers who nurture Munoo along his route, including the wife of the owner of a pickle factory and most successfully, the wife of another coolie who "adopts" Munoo and works with him in the cotton factory. This last woman, Lakshami, functions as Anand's ideal mother. Her extreme modesty is inversely related to the ultimate sign of her nurturing capacities: her willingness to answer Munoo's adolescent desire by taking him to bed with her (215–16). This union between Munoo and Lakshami seems very odd because it completes a pattern where the more modest the novel's Indian women are initially, the more sexually involved they will become with its doomed hero. Ultimately, they are revealed by the narrator and judged by the readers to be Anand's good mothers. The novel obscures the scandal of its incestuous ideal of the perfect mother-lover by ensuring its sexually good mothers are lost or sacrificed before the book's end.

This brings us back to Mrs. Mainwaring, a decidedly bad mother, and the questions that I posed above: What made the weaknesses of Mrs. Mainwaring and her light and dark cookie-cutter sisters invisible to Anand's early readers? What difference does it make that she is to be judged by the same criteria of body and voice that determined the worth of

Anand's Indian women? And what can readers learn about the end of empire and its relation to intermodernism given Anand's value of masculine supremacy within his Marxist-humanist protest novels?

My theory is that the similarities between Anand's Anglo and Indian women, their division into two camps of perversely sexual virgins and frigid whores, appealed to his readers' need to limit the logic of his critique of power structures. While they might be willing to see how these structures sustain the evils of imperialism, racism, and caste-exclusion, apparently they did not want to see how the same structures also characterized what Virginia Woolf would have recognized as patriarchy. Anand's women encouraged English readers to agree with the narrator's judgments about the moral meanings of their light and dark bodies. This abstract union of the protagonist with his English, Indian or Anglo-Indian readers, constructed by the narrative as male, was particularly important given that Anand's ignorant, poverty-stricken heroes, in their ambition and complexity, would have threatened the values about empire or caste held by most of those same Anglo-Indian or educated Indian readers.

A reading of the structural function of two of Anand's most hateful women in *Coolie* supports my argument. The horrid May Mainwaring is strategically, symbolically brought to whorish life at the very end of *Coolie*. Her sexual "dissolution," to use Anand's word, seems to cause the literal dissolution of Munoo. Positioned at the end of the narrative, her feminine transgressions, her failures of mothering, gain a disproportionate weight. This weight is counterbalanced, however, by the equally significant position of Munoo's shrewish aunt, Gujri, at the very beginning of *Coolie*. Readers open the book to the aunt's calls of "Munoo ohe Munooa oh Mundu!" She curses Munoo again and again, eventually "raising her voice . . . to the highest pitch to which, in her anger and hate, she could carry it: 'Where have you died? Where have you gone, you ominous orphan? Come back and be gone!' " (1). In her bitterness over her own childless state, Gujri is interchangeable with Bibiji, Nelly Thomas, Gulabo, and Anand's other bad mothers. Her hard, barren voice expels Munoo from his rural paradise among the hills; May Mainwaring's soft, seductive glances end his coolie's journey toward inevitable sickness and death.

As the novel's bookends, one dark, the other light, Gujri and May threaten to absorb the reader's anger over the hero's sufferings due to institutional structures of colonial economies and the injustices of imperial culture. Bad mothers seem to become the ultimate arbiters of imperialism's wrongs.[25] The reader can finish *Coolie* with the impression that it is women who condemn Munoo to death. This is not to suggest that *Coolie* and *Untouchable* don't convey real and powerful critiques of British imperialism and Indian social hierarchy. They do. But this critique is advanced at the expense of the novels' women characters and humanist logic. The most discomforting possibility suggested by my analysis of *Untouchable* and *Coolie* is that Anand's women, in all their stereotypical, hollow failure, are necessary to the books' successes as celebrated 1930s novels. Anand's reputation as the best Indo-Anglian writer of the period may be established, in part, on the compliant bodies of several invaluable minor female characters.

There is no evidence that Anand's disturbing representations of women characters in his 1930s novels cost him his friendships with many of the prominent modernists and intermodernists in the early 1940s. Certainly Smith and Holden do not record any disappointment with his treatment of them or ever suspect him of regarding women, fictional or actual, as inferior creatures. Rather, Anand's Marxist, anti-imperialist, pro-Indian independence politics seem to be the cause of his increasingly weak connections to English leftists. Orwell is just one of many Englishmen who distanced himself from Anand during the war. Although he was working very closely with Anand at the BBC and maintained a cordial, professional correspondence with him, Orwell's private diaries show an irritation with Anand's politics that suggest the relationship was strained. Such strain was not unusual. Cowasjee points out that "Anand's attitude toward his contemporaries was chiefly determined by their stand on the question of Indian freedom" and that he tested the limits of their revolutionary commitments most pointedly in his 1942 *Letters on India* (*So Many* 29).[26] This "test" followed his unpopular 1940 novel, *Across the Black Waters*, which is about the misadventures of a group of Indian mercenaries in the British Army during World War I. As Graham Parry points out in one of the few scholarly treatments of this unusual and compelling novel, Anand's timing could not have been worse. Published at a low point of English morale during World War II, *Across the Black Waters* is an undisguised attack on a British government at war (Parry 32–33). For those leftist writers whose feelings of patriotic nationalism intensified in the conditions of world war, Anand's "low blow" was reason enough to exclude him from their lives.[27]

The same Bloomsbury leftists and artists who in the 1940s rejected Anand along with his literature, had, several years before, received *Untouchable* as an important novel by one of their own. They welcomed its attacks on caste and class discrimination and took pleasure in its offense to people they perceived as antagonists, Anglo-Indian loyalists and committed British imperialists. They would not have predicted that, many years later, it would prove equally offensive to Arun P. Mukherjee, a postcolonial critic who shares postmodern versions of Anand's professed goals and commitments. Mukherjee's essay, entitled "The Exclusions of Postcolonial Theory and Mulk Raj Anand's *Untouchable*: A Case Study," places analysis of Anand's work at its center as a means of criticizing the homogenizing tendencies of postcolonial theory. Mukherjee claims that postcolonial theory's most influential spokespersons—Bill Ashcroft, Gareth Griffiths, Helen Tiffin, Benita Parry, Fredric Jameson, and even Rushdie—flatten out the "Indianness" of India's literature because their theoretical writing "thematizes India's literary texts only in terms of search for identity and resistance to the colonizer, entirely overlooking collaboration" (32).

This last objection about collaboration leads Mukherjee into his critical case study of *Untouchable*. He sees Anand as a writer with a "radical cognitive intentionality" whose fiction is not, finally, radical or subversive and requires from leftist critics a "hermeneutic of suspicion . . . like any other text" (35). Among other things, Mukherjee recounts the political history of activist untouchables whose leaders articulated demands that often ran counter to the Indian National Congress Party positions that Anand echoes. Mukherjee finds it "absolutely astounding" that "Anand does not refer at all either to the oppositional acts or the oppositional discourses produced by untouchables at this time period all across India" (46).[28] Although the Government of India found *Untouchable* threatening enough to ban it, Mukherjee concludes that Anand's *Untouchable* "successfully contains the realities of the volatile social order at this period of Indian history" (42). He asserts, "It reassures its bourgeois readers, both in India and in Britain where it was originally published, that the simmering unrest among the untouchables would not lead to a violent destabilization of the *status quo*" (42).

It is this mention of *Untouchable*'s reception, and particularly its reception in Britain, that inspires the next section of this chapter. Taking as my starting point the idea that Anand's 1930s fiction is divided between a radical intentionality and collaborationist effects, I examine the political and aesthetic implications of Anand's "ambiguously non-hegemonic" position in two nonfiction texts of the 1940s, in order to complicate Mukherjee's reading and advance Anand's reputation as an intermodern radical writer.

No Apology for Heroism

Anand's many autobiographical writings document his divided position in India—a division that is evident on the micro level of family politics as well as the macro level of caste allegiance. Anand grew up in the cantonments of northern India. His father had given up the traditional coppersmithing trade of his ancestors and had devoted himself to secular advancement in the British–Indian army (*Apology* 29–31). Anand characterizes his mother as a simple, silly woman of peasant origins whose vague pantheistic religious practices were a source of amusement and mockery for the men in his family. As a boy, Anand earned shiny silver coins from male relatives who admired his "prodigious feat of mimicking [his] mother reading the Gita" (*Apology* 30). The divide between father and mother symbolizes Anand's larger social, political divisions as an Indian and a writer. This divide is more dramatically illustrated by Anand's description of his immigration to England. He writes in *Apology for Heroism*, "The immediate cause of my impetuous decision [to leave for England] was that my father hit my mother in an argument about my having gone to jail in the Gandhi movement and having fallen in love with a Muslim girl from Lahore" (45). This is a painful but perfect example of the way family politics introduced Anand to the contradictory claims of his social position even before he left India. He was nearly torn apart by divided loyalties to masculine power and feminine nurturing, collaborationist advantage and revolutionary practice, social privilege and religious oppression.

If we consider Anand's situation in England during the first years of his residence there, it is obvious that his flight westward merely allowed him to exchange one set of contradictory social and political experiences for another. In *Conversations in Bloomsbury*, the contradictions become a source of comedy and literary anecdote, illustrating how the young Anand was important rather than eccentric to intellectual life in the Empire's center. Yet in *Apology for Heroism*, which he wrote while working for Orwell at the BBC, Anand emphasizes his *distance* from his English colleagues and peers. Published two years before Indian independence, this document accuses almost all the intellectuals of the 1930s of lacking a centrality of vision. Anand, in contrast, was trying to find a comprehensive theory that would allow him to understand "human values" in terms of the "problem of politics and economics, particularly the wretchedness of the human beings in India" (82–83).[29] His reflections on this period of his intellectual and spiritual life lead him to "confess" to feeling "a considerable gap" in his relations with English writers (83). While he admits to being grateful for their loyal friendships, he also admits to "a certain kind of self-consciousness in [his] . . . discussions [with them] about India" due, in part, to his own "inferiority complex" but also certainly due to what he calls "the acquiescence (conscious or unconscious . . .) by most British writers I knew at that time, with the status quo and with the arguments used even by the most obtuse of publicists against the advancement of the under-privileged both in Britain and the Empire" (83).

Curiously, Anand here accuses British writers of doing precisely the same thing Mukherjee criticizes Anand of doing: maintaining a cowardly allegiance to the status quo. In each case, the earnest, liberal intentions of the accused only intensify the critic's accusations. Although Anand writes,

"I don't want to exaggerate the significance of such differences of opinion [between himself and English writers]," in the next breath he declares,

> I was also firmly convinced that there could be no dignity in the personal relations of British and Indian intellectuals unless British writers realized that the freedom of speech and opinion which they took for granted was denied to their friends in [India], and unless they saw to it that intellectuals everywhere enjoyed equal rights of citizenship. (84)

The phrase, "no dignity in the personal relations of British and Indian intellectuals," throws into question the reality of the friendships Anand confirms elsewhere in *Apology for Heroism*. This strikes me as an important declaration of difference, his confession in the 1940s that the friendships of the 1930s were, all along, only pseudo-friendships. *Apology* mentions favorably only Bertrand Russell, H. N. Brailsford, Lowes Dickinson, E. M. Forster, Edward Thompson, and Leonard Woolf (the last an odd choice in light of Woolf's criticism of *Letters on India*) (85).[30]

Given the high moral tone of the autobiography and its strikingly *un*apologetic critique of English intellectuals as "selfish," "petty," "egotistical" betrayers of the ideals of European culture (87), one must wonder about the actual contents of the apology. Suspicions that Anand is offering nothing but the *forms* of apology are confirmed by the end of the sixth and central chapter of *Apology*. Here Anand writes, "If it is not a simplification, I may say, generally, that the youth of India during the last quarter of a century had been going through a kind of heroic age. All our gestures, all our thoughts, all our talk—everything that we did—had been inspired by the belief that we must create a new India, build a new world" (96). Asserting nothing less heroic than building a new world, Anand offers only the appearance of apology for thinking too boldly or crudely about the artist's role as a political agent of history.

The strength of Anand's belief in his generation's heroism is contradicted by the title, "Apology for Heroism," which he chose for his political autobiography.[31] Perhaps it is a concession to the book's anticipated readership: members of a leftist English community who, despite their socialist leanings, could not separate themselves from the fate of a nation shaken by years of economic crisis, class division, Blitz bombings, and the ongoing and very real loss of Empire. In this English context, in which Anand is both insider and outsider, privileged spokesperson for the intellectual elite and disempowered representative of Britain's colonial subjects, trusted friend and contentious revolutionary, the ambiguous and even contradictory nature of his apology begins to make sense.

Another source of the contradictions of Anand's *Apology* is its generic status as autobiography, which inevitably affirms individualism no matter how much autobiographers wish to advance revolutionary collectivist causes. Anand's readers are entirely justified in asking how far, really, he moves from the "egotistical," "selfish," nonheroic performances he associates with the majority of English radical writers of the period given his celebration of self in *Apology*. Answers to this question about Anand's difference will depend, in part, on whether of not readers take into consideration his earlier *Letters on India*. In contrast to Anand's other, possibly "collaborationist" fictions of the 1930s or "egotistical" nonfiction of the 1940s, *Letters on India* generously takes up an unpopular, minority stance on behalf of poor and oppressed Indians (and by association, poor and oppressed English), announcing a radical departure from the politics of mainstream English culture and the liberal, leftist politics of Anand's Bloomsbury friends.

Letters on India is a remarkable book to read in the context of British wartime activity since it vigorously accuses the British government of the crimes of murderous exploitation that the British were accusing the fascists of committing. The epistolary form Anand adopts to mount this criticism is calculated to earn the sympathies of activist workers in England. It announces itself as the edited version of an exchange of letters from one Tom Brown, factory hand, and Anand, local expert on the "India problem," that followed from Anand's first public letter on India to *The Fortnightly* in June 1942. Anand's ninth chapter-letter, "Is This a Human Being?," is typical. Documenting the findings of Royal Commissions sent to India to investigate the state of the industrial workers, he answers with devastating detail his correspondent's inquiry, "Surely our rulers, the masters of India, are not ignorant of what has happened to India? I should like to . . . know whether these people are ignorant or just heedless of the misery they have caused . . . ." (78). Beginning with the claim that "The report of the Royal Commission on labour, familiarly known, after its chairman, as the Whitley Report, is one of the most damning indictments of British rule in India," Anand sets out to prove that "the condition of the industrial workers in India are about the worst in the world, except in the West Indies and Africa" (78–79). Indeed, Anand shows again and again that imperial heedlessness, not ignorance, is the cause of working conditions in India's industries—its mines, textile mills, cigarette factories, tanning sheds, merchant ships, and tea plantations—that rival anything recorded in the Blue Books or Engels's *Conditions of the Working Class*. Anand concludes his chapter-letter with words that must have scalded most English folk who read them:

> [W]ell-intentioned folk appeal to the "protector of the poor," the British Sarkar, to do something, or beg the new "father-mother," the employer, to offer humane treatment to the coolies. But we can as little expect tenderness

from the king of the jungle as hope for comfort from a reactionary State and its allies, the capitalists [this, in 1942!], who control industry and sit pretty on their gains, while fresh enterprise is barred, unemployment continues, cheapening the price of labour and lowering the standard of living to still lower levels. (86)

Published by the Labour Book Service, this letter and seventeen others are preceded by Leonard Woolf's introduction to the book. Woolf, famous for his socialist and literary credentials, must have been asked to write the introduction because of his service in Ceylon from 1908 to 1911. Although Woolf begins with the affectionate salutation, "Dear Anand," he almost immediately springs into an argument against the very book he has agreed to support. Woolf defends his iconoclastic departure from the conventions of introductions by noting, "It will not be the usual kind of introduction, which seems to me nearly always impertinent, in both senses of the word, for in it a distinguished or undistinguished person irrelevantly pats the author on the back. Even if I wanted to—which I do not—I would not dare to pat you or any other remember of the Indian Congress Party on the back" (vii). He goes on to characterize his friend as an untrustworthy advocate of the " 'extreme' Congress case" who has produced a book that is "dangerously biased" and full of "a lot of nonsense" (vii). Woolf's objections boil down to one thing: he believes Anand is not fair to the British. He complains, "[The British] record in India is not as black as you make out, black though it may be" (viii).[32]

Anand's published reply to Woolf's introduction only hints at what must have been his profound astonishment upon reading the hostile beginning to his book. After modestly noting that he was "rather disturbed" by the introductory letter, he objects,

That a socialist publicist of your experience, and a person whom I respect, should, in spite of my obvious socialist analysis, accuse me of being a prejudiced extremist, made me say to myself: "Either I have failed to convey my real point of view, or Woolf is showing his own particular prejudices in warning people against my alleged bias." On reflection I am convinced that in your zeal to warn Tom Brown against my one-sidedness you have almost gone to the Amery extreme. (x)[33]

Fortunately for scholars of the end of Empire, Anand gets the last word in this battle between leftists. His defense against Woolf's attack is sure, specific, and unapologetic, as is his extended and persuasive critique of British imperialism in the rest of the book.

Anand's response to Woolf is one of the reasons that *Letters on India* should be seen as providing the kind of uncompromising Indian hero that

Mukherjee finds missing from Anand's most famous novel, *Untouchable*. My analysis of the relation between Anand's (ambiguously) non-hegemonic social positions and his literary productions modifies, while not eliminating, Mukherjee's claim that Anand's fiction collaborates with bourgeois imperialist agendas. Mukherjee warns that if we take at face value the versions of nationalist historiography advanced by Anand's *Untouchable*, "we run the risk of being caught off guard by history" (43). Fair enough. But we can be caught off guard by literature too. Mukherjee's case study of Anand is impoverished by an inattention to literature—specifically literature by Anand. Two nonfictional texts of the 1940s, *Apology for Heroism* and *Letters on India*, illustrate better than his fictional texts of the 1930s the importance of literary form for analyses of authors' social positioning and their fiction's ideological effects.

Anand's nonfiction presents more thoroughly, consistently radical heroes than his fiction, in part because his autobiographical narratives are freed from the constraints of modernism. Instead of emerging from the tradition of the stream-of-consciousness novel, with its debt to the alienated, romantic hero of bourgeois realism, Anand's nonfiction heroes are, ironically, empowered and enlivened by the more prosaic generic claims of their narratives. This conclusion implies that critics must ask questions not only about Anand's ambiguous positioning in various social contexts and the "real" history of India, as Mukherjee would insist, but also about the traditional materials of literary study: form, style, genre, and language. The last of these formal literary qualities, language, is the subject of one of Anand's most powerful and insightful pieces of political writing, a slender book or pamphlet called *The King-Emperor's English* that he published in 1948, the same year Orwell was completing *Nineteen Eighty-Four*.

The King-Emperor's English

Like this chapter, Anand's passage through Bloomsbury ends with a return to India. While Orwell, Smith, and Holden were struggling in a grey, postwar, postimperial London that provided *Nineteen Eighty-Four* its memorable setting, Anand was in Bombay, contributing to the political and literary discourses of the new nation. His writings of the late 1940s show their debts to English intermodernism, but unlike the postwar writings of his English friends, Anand's publications are energized by the chaos of new beginnings. Celia's paralyzing grief, symbolized by the tears flowing through *The Holiday*, is entirely missing from the pages of Anand's books. *The King-Emperor's English*, with its directness, energy, and youthful defiance, stands out among the contemporary productions of the English radical eccentrics as well as Anand's self-congratulatory, over-written, avuncular postcolonial writings. It is as pointed and sarcastic as Orwell's political journalism of the same period, as aware of the force that prewar culture exerts on a postwar world, and as concerned with the defense of national culture in the face of aggressive American capitalism and hyper-industrialization. Arguing passionately for the continued support of English and English-language literature in free India, its concerns will strike twenty-first-century readers as more relevant and its conclusions more insightful than any other text by Anand examined in this chapter.

In this slight volume, which vibrates with righteous anger, nationalist vision, and hard-won literary pride, Anand takes up a radically eccentric position in the debates on English in India. Making his way between cultural–political groups, looking both Left and Right, he advocates unashamed study of literary English and recognition of Indo-Anglian writers who have produced "a kind of regional branch of English literature" that is yet "a part of the Indian cultural development and has its value, if only as an interpretive literature of the most vital character" (16). Before presenting his case for retaining English for Indians, Anand asks a crucial question: "What kind of English are we talking about?" The "King's English, supposed to be spoken and written in Britain" or "John Company's English, the King-Emperor's English" or finally some other variety (1–2). Of the first, he says that whatever the King's English is— amid the vast variety of Englishes spoken in the British Isles—"most people in Britain recognize it when they hear it" (2). He has more to say of that other English, what he calls the King-Emperor's English, "the copious prose (and verse) written in the erstwhile Indian Empire of His Britannic Majesty." About the history of this King-Emperor's English he claims little is known outside the voluminous files of the pre-1947 Government of India; its public results he limits to the creation of the "Babu," a despised and ridiculous figure, "Mr Punch's friend, with thick glasses, a pen behind his right ear, sporting an odd mixture of Indian and English habiliments, and loaded like a donkey with numerous files and ledgers as he dragged his tired limbs along the corridors of Government offices" (8). The third form of English that Anand defines and defends is his own, the English of Indians who have, during the last century, struggled against the constraints of "Babu English" taught in the schools and have written against the odds set by cynical and contemptuous critics a distinctive Indo-Anglian literature (3). Rather than throwing the books by Indo-Anglian writers into the sea or exiling them to Britain, actions he claims some patriots recommend, Anand argues that Indians should value the works of the Indo-Anglians because they "bring the techniques of European literature to our country whilst contributing Indian idiom and metaphor to English literature" (x). Making predictions that, in retrospect, seem eerily visionary, he expresses confidence that in the future younger Indo-Anglian writers will "compete in quality of attainment with any other literatures of the period before the Second World War" (19). He predicts that their success will arise from their freedom from the King-Emperor's English, their conscious reorientation to English language, and their synthesis of Indian and English values. These influences will inspire a literary movement that will be counted as one of the "most important parts of Indian literature" (20).

Anand's insights emerged out of the needs of contemporary culture rather than any prophetic qualities. Published in Bombay the year after India gained independence, *The King-Emperor's English* is influenced by the same dynamic sociopolitical context that produced the gentler *Bride's Book of Beauty*. Both books attempt to isolate and preserve cultural discourses from India's past that can be reshaped to suit the needs of a populace torn by nationalist triumphs and griefs, although of the two, only *The King-Emperor's English* engages with the meaning of India's legacy of English rule and language for nationalist debate. Anand's peculiar intimacy with England, shaped by his changing public roles as Bloomsbury intellectual, acclaimed London novelist, English socialist and mistrusted Indian Congress Party nationalist, lead him to defend the English language in the face of those Indian critics who want to "apply a kind of 'Quit India' resolution against the English language" (3). He claims that his English, the English studied by Indo-Anglian writers, is a wondrous, supple, powerful thing to which all Indians should feel entitled. Anand encourages his readers to take up the real, as opposed to "perverted" King-Emperor's English, "as a good second language without any fears or inhibitions" so they may "receive the classics of English literature with an open mind, for these were written, mostly, not by hardened imperialists of the Tory brand . . . but by the finest minds in England, by men who were sensitive, independent, humane" (21–22).

Anand's defense of English is accompanied by an attack on those preservationists who want to retain "the King-Emperor's English," labeling such desires "stupid, antiquated and absurd" (3). His second chapter is titled "A potted history of the imposition of King-Emperor's English in India," and emphasizes the compromised motives of the colonizers who mandated that this limited, distorted English become the language of the schools and universities. Anticipating late-twentieth-century critics of the educational system that taught generations of Indian men "inadequate English for reasons of policy," he describes the principle result in outraged tones: the creation of the "Babu," a butt of caricature, a "montage man" whose fragmented intellectual and spiritual life left him an exile from the heritage and family that produced him as well as the Anglo-Indians he served.[34] A snobbish, lost creature, the "Babu" had "the assurance, the complacency and the superciliousness of a man who could not fit into any society, who did not know where he belonged" (11).

Anand's description of the "tragedy" of the "Babu" is haunted by signs of his regret over his own early exile from family, country, and language. Shaped equally by compassion and shame, his ironic "potted history" becomes poignant to the reader who sees in the following generalization a version of the young Anand in Bloomsbury, striving to earn the respect of English and Indians alike:

> Our rulers were moved to supercilious laughter by the bad grammar and faulty syntax of the "Babu" English of the Indian clerk whom they had trained through a barren and vicious system of education. In consequence of this, and the humiliating position in which the "Babu" was placed through the initial folly of the British Imperialist, all Indians who speak or write English have been under a stigma, however well they might have mastered the language. (4)

A stigma realized in England or India? The context of the passage and more broadly, the Indian context of the book's production and reception, suggest that Anand means the latter, but his bitter experience in the 1930s trying to get *Untouchable* published in England and his confrontations in the 1940s with English leftists who would not support his literature of nationalist aspiration complicates the scene of humiliation and failure. Condensing into the figure of the "Babu" the different kinds of social, linguistic, and cultural alienation experienced by "all Indians who speak or write English," Anand simultaneously invokes and distances himself from the clownish figure, uncannily like his younger self, through the voice of the mature, English-educated, English-speaking repatriated Indian writer.

Having established the terms that grant him authority to speak in English on behalf of English in India, Anand can risk criticizing what we now call high modernism. The "effete and literary" English of contemporary writing he blames on rigid class barriers, arguing that members of Britain's working classes were prevented by social hierarchies from contributing their "vital and homely influence" to the most prestigious English prose of his day. As an alternative to this desiccated, effete literary language he points to the English of Orwell, Forster, Herbert Read, and V. S. Pritchett because these men have managed to integrate working-class conversation into their literature.[35] Locating in English class hierarchies the origins of the difference between the "effete" language of modernism and "blended" language of Orwell, Forster, Pritchett, and Read, Anand bemoans the inability of Indian writers to contribute to the latter due to their inheritance of only the "Mandarin prose of old text books" and consequent discomfort with colloquial English Ironically, the man who I am treating as an exemplary voice in English intermodernism throws into doubt his suitability for this role by implying that even *his* Indian English is too formal for the necessary "blending" of Mandarin, upper-class and working-class styles that characterize the contemporary English novels he most admires.

Anand's list of favorite authors lets us see his eccentric bias: intermodernism, not modernism, is the inheritor of the "great" literary tradition of English Romanticism and protesting English Victorianism. Again and again, his defense of English for and of Indians comes back to the paradox that the "best" English literature of the last two centuries—poems by Wordsworth, Coleridge, Shelley, Byron, and prose by Thackeray, Dickens, Ruskin, Morris, Arnold, Hardy, and Lawrence—has been dedicated to criticism and even destruction of the dominant values of the machine age. Anand argues that this English and its critical literature should be cherished rather than despised by Indians because it is most likely to inspire them to reevaluate their society "while it is face to face with the dangers that threatened Britain only a century earlier" (28). Adopting the logic of liberal protest to his own purposes, Anand makes this catalog of great English authors—the elite voices of English literary history—the guarantor of democratic Indian statehood. Admitting that India's course toward statehood has brought with it confusion and anarchy, Anand urges Indians to immerse themselves in the English of Shelley, Wordsworth, Byron, or Dickens not because it will help them impose order upon such anarchy, but because it will stoke the fires of change in ways that prove "man can transform his destiny" (45).[36] Anand's Marxist-humanist politics are consistent with this statement of faith, but the vision in *The King-Emperor's English* of India as a modern nation, free from and equal to Britain, seems to depend more on Indians' acceptance of English literature and literary language than any particular political ideology. Literary English, especially when it incorporates the riches of working-class speech, becomes "a basic preliminary to the task of reconstructing the minds of the [Indian] intelligentsia—itself the first step in the task of educating the people for a free society" (45). In other words, English literature and literary language is invaluable for and perhaps inseparable from the social, political work of Indian nation building.

Anand's belief in the value of English for Indians and Indian statehood does not lead him to believe that English is necessarily destined to become "the *Lingua franca* of India" though he believes English will probably become the language of the world (49). Noting that the usage of Hindustani and Urdu has increased dramatically since the emancipation of India, Anand proclaims that those who see beyond the immediate anarchic situation know that

> The utmost integrity lies in not checking the local dialects and languages of India. Anyone who knows anything about languages is aware that they seldom flourish if they are organized through ordinances issued by some central authority or Dictator, but grow up simply through the flowering of the human spirit in the ordinary exchanges of life. . . . the safest course lies in giving equal opportunities to all to learn, to read and write their own mother tongue, and at least one or two foreign languages as well, through which the wealth of various literatures can be made available to people in our small world. (50)

Taking his metaphors and images from the literature of English liberalism, Anand prepares a place in India for a kind of English that does not belong to Britain, but to the world. Indians who write in English even have a special role in nationalist propaganda efforts through their ability to publicize the "truth" of India, known to many inhabitants only through their mother tongues, in that English world language. Anand speculates that "it may be necessary, in the period that stretches before us, to increase the output of English writing, to give the outside world a better idea of our culture or, at least, to neutralize, through imaginative work, the anti-Indian propaganda of generations, both in Britain and America" (23).

Anand's interest in using English to attract and educate a world audience on Indian affairs has parallels to other intermodernists' interests in world-language movements, including the Basic English movement that Orwell once advocated and then satirized.[37] Anand may be alluding directly to Basic when he suggests that at some distant future date, if the major nations of the world surrender their national sovereignty to a supranational authority, "an artificial code language will be adopted as a means of world communication" (47–48). With one eye on a possible future global community united by a code language and one eye on the political implications of diverse forms of English used in India, Anand still has enough sense left to argue for acceptance of the local languages of India. He shares with readers what this attitude means for his writing:

> I for one, would plump for the vernacular and, though continuing to write in English, would like also to write in Punjabi and then render it into English more realistically and adequately than I do at present, for now I literally translate all the dialogue in my novels from my mother tongue and think out the narrative mostly the same way. (23)

English, when it is not the King Emperor's English and when it is not learned in the shadow of the unwritten fiat, "'Learn English or die,'" is already an Indian language (48). And Indo-Anglian literature is not simply English literature with an accent, but, in Anand's case, Punjabi–English literature. The Indo- in "Indo-Anglian" is ideologically, historically equal to the Anglian.

Anand's Anticolonialism and Postcolonial Critique

In her introduction to *Dissenters and Mavericks: Writings about India in English, 1765–2000*, Margery Sabin explains why liberal arguments such as the one Anand makes on behalf of English in *The King-Emperor's English* are worth recovering despite a late-twentieth- and early-twenty-first-century intellectual climate that favors a postcolonial criticism that is deeply skeptical about the possibility or meaning of individual dissent (7). Sabin's defense of the methods and interests of study of the "language and designs of individual writers and texts" is intelligently and at times irreverently argued in the face of this skepticism. Whether she intends it or not, her introduction functions as a manifesto for other scholars seeking support for their literary studies of the motives, methods, and historical impacts of many kinds of individual dissenters and mavericks. Sabin's defense of her practice serves as my own:

> I in part follow the models and benefit from the methods developed in what has come to be called cultural studies. But only in part, because as a literary critic I am always also on the lookout for something special, something qualitatively better than the norm, and worth reading not primarily for more evidence of general discursive patterns but for its own value and as stimulus to further and different questions, such as "Look at this! Who wrote it? What makes it special? What else did this author write?" . . .
>
> The discovery of exceptional writings in unexpected places does not invalidate the concept of a colonial discourse; its value is to loosen the grip of cultural generalization . . . . The exceptional text resists that mastery [of the object that possession of a theory or method or set of hypotheses provides the interpreter] and, if the critic is willing, offers the different satisfaction of an experience that baffles and even contradicts expectations. (4–5)

In support of her distinctly literary-critical intervention into postcolonial studies, Sabin cites Edward Said's President's column from the spring 1999 *MLA Newsletter*. She points out that in that context, weighted with the history of a dominant, inherently conservative academic literary culture, the most influential contributor to the field of a dissenting postcolonial discourse criticizes his own radical followers, objecting to the proliferation of "All manner of fragmented, jargonized subjects of discussion" and calling for "a reinforced sense of intellectual responsibility . . . to what in fact we [in literary studies] ought to do, namely, the interpretation, analysis, and serious consideration of literature in its historical and social environment" (qtd. in Sabin 7).

Sabin's approach to the study of writings in English about India, thoroughly indebted to Said's early postcolonial critique of English literary studies and his more recent criticism of the departure of postcolonial studies from literature, bears directly on Anand's reputation and visibility in English and cultural studies. Sabin's sensitivity to the political vulnerability of literary studies in the face of a powerfully articulated field of postcolonial studies helps readers of intermodernism or Indo-Anglian literature realize that after they have responded to the question that motivates this chapter, "What is Anand's place in English literature?," they should consider the following: "What does Anand's writing offer to postcolonial discourse?" If literary scholars leave this question to postcolonial critics, Anand's writing, with all its distinct challenges and pleasures, will disappear from discourse about English cultural history at the very moment his work is getting renewed attention from revisionist literary scholars. Discredited by the very words that distinguish him, "Indo-Anglian," "radical," "eccentric," Anand's peculiarly English context and language of dissent becomes a liability, the sign of the tainted legacy and continuing dominance of English language and liberalism for members of India's cultural elite. This taint, easy to spot, promotes the agendas of postcolonial critics who can quickly apply their theoretical tools, master, and then dispatch with Anand's writing.

This chapter and its subject may appear suspect, even degenerate, in the context of postcolonial literary analysis by Arun Mukherjee or postcolonial theory by Ranajit Guha, the founder of the Subaltern Studies Collective. For example, in *Dominance without Hegemony*, Guha argues that during the time Anand was writing his intermodern fiction and traveling to India to advocate for workers during the Gandhi movement, the very collective bodies he championed, the trades unions and *kisan sabhas*, were not vehicles of sincere or effective protest, but "instances" of the compromised "British idiom of R (Resistance)," or what may be called "Rightful Dissent" (55). Guha emphasizes the limitations imposed by this British idiom on collective Indian voices, citing as the results "systematic misrepresentation, abuse and exploitation by foreign and indigenous elites" of the "peaceable aspect" of some forms of collective Indian protest. Guha's sense of dissent, so different from Sabin's and so different from mine, makes shame and loathing, rather than careful contemplation, the due of Indians like Anand who relied in part on this "British idiom of R (Resistance)." Anand's status as a member of an English-speaking, English-educated elite puts him into the wrong camp, the camp made up of groups including the Congress Party, Communist Party, and followers of Gandhism generally, that Guha rebukes. However, both Guha and Anand agree on one thing: the value of the idiom of English liberalism and thus English language for Indian anticolonial protest movements. They would disagree on the character of that value, Guha arguing passionately that it is a negative value, Anand arguing at least as passionately that it is positive.

Sabin's book implicitly supports my call for future study of Anand as radical eccentric by describing an as-yet-to-be written "survey of writings critical of the British-Indian relationship" in such a way that Anand appears a necessary addition to her collection of English-language dissenters and mavericks (3). She suggests that Edmund Burke, who is featured in her book, would probably head such a survey, and that, among other late-twentieth-century writers like Salman Rushdie, early-twentieth-century writers Gandhi, Orwell, Forster, and Leonard Woolf would require treatment. Anand is an obvious addition to this last group of dissenters, but he, like the others, must be defended as a subject of study in the face of postcolonial criticism of liberal colonial dissenters. Sabin prepares the way for such defense by opposing Guha's argument in the following terms:

> Prevailing postcolonial critique offers little space for literary reading as I am describing it because it denies individuation: every text is made to be representative of collective discourse . . . . Such reduced differentiation invites no exploration of the specific questionings and self-questionings that give distinction to particular voices, nor is it responsive to history in attending to the varying pressures of different historical moments. (10)

This chapter attempts precisely what Sabin thinks is missing from postcolonial critique: an exploration of the "specific questionings and self-questionings that give distinction to [Anand's] particular voices," an exploration that is sensitive to "the varying pressures of different historical moments" during his intermodern career in London and Bombay.

Given Sabin's focus on English, rather than Indo-Anglian writers, it is interesting that she ends her literary-critical manifesto with a list of Indo-Anglian novelists, or what she describes more specifically as the "writers of current fiction in English by writers of South Asian location or origin." This list includes names that are more or less familiar to most readers of popular new twentieth- and twenty-first-century English-language fictions (for example, Vikram Seth, Arundhati Roy, Rohinton Mistry, Pankaj Mishra) and represents what Sabin regards as "the greatest challenge to the inert categories of academic postcolonial criticism" (11). She speculates that the English writings of the young South Asian writers who pose this challenge may eventually lead to a revision of not only postcolonial academic criticism, but to "interpretations of earlier writers, such as Nirad C. Chaudhuri, V. S. Naipaul, and Salman Rushdie" (11). While Sabin does not mention Anand here or elsewhere in her study, Nirad C. Chaudhuri, the first of the three men who represents Sabin's category of the "old" Indo-Anglian writers, is Anand's contemporary.[38] Sabin limits her analysis of Indo-Anglian literature to an epilogue that examines the works of the young Pankaj Mishra, a decision based more on her attraction to him than any prediction of his future eminence. Her purposes, if not her tastes, could have been served equally well by analysis of texts of Chaudhuri or Anand. Interpretation of literature by Anand and other "old" Indo-Anglian writers is so limited we have yet to discover whether, with their intermodern values and contexts, they could challenge the postcolonial academic criticism of a Ranajit Guha as cleverly and powerfully as a Vikram Seth, Arundhati Roy, or Pankaj Mishra. I end this chapter with two invitations. The first asks scholars who thrive on theoretical debate to take on the project of analyzing the specific forms of Anand's challenge to postcolonial critique. The second asks more traditional scholars of English and English-language literature to engage in new but recognizably literary ways with Anand's texts because, at their most exceptional, they resist theoretical mastery, stimulating interest and analysis to the degree they baffle and even contradict expectations (Sabin 5).

Chapter 3

Inez Holden: "Adventuress" to Socialist

The writing and working history of Inez Holden confirms an unfortunate paradox; although Holden was socially the best connected of the writers I discuss in this book—the daughter of gentry, she was painted by Augustus John, appears in memoirs by Evelyn Waugh and Anthony Powell, lived in H. G. Wells's mews flat during the Blitz, was George Orwell's friend until his death in 1950—she remains the most obscure figure in my group of radical eccentrics. Only with the publication of Jenny Hartley's feminist study, *Millions Like Us*, did Holden's name come to the attention of a wide audience. This chapter expands on Hartley's recovery of Holden, demonstrating how Holden's voice counted for Orwell, Smith, and Anand, and arguing that it should count for anyone intrigued by literary London of the 1930s and 1940s. Scholars of intermodernism, in particular, should find Holden interesting in part because she transformed herself from a high-jinx party girl, the Lopez of Smith's *The Holiday*, into a writer of wartime documentaries praised by H. G. Wells and J. B. Priestley. The story of her shifts from interwar frivolity to wartime seriousness provides scholars with invaluable representations of classic intermodern obsessions: workers, work, and total war. A writer of comedic fictions about labor, war, and Englishness, Holden is of special value to critics who are frustrated by the relatively low numbers of women writers who are cited in surveys of English industrial or working-class fiction, war writing, or comedy.[1] This chapter attempts to sort out the lessons of Holden's exclusion from these histories by analyzing her patriotic socialist satires, written shortly before her close friend Orwell composed his fantastically popular and fantastically pessimistic satires, *Animal Farm* and *Nineteen Eighty-Four*.

Holden, born into a gentry family, was one of many writers and artists who found the lives of workers on the home front compelling. Her most memorable intermodern narratives fulfill the ambitions that the scholar Constance Reaveley describes in her *Spectator* article of 7 April 1944:

> I watched the life of the factory. I thought a good deal went on that ought to be more widely known about and understood. I thought I would write to the Bishop, and urge that young men in training for Holy Orders should work for six months or so in a factory (or a mine or a shop) to get an insight for themselves into the way people live and work . . . Again, it seemed to me that the girls I knew at the works needed a better literature to feed their minds. Fiction, like poetry, should be an interpretation and criticism of life . . . I thought I would write to the head of a women's college, and suggest that a girl who wanted to write, and would work in a factory for a few months, could produce stories for factory girls about factory girls, which would give them a lot more interest than anything there is on the market for them at present. (Hartley, *Hearts* 148–49)

As Reaveley admits, she did none of these things. Holden, without the incentives or prospects of university students, took up where Reaveley left off, writing fictions that could appeal to working-class readers who wanted "stories for factory girls about factory girls." The narrative style of her fictions also would have appealed to readers of the *TLS*, *Spectator*, and other middlebrow journals that reviewed her books. Holden's readers would have recognized in her representations of working-class people an invitation to work for the leftist ideals of the Thirties, long after the most prominent writers of the Auden Generation had given up on them.

In the process of introducing Holden's literature of the 1930s and 1940s, this chapter provides my book's best evidence of the need for widespread adoption among scholars of twentieth-century literature of the category of intermodernism. Exploring relations between Holden's fiction and the dominant narrative aesthetic of the 1930s, the documentary movement in English literature and film, the chapter shows how consideration of women novelists and short story writers breaks down the divide between the period's categories—"the Thirties," "the War," "the Forties"—that still structure knowledge about English literature in the intermodern decades.[2] It also shows how Holden's gradual movement from upper- to working-class identifications resulted in a body of writing that differs in subject and form from the writings of bourgeois males who "went over" during the same period, challenging old values as it infuses new vigor into critical accounts of the Left literature of the period. Aiming to change the way critics define politics, literature, and their relations in the intermodern years, this chapter never loses sight of a more immediate goal: to create a memorable, inspiring story out of Holden's radical border crossings, from adventuress to socialist, party girl to novelist, writer to worker and back.[3]

To describe Holden's movements in terms of border crossing is to employ a metaphor that preoccupied many of the members of Orwell's generation and the critics who have written about them. For example, Cunningham uses this metaphor to figure his critical enterprise as he attempts to provide a fuller account of the period by breaking down distinctions between literature and society, text and context. He frames his study with the following questions: "Admitting, then, the fluidity of the '30s bounds, what of the decade's contents? How is one to decode the plurality of signs, to read the multiplicity of texts within, and comprising, the larger period text, how to map this terrain . . . ?" (16). Boundaries, signs, maps, terrain: Cunningham's journey in many ways takes its language from the poetry, plays, and memoirs of the prominent writers it comments upon, repeating their enthusiasms and blindnesses even as it strives to revise our understanding of their achievement.

Cunningham's interrogation of the accepted bounds and contents of the 1930s leads him to conclude that, despite the "strong presence" of Auden, "It is even more obviously the case . . . that the '30s are greatly straitened when they are defined only with reference to Auden and his closest contemporaries" (21). The writers he lists as "roughly the same age as Auden but not actually in the inner circles" include Orwell, V. S. Pritchett, Christopher Caudwell, and Samuel Beckett. These men he designates "maverick authors" who "attended neither Oxford or Cambridge" (21). It isn't until he discusses the critical bias against the 1930s novel that he mentions multiple names of women writers who, like the mavericks (and worker-writers) also didn't attend Cambridge or Oxford. However, the women writers' lack of an Oxbridge education does not earn Cunningham's commentary and he rarely discusses their work in any detail. This inattention to a vital source of the period's "multiplicity of texts" belies his comment that, in addition to novelists like Rosamond Lehmann, Naomi Mitchison, and Winifred Holtby, "previously well-known women novelists like Virginia Woolf, Elizabeth Bowen, Jean Rhys, Ivy Compton-Burnett, and Dorothy Richardson . . . cannot be simply left, as most books about the 1930s leave them, out of the account" (26). Cunningham's assertion that it is enough for him to identify "the gap that commonly denotes [women writers'] absence" implies that only in the case of male writers will the contents of the map of the Thirties fundamentally alter once scholars look beyond the "Auden Generation" (27). Women writers are presumed to have a single "place" that can be "marked on the '30s map for future reference" (27). The study of women's fiction may require a shift of a boundary here and there, but will not lead to startling discoveries about the underlying character of the 1930s terrain.

The more recent books on 1930s to which I've referred in previous chapters challenge this assumption. To a greater or lesser extent, each of these studies demonstrates that consideration of women writers actually matters to our configurations of the period's literature and history. Yet the study that helps us see best how Inez Holden's fiction demands a new map of the 1930s, readers should initially consult Andy Croft's *Red Letter Days*, a revisionist study of the period's fiction, which provides the most direct challenge to Cunningham's vision of the connections between literature and politics.

Adventures in Commitment

Croft sees the 1930s as a "generous moment" and celebrates what he sees as the alliance between imaginative writing and leftist, socialist politics. His portrait of the decade invites Holden into the mainstream of literary activity insofar as it claims the 1930s are "The one moment in the twentieth century when . . . the causes and concerns of the Left were genuinely popular, forward-looking and culturally dominant" and the "the novel the most popular literary form among readers of all ages and classes" (24, 25). In contrast to Cunningham, Croft does not see the redness of the Red Decade as a false tint that represents either the transitory sympathies of "a small number of young upper-middle-class poets" for the Communist Party or the mind-numbing orthodoxy of a Marxist literary establishment. Instead, he describes leftist novels as "the characteristic achievement of a developing political and intellectual alliance, between the literary intelligentsia and the organized working class, between professional and amateur writers, metropolitan and provincial" (28–29).

Croft provides an appropriate frame for interpreting the writings of Holden, an ambiguously classed, non-activist writer, in part because he argues that most of the 1930s leftist writers "belonged to no political party, few would have seen themselves belonging to a 'Red Decade,' some would not necessarily have described themselves as socialists" (27). He disputes the belief that the 1930s was a decade of inhibiting leftist orthodoxy, an idea he associates with the legacy of exaggerated panic about the Communist Party inspired in part by Orwell's misguided comments in "Inside the Whale":

> Communists and near-Communists had a disproportionately large influence in the literary reviews. It was a time of labels, slogans and evasions. At the worst moments you were expected to lock yourself up in a constipating little cage of lies; at the best a sort of voluntary censorship ("Ought I to say this? Is it pro-Fascist?") It is almost inconceivable that good novels should be written in such an atmosphere. (Orwell, *CEJL* I: 519)[4]

In contrast to this vision of Communist-dominated culture industry, Croft argues that even an overtly political journal like the *Left Review* avoided any single position and was crowded with talent—with established and experimental writers, working class and middle class, famous and new (26). This view of who matters for 1930s writing demonstrates why Croft should be seen as making a new map of the period rather than redrawing boundaries on the old one. He recognizes and prioritizes new names in the decade's cast of writers, rather than simply reshuffling the standings of the same familiar figures. Holden might be one of the writers who Croft anticipates with his generous speculation about "how many more wondrous fictions are still lost, how many more unquestionably await rediscovery" (10).

Although Holden's fictions display her special talent for capturing the absurd pretensions and fixations of characters from the wealthier strata of English society, this chapter argues for her rediscovery on the basis of the relations between her satires of bohemian and upper-class life and her treatments of working-class characters in her short stories and her two wartime novels, *Night Shift* and *There's No Story There*. Like Orwell, Isherwood, Henry Green, and other celebrated middle- or upper-class writers who wrote convincingly about the working class, Holden entered the worlds of the working-class people she wrote about.[5] She shared the conditions of their lives before pushing for change through documentary fictions that, in Reaveley's words, provide "an interpretation and criticism of life." In Holden's case, however, immersion in working-class life was motivated as much by financial desperation as literary ambition or socialist commitment. She wanted the salary for her labors as well as the commissions that might come from writing about it. Without a family, profession, or education to fall back on, Holden's hold on the privileges that distinguish the typical writer's life—food, paper, books, a room (or desk) of one's own, and time to write—was unstable. Her deviations from intellectual, financial, and what some might have regarded as respectable sexual conventions may have enabled her to represent with more sensitivity than her celebrated contemporaries the frustrating contradictions and illuminating gaps in dominant ideologies about class and gender, particularly as they emerge in discourses about an idealized England and heroic Englishness.

Holden's background makes her an unlikely candidate for the role of path-breaking author in English working-class and war literature. When in her twenties, Holden was noted for her beauty, and aging millionaires and bohemian artists alike found her attractive. The three novels she wrote during those years record the frivolous, absurd lives of privileged characters who could have stepped out of *Vile Bodies*.[6] In a short memoir of Holden written after her death in 1974, Anthony Powell claimed that the rich world described in her second novel *Born Old, Died Young* (1932), was not invented, but rather satirically drawn from Holden's experience. He also claimed that the novel's heroine, Virginia Jenkinson, was Holden's fiction-alized self-portrait ("Memoir" 91). Powell notes that Holden, like Virginia Jenkinson, lived "fairly dangerously in a rich world of a distinctly older gen-eration" ("Memoir" 91). Musing on Holden's appeal, the "consumptive charm" that led to her being known in the Sitwell circle as "Gallopers" (89), Powell is drawn into speculation about the nature of Holden's shadowy love affairs. While he admits that his portrait makes Holden seem a "poule de luxe," he softens that judgment by noting, "I don't think I can recall any-one upon whom less could ever be pinned (among ladies who, like Virginia Jenkinson, were admittedly adventuresses) than Inez" (92). Of her fiction, the stuff that really mattered to Holden, Powell has this to say: "In a strange way it was herself, rather than her books, that marked her out. Her novels, like her talk, full of wit and original ideas, never quite came off. They lacked construction" ("Memoir" 88).[7]

I cite Powell's dubious tribute at some length to illustrate a common pat-tern in portraits of Holden that appear in literary memoirs or biographies. Emphasizing the unusual, indeed mythical nature of the story *of* her youth, these materials are careful to register critical disappointment for the stories she produced *in* her youth. I examine her youthful productions with fresh eyes, concentrating on relations between Holden's first novel of 1929, *Sweet Charlatan*, her experiments with Basic English published as the col-lection *Death in High Society* in 1934, and her satires of high society pub-lished in popular, mass circulation magazines throughout the 1930s. Rather than lacking construction, Holden's early fictions should be seen as intro-ducing readers to literary–political territories that demand better-constructed maps. They are the unlikely materials that supported Holden's transformations of consciousness and circumstance that, by the 1940s, complement and complicate the conversion stories told about bourgeois socialist writers of the 1930s.

Of relevance to interpretations of Holden's journey are Croft's stories about Jack Lindsay, a young Australian poet and dealer in fine prints, who roamed the circles of London's demimonde in 1927 hoping to meet the likes of Augustus John. According to popular anecdote Lindsay was accom-panied by Aldous Huxley on one of his trips and was rewarded by his caricature in *Point Counter Point*. Ten years later, Lindsay wrote *1649*, his most famous socialist novel (Croft 127). This thumbnail sketch leads Croft to ask, "What had happened in these ten years to turn a minor character in a late Bloomsbury novel of ideas into a major political novelist?" (128). With some alteration, we can ask Croft's question of Holden: "What had happened in ten years to turn a minor character in Bloomsbury artists' cir-cles into a powerful political novelist?" How could Holden—quintessential

girl-about-town—be the author of *Night Shift*, a novel that impressed
H. G. Wells as "First rate" and earned J. B. Priestley's jacket comment,
"The most truthful and most exciting account of war-time industrial
Britain"?[8]

Documentary in form, *Night Shift* gives an account of Holden's wartime
work at an aircraft factory in North London. Its compassionate, humorous
renderings of the workers' conversations amid the noise, danger, and routine
of the factory demonstrate that for Holden the arrival of war did not
diminish the importance of the political goals of the 1930s. Holden's choice
of the popular forms and contents of the 1930s in her first novel of the
1940s is not a sign of her lack of imagination or capacity for narrative construction, but rather her commitment to a still unrealized social vision. It
is worth remembering that as late as 1937 Storm Jameson was writing in
Fact that "The conditions for the growth of a socialist literature scarcely
exist" and was calling for a "new literature" built on documents (Deane
314). Her description of a realist fiction modeled after documentary film
perfectly describes the aims and effects of *Night Shift*:

> As the photographer does, so must the writer keep himself out of the picture
> while working ceaselessly to present the fact from a striking (poignant,
> ironic, penetrating, significant) angle. The narrative must be sharp,
> compressed, concrete. Dialogue must be short—a seizing of the significant,
> the revealing word. The emotion should spring directly from the fact. It
> must not be squeezed from it by the writer . . . His job is not to tell us what
> he felt, but to be coldly and industriously presenting, arranging, selecting,
> discarding from the mass of his material to get the significant detail which
> leaves no more to be said, and implies everything.
> And for goodness' sake let us get some fun out of it. (Deane 316)

Once we read Holden's war novel in terms of Jameson's call for a new literature, it becomes an interesting, "fun" book to consider in accounts of both
1930s and 1940s writing.

Night Shift invites comparisons with other documentary accounts of
factory life in wartime, especially Amabel Williams-Ellis's *Women in War
Factories* (1943) or Mass-Observation's *War Factory* (1943), while its title
also reminds us of its debt to peacetime documentaries such as Jack
Common's volume of worker-writers' prose in *Seven Shifts*. Each of these
four books shows a shared belief in the value of workers' lives and the ability of documentary prose to win for the workers their readers' support.
However, the wartime documentaries by Holden and Williams-Ellis focus
on exactly that which is omitted from Common's collection: descriptions of
and by women workers. In fact, Common's book begins with an apology
for "one serious omission: [my book] does not include any contribution

from the women's side of the world of work." The apology is followed by a promise, "to make good [the lack] in a subsequent volume, which the women will have to themselves." For unknown reasons, this promise went unfulfilled. Wartime socialist fictions by women writers are also invisible. They probably lie buried beneath what Tom Harrison described in a December 1941 *Horizon* review as "right wing" productions of "lady novelists" (qtd. in Hartley, *Millions* 7), or grouped with other wartime socialist fiction that was reviled as old fashioned and boring and was swept out of public view (Croft 340).

The six chapters of *Night Shift* are far from boring although they represent six monotonous days in the lives of workers who are making camera parts for reconnaissance and bombing planes. The novel has an anonymous third-person narrator who is described in the jacket copy as "having no very definite personality, acting rather as the lens of a moving camera." A reviewer agreed with the jacket copy's implied grouping of *Night Shift* and prewar "camera-I" socialist realism, describing Holden's novel in the 15 May 1942 *Spectator* as a documentary and praising it for having "the assured interest of good reportage." Edwin Muir in *The Listener* emphasized the novel's "feeling of reality" and concluded that "This little book is perfectly conceived and executed; it compresses into a small scene a great mass of life," and Rebecca West praised the last chapter as "a masterpiece of descriptive writing," adding, "the factory workers, even when they are described in a few lines, are three-dimensional figures."[9] In other words, Holden achieves in 1942 what others found so compelling (or irritating) about *Down and Out* or *The Road to Wigan Pier* in the mid-1930s: an upper-class writer's ability to render social and political truth about working-class lives through fictionalized autobiography. No less ingenious than Orwell, Holden achieved her documentary truth-effect by displacing her class origins and identity from the novel's first-person narrator to a character named Feather with whom upper- and middle-class readers would presumably identify.

Her narrator tells us that Feather is "the sort of girl who would have been 'ladying it' at a First Aid Post attached to some auxiliary service" and wonders if "something had happened to shake up her journey in the slow coach of security" (13). The narrator ends her speculations with the observation that "Anyway, her hair was still sleek and well brushed like the soft coat of a luxurious pet animal" (13). Holden treats her less fashionable characters with equal care, using a spare description and dialogue to bring to life the novel's more numerous working-class women such as Mabs, Nan, Mrs. Lloyd, Mrs. Chance, and Ma, or its managerial men, the Jewish foreman, Dick Strauss, or the engineers like old Sid or Flash Jack.

Typical of Holden's style and concerns is a scene that records the reactions of the workers to a conversation between Mabs, who is humorously protesting the tedious demands of their work, and the unpopular Mrs. Lloyd, who primly objects, "We have to work to produce the arms for the airplanes to fight the Nazis":

> "We know that," answered Mabs. "But it don't prevent you getting tired, do it? Besides, although it's war now, I worked in a factory very much the same as this, in peace-time, see." Everyone frowned on Mrs. Lloyd, there was a convention against easy heroical talk and pat-off patriotism in the workshop; that way of yapping-out was all right for people who did not work at all . . . sitting well back in their arm-chairs and thought, "We are all in it together" because they listened to the radio news four times a day. "After all," said Mrs. Chance, "we work here to get away from thinking about the war, so what does she want to start in talking about it like that for?" (109–10)

This exchange, which characteristically honors the differences between working-class individuals as well as those individuals' differences with nonworking patriots, takes place at the end of a shift on a Friday, the fifth day of the week. When nearly all the workers are killed in an air raid during the next night shift, the reader is shaken by the loss of a predominantly working-class community. The political meanings of this ending clearly connect *Night Shift* to other working-class, industrial, or Popular Front novels of the intermodern period, but they appear to distance the novel from Holden's earlier work.[10]

It is hard to imagine a novel more different from *Night Shift*, with its sincere, tragic representations of wartime factory work, than Holden's first novel, *Sweet Charlatan*. An absurd, comic ghost story, it inspired one irritated *TLS* reviewer to complain, "Miss Holden could, if she wished, write quite well and lucidly. Instead she is clever." *Sweet Charlatan*'s most memorable innovation is a witch character named Rose Leaf, whose roles as hostess and murderess seem to demonically attract the young "hero," Cedric Dorn. The only sympathetic character in the book's cast of absurdities is Cedric's young wife, the bohemian waif, Autumn. Rose Leaf takes care of the various human impediments to her union with Cedric by magically killing them off. Only Autumn escapes because she has abandoned Cedric before Rose's evil spells can catch up with her. Although Autumn is herself abandoned by her author at the end of the book, we are able to imagine some positive fate for her given the following revelation:

> Once she [Autumn] had been enslaved by the frail affectations of Cedric, the belated Beardsley gesture, the sweet superficiality, . . . the epigrammatic out-look on all that could be considered scholastically sound. . . . The talented versatility that made of Cedric poet, painter and actor in parody; all this silly brilliance had ceased to hypnotise, and Autumn herself had returned to

almost schoolgirlish simplicity of speech and thought and was even now considering the importance of doing what one liked. (181–82)

The language of this passage provides a taste of Holden's "social" (versus
socialist) style at its flippant best, with all its signs of a witty, Wildean satire
and sensibility.[11] Yet the subdued earnestness of Autumn's escape from
superficiality and the affirmation of her desires suggests that Holden might
have maintained a latent sympathy for her young female character that
arose from her own changing goals and identity.

Basic Experiments

Autumn's repudiation of the epigrams of the young bohemians in favor of
simplicity of speech points toward Holden's movement in this same direction.
The best examples of Holden's new style are the stories that she collected in
a volume titled *Death in High Society* (1934). It is the form of these stories,
rather than their contents, that sets them apart from other writings of the
day. Each is written in Basic English, C. K. Ogden's experimental language
that became famous as the "real" basis of Newspeak. In contrast to Orwell's
frightful parody language, which is intended to insure total Party dominance
by limiting all of Oceania's residents to thought consistent with the principles
of Ingsoc (English Socialism) (303), Basic was intended to facilitate communication between different classes and nations. Limited to a vocabulary of
850 words, Basic was designed so anyone with a phonograph could teach it
to themselves in thirty hours (Ogden 4). As Ogden explains in the foreword
to *Death in High Society*, "[Basic English] is an all-round language for everyday use, which may be turned into a language for the expert by the addition
of short special lists" (8). When it comes to literature "at its highest levels,"
Ogden acknowledges that Basic "is able to do little more than give an outline
of what the writer said," but he insists that it is still important for "the experts
to see what sort of [imaginative] books go best into Basic and why" (8, 9).
Holden is Ogden's expert on the short story, and after noting that her stories
or sketches appeared first in standard English in such publications as *Harper's
Bazaar, Nash's,* and *The Evening Standard,* Ogden assures us that Holden's
stories "are representative of an important part of the reading material on
which the value of Basic for general purposes has to be tested" (9).

It would be easy to interpret Holden's willingness to participate in
Ogden's project as a sign of her commitment to leftist movements that promoted an egalitarian, nonelitist language. However, Holden never
announced her motives for translating previously published stories into

Ogden's nonliterary language. The lack of any record of her interpretation of Basic's goals and impact may go part way toward explaining her absence from critical accounts of simplified language movements of the intermodern period. We should keep in mind that Basic was popular long before Orwell wrote *Nineteen Eighty-Four*, at the time Michael Roberts was writing a characteristic leftist retort to T. S. Eliot's call for complexity and difficulty in modern poetry (Cunningham 298–99). Roberts declared in his "Preface" to *New Country* that as the writer

> sees more and more clearly that his interests are bound up with those of the working class, so will his writing clear itself from the complexity and introspection, the doubt and cynicism of recent years, and become more and more intelligible to that class and so help in the evolution of a style which, coming partly from the "shirt-sleeve" workers and partly from the "intellectual", will make the revolutionary movement articulate. (Roberts 18)

Ogden's, Holden's, and Roberts's efforts can be seen as contributing to one characteristic cultural movement and they deserve to be read as such. Politics, more than aesthetics, determines the significant differences between their contributions to that movement.

In contrast to Roberts (and Roberts's critical commentators) neither Ogden nor Holden imagined that simple vocabulary and syntax would necessarily facilitate a Marxist political program. Far from it. In Ogden's early texts on Basic he never associates his simplified "miniature" language with revolutionary goals and rarely explores political implications or mentions contemporary political contexts. In fact, one of the first instances of a statement from Ogden that approaches political interpretation of Basic's motivation or effects appears in his obscure volume of 1931, *Brighter Basic: Examples of Basic English for Young Persons of Taste and Feeling*. Arguing that international pressures urge the immediate adoption of Basic as a world auxiliary language, Ogden makes the following prediction:

> [The Great War was, in fact], only a little one—a sort of one act play before the curtain is lifted on a more serious military outburst. . . . Something has to be done for the development of international feeling, or another War will take our breath away in more sense than one. Where there is no breath, there is no language—only a system of signs or marks on paper; but where there is no international language, the breath even of nations may be turned into some new chemical substance by gasses of such power that there will be no signs of the British Museum, or the committee for the Study of International Relations, having ever been in existence.
>
> What is chiefly necessary at the present time is some new Idea, by which the mind of man may be lifted out of its narrow prison-house. . . . If the

nations get at one another's throats again and secretaries make more tea in
Government offices, money will go down in value so far that families may
no longer be supported, and the Earth may go up in smoke. What makes a
nation is a common language. What will make men international will be a
common language. That is the great Idea.
     Basic is the only chance. (26–27)

While Ogden's humanitarian conviction that the immediate adoption of
Basic is necessary to save nations from massive acts of destruction is as clear
as it is naïve, it would be difficult to find in this expression of internation-
alist sympathies anything approaching a political or party platform. Only
in 1934, after Hitler had assumed power and fears of losing the British
Museum would have been shared by a wider public, does Ogden directly
address the question of Basic's political uses. Admitting in his introduction
to *The System of Basic English* that "the moment is perhaps not altogether
unfavorable to the demand for a new linguistic conscience in the new
generation whose social experiments may otherwise be frustrated by
outworn verbal formulae," he also points out that "Basic is not unduly
revolutionary." He notes that in its attempt to "preserve the essentials of a
great tradition . . . [Basic] may even be regarded as conservative by those
who advocate a complete break with the past" (vi).
     Ogden's awareness in 1934 of the ambiguous political implications of
adopting simple prose contrasts with Roberts's assumption that simple style
and "shirt sleeve" concerns are inherently linked. It also contrasts with
Cunningham's conflation of simple prose movements with Marxism and
Socialist Realism. Impatient with middle-class writers who attempted to
"go over" to the working class, Cunningham proves Orwell's match in his
contemptuous dismissal of committed prose fiction of the 1930s.
Discussing the effects of the "Party dogma" implemented at the 1934
Soviet Writers' Congress, Cunningham concludes that in Britain Socialist
Realism "helped to slow down literary experiment and to smash up modernism especially in the novel, thus pushing the novel back beyond Henry
James into the arms of nineteenth-century bourgeois naturalism" (299).
Study of Holden's intermodern experiments with Basic remind us that simple language movements predated the 1934 Writers' Congress and that the
"smash up" of modernism occurred because there were real and widespread
cultural and political shifts in English culture, not because hordes of nas-
cent modernist poets and novelists were brainwashed by Karl Radek or
Michael Roberts to adopt the aesthetic of Socialist Realism. Since this study
celebrates what Cunningham mourns, it is inevitable that its vision of
1930s intermodernism departs markedly from Cunningham's. Rather than
characterizing intermodernism as a regression to nineteenth-century

naturalism, I argue that scholars should see it as a distinctive space or movement in English literary history that grew out of particular twentieth-
century historical and political pressures. Its literature appeared in diverse
forms advanced by several aesthetic movements, some of which were influenced by leftist, though not typically or necessarily Marxist, ideologies.
Basic English is just one of those movements. Basic's widely publicized
debates with rival artificial languages Esperanto, Ido, Interglossa, among
others, provide additional evidence of the cultural and ideological breadth
of the move toward a non-modernist, non-Marxist aesthetic of simplicity.

Abiding by Ogden's rules, Holden's Basic stories are always funny, often
absurd, and occasionally grotesque, employing the techniques of comedy in
order to avoid what Cunningham sees as the worst danger of simple prose:
dullness (302). Holden's publications of the 1940s continue her penchant
for comic writing, first indulged in her satirical novels of the 1920s and
early 1930s. Despite her increasingly sophisticated political consciousness
and newfound dedication to an Orwellian nonrevolutionary socialism,
Holden depended as much on the forms and spirit of comedy as techniques
and contents of documentary to work for transformation of oppressive
institutions of intermodern English culture and society.[12]

Glen Cavaliero's book on comedy in English fiction provides a theoretical framework for assessing the potential political effects of Holden's intermodern comedies. Cavaliero's emphasis on the reception of textual comedy,
the peculiarly social dimension of the private practice of reading comedic
novels, recalls the explanation of the social contexts of humor, comedy, and
jokes proposed by one of the best early-twentieth-century theorists on the
subject, Sigmund Freud. Discovering in structures of reading resemblances
to the social situation Freud associates with the telling of jokes, Cavaliero
implicitly invites us to incorporate Freud's political analysis of a triangular
joking situation into our interpretations of narrative comedy. The degree of
critical attention traditionally paid to the political contents of 1930s and
1940s fictions makes investigation of the political meanings of the structures
of intermodern comedy all the more important. Cavaliero ascribes to the
author of a novel a role structurally akin to Freud's joke teller; his novel
reader is akin to the recipient of a joke; and the occasion inspiring narrative
comedy—what Cavaliero terms the "monolith"—is akin to the butt of the
joke, the third person in Freud's analysis whose passive, but evocative body,
invites the joke and calls up the social laughter that proclaims it a success.

For Cavaliero's description of the relations between author, reader, and
comedic occasion to prove useful for understanding of the structural politics of Holden's comedies, one must first understand his symbol of the
"monolith," the thing that generates comedic process or action. Describing
the monolith in ways that recall another term from classic comic theory,

Henri Bergson's "mechanical inelasticity," Cavaliero argues that the monolith symbolizes

> personal beliefs and institutional behavior of an absolutist and authoritarian kind which form the primary material for the imaginative process of comedic transmutation, a process which enlarges human understanding and perspectives, and of which the several categories of comedy (celebration, parody, satire, farce, irony, burlesque and wit) each form a part. (x)

Cavaliero's hopeful emphasis on the transmuting, enlarging powers of comedy assumes that novels can change their readers and the societies in which those readers learn and act. He characterizes the action of narrative comedy or more precisely, "comedic novels," as a "living process, an experience *of* experience, a way of contending with the enigmas, frustrations, contradictions and misfortunes that are the external obstacles to happiness—and also with the vanities, follies and sheer wickedness that human beings breed within themselves" (ix). If a comedic novel is also a "way of contending," reading comedy becomes an opportunity to participate in a kind of politico-religious experience and each comedic novel an invitation to readers to understand and analyze conditions that can be "resolved by laughter" (15). Cavaliero sees celebratory comedy as the pinnacle of comedic achievement because it permits the most thoroughgoing transformation and resolution.

The extent of comedy's transformative or resolving effect depends, in Cavaliero's theory, on the formal procedure the novelist takes up in response to the monolith. Satire, the procedure of comedy that Holden most favored through the 1930s, confronts the monolith openly, often aggressively, and usually with an appeal to a broadly popular laughter (Cavaliero 5). It supposes a "congenial audience," readers who share the narrator's motivations for attacking the third party, the blocking, obstructing monolith that in Holden's 1930s satires is usually identified with protected members of England's pretentious upper-classes and in the 1940s fictions, with the English class system itself (Cavaliero 5). Cavalerio's emphasis on the unyielding, institutionalized nature of the monolith tends to suggest that the satirist and her audience are inherently and heroically rebellious, seeking to transmute an authoritarian, oppressive reality through comic critique and belittling laughter. But it is important to acknowledge the flip side of this comedic power-game; "Where satire is concerned, the reader, through his involvement in the matter under scrutiny, is both the judge and the potential victim of the process" (Cavaliero 33). The potential victimization of the reader reminds us of the political instability of the satirist's position—his or her power to encourage social or political acceptance or exclusion, freedom or constraint, within specific historical, cultural circumstances.

Critics who examine comedic writings by members of socially oppressed groups sometimes express doubts about comedy's real transformative power because they recognize the ambiguous political effects implicit within comedic structures. In her study of British women's comic fiction, for example, Margaret Stetz surveys the feminist literature on humor theory, finding some theorists championing the view that comedy leads inevitably toward personal and political liberation while others warn that it can "defuse anger and undermine action," weakening the will to change (Stetz xi). Such division points to the always dynamic relation between aesthetics and politics, the need to ground theory in specific readings of comedic texts and categories and in specific historical circumstances.

During the intermodern years, specific historical circumstances inspired many novelists to write novels of dark humor. As Lisa Colletta notes,

> The real circumstances between the wars were shockingly unkind. Violence on a grand scale, the loss of identity, and the increasing mechanization of society left the modern individual in a dilemma. Traumatized by recent historical events, there was the fear that some incalculable and horrible catastrophe awaited, yet, deprived of a sense of forward movement, there was the equally terrible prospect that nothing at all would happen. (9)

Colletta's study of modernist dark humor novels helps readers measure the aesthetic, political distance of Holden's 1930s fictions from those of her better-known friends, Powell and Waugh, and contemporaries Woolf and Compton-Burnett. Holden's Basic and standard English stories of this time clearly affirm the satirist's belief in a solid moral ground against which absurd, wicked, or excessively antisocial behaviors can be measured and judged. Unlike the dark humorists Colletta discusses and unlike her friend Orwell, Holden never seems to abandon hope of understanding the world or of correcting human behavior (Colletta 2, 5).[13] More to the point, Holden's Basic stories, in all their simplicity, have the potential to oppose monoliths just as effectively as her standard English satires of high society.

We see this potential in Holden's Basic story "The Value of Being Seen," which was first published in standard English in the August 1933 issue of *Nash's* as "The Importance of Being Seen." In both its mainstream and Basic versions, the story satirically traces the inauspicious career of Daphne Astor, debutante, who fails so spectacularly to achieve the key note of "being seen" that she literally becomes invisible. In both stories, Daphne mistakenly ends up at a naughty bohemian party where she is pushed out of an upper-story window by a young man who thinks her disembodied voice is a hallucination. In both stories, Daphne crashes to the pavement below and loses consciousness. But there the similarities end. In the mainstream version published in *Nash's*, Daphne regains consciousness due to the ministrations of a young man in evening clothes with a "strong and sympathetic" voice. Having earned the upper-class male gaze, Daphne is rewarded with the last words in the story: "It is still early . . . Did you know that there are over two thousand night-clubs in London?"

With this statement, the story's scathing satire of the patriarchal aristocratic ritual of coming out is blunted. The suicidally respectable heroine may have been replaced by a naughty Bright Young Person, but she has returned to the fold of her class and all is well. Such reclamation is noticeably missing from the ending of the Basic version of the story. "The Value of Being Seen" sustains its satire of class privilege and the sale of women that underlies it because there is no gentleman in evening clothes to rescue Daphne. After her fall she remains prostrate on the pavement while the bohemian partiers continue their "one long, unending night out." In other words, this Basic story rewrites the non-Basic story in order to enact a more vigorous critique of monolithic social forms.

Holden's short stories show her delight in perverse endings that, like the endings of Stevie Smith's poems, finally disclose the social motivation of their comedy through a sting in the tail. Daphne's pathetic death at the end of "The Value of Being Seen" mocks women who would allow themselves to be emptied of character, voice, and visibility, who are complicit with the processes of social division that sustain snobbery like Mrs. Astor's. Yet some readers might feel a twinge of guilt at finding themselves enjoying the demise of such a victimized representative of social privilege. No such ambivalence disturbs the comic effects of Holden's wicked title story, "Death in High Society."[14] This story begins with the departure of two nameless cleaning women from the London home of Esmee Earnshaw, who watches them secretly and vindictively from the comfort of her long, elegant gray sedan. Esmee's sense of entitlement and her distance from her employees is revealed by her belief that "the chance to go into [her house] at all was, even to her friends, a sort of special reward. For this reason it would have been natural if the brushing and cleaning of this house had been a special event, valued in the memory of such women" (*Boating* 113). "Such women," working-class women, are vital to the story's plot, although the narrator concentrates on Esmee. We witness Esmee sneaking into her own house in order to check up on the thoroughness of her cleaning ladies and, as it so happens, her husband's letters, before she gets trapped midfloor in the elevator that she'd installed in order to "get more work done in less time" (*Boating* 118). Since Esmee is cheap and mean as well as rich, she has sent away her cleaners for the next three weeks to save on caretaking costs during the time she is supposedly down south relaxing in the sun. The story ends three weeks later with a satisfying, if macabre, form of retribution that gives the cleaning ladies the last word. "Well," says the first, "here we are again, dear. Where is she now, eh?" The second replies, "Keep your nose out of other cats' milk" while she makes her way with "slow, stiff feet . . . in the direction of the lift" (*Boating* 119).

The Interrupting Classes

Holden's delight in wicked endings is evident in her standard English stories that appeared in popular magazines and newspapers throughout the 1930s. "Blond Hero" is typical. Published in the February 1934 issue of *Harper's Bazaar*, the story features a shrewd, young manicurist named Miss Mason who never interrupted her clients' stories of their love affairs because she did not come from the "interrupting classes" (30). Miss Mason listens to the absurd fantasies of Miss Henrietta who agonizes over the affections of a man so indistinct, and so obviously in love with one Mrs. Talbot, that Miss Mason can only refer to him as the Blond Hero. Catering to Henrietta's vanity, desire, and bad habit of biting her nails, Miss Mason earns generous tips while her husband, a florist, delivers the Blond Hero's costly bouquets to Henrietta's unknown rival. The story satirizes the familiar vices of society ladies and leisured femininity in general, but does little to compensate its hard working, cynical heroine with anything other than laughter and the dominant and final perspective in the story: "Only Mrs. Talbot's eyebrows to pluck and then she could go home, see her husband, drink some gin and have a good laugh" (94).

Readers of *Harper's Bazaar* may laugh with Miss Mason at the particular foolishness of Henrietta, but they would be likely to also laugh off any more trenchant critique of the economics of idealized femininity that are implicit within representations of Miss Mason's intimate, demeaning work and dependent position. Holden's favored comic techniques of satire and burlesque give definite shape to the story, although her politics are, as in her Basic English stories, undetermined. There is no threat that Miss Mason's knowledge of the illusion of feminine beauty, its parasitic relation to masculine capital and feminine service, will ever inspire collective action against social and gender inequity, or even point toward the limited haven of liberalism, individual economic (and perhaps social) success for the deserving, intrepid heroine. The story's potential for upsetting the cultural politics of idealized leisured femininity is best measured through ironic tensions that emerge from its placement between columns of ads promoting luxury services and commodities—the very things the story requires us to mock, diminish, and reject if we are to enjoy its literary, aesthetic pleasures: "Marie Louise presents new hairdressing and beauty ideas"; "Look Happy!" through Irene Leslie's abilities to "bring your loveliness to its best" with "the most soothing, revitalising treatment in London"; study at Brown's Paris school of fashion where you can take "short and long courses in every high-salaried profession in the most popular businesses to-day"; or follow the advice of the Norway winter sports bureau and head to the Scandinavian slopes if you want an "ideal winter sports ground" where "you don't feel the cold" or, presumably, the pain of worldwide depression and developing political crisis.

The ambivalent political work of Holden's stories and sketches in popular magazines is best measured through casual, humorous pieces that explicitly cater to the fantasies for upward mobility that *Harper's Bazaar* advertisers depend on and sell to the magazine's readers. Making explicit the achieved, rather than natural, signs and styles of upper-class member-ship, Holden's pieces, "Country House Bridge" and especially, "Foxhunting—Is it Human?," blatantly trade on Holden's insider knowledge of upper-class ritual for their humor and her paycheck. Holden's sketches assume that *Harper's Bazaar* is attracting more readers who fantasize about joining the upper class or at least mastering its outward forms than readers who already have intimate knowledge of, let alone ancestral membership in, the upper class. In other words, her narrative voice assumes a feminine audience com-posed of adventuresses or more prosaically, dutiful students attending Brown's Paris school of fashion, rather than an audience made up of young society women like Miss Irene Cholmondeley, with her "defiant checks," whose picture appears at the bottom of the page containing Holden's "Country House Bridge" essay.

Satirizing anyone who might take seriously *Harper's* authority as a conduct manual, Holden yet depends on her ability to give instruction in upper-class manners for acceptance of her essays into the magazine. The humor of these essays is their principle value, for without it Holden would not be able to both mock and enchant readers aspiring to upper-class inclu-sion. Having inherited knowledge of the gentry's style and culture, Holden is disaffected enough from her class of origin to be able to expose to the public the absurdity of its prestigious traditions and exclusions. But her commitment to demystifying the signs and rituals of upper-class prestige is diminished by her role as salesperson, one hired to entice *Harper's Bazaar* readers with a secret class knowledge that makes the Cinderella fantasy of class infiltration seem attainable. Holden fashions herself as an actress, or as she describes herself in "Country House Bridge," a player, whose actual and acted roles are indistinguishable. She makes clear to her various constituencies that she can pass among the upper classes, but then shows her cards often enough to prove she cannot be relied upon to play by the house rules.

"Country House Bridge" begins with general comments on the ubiquity of the fashionable card game, before placing its author-narrator within the inner circle of its most rarified English practitioners. "Bridge is played all over the world, in all weathers and in different languages, but this summer it seemed to me that it was being played most in England, in English, at country house parties" (67). Holden then points to her eccentric position in those parties, admitting that she's been taught the elementary rules and complicated conventions of contract bridge innumerable times, but does not know the "real meaning and object of the game" and still has no ambition to learn (67).

The article's focus on the society that demands and sustains the complicated conventions of contract bridge makes it abundantly clear that "the game" Holden professes not to care about is both contract bridge and the game of upper-class socialization. The class meaning of the game becomes more obvious in Holden's commentary on the preliminaries of card playing. Describing these preliminaries as "a kind of guerilla warfare," she describes how the

> prospective players try, without any direct questions or answers, to find out the class of play of their partner and opponents. It is possible to say "I am a bad player," but it does not help the others, because they then have to set about finding out whether or not you mean it. On the other hand it is impossible to say, "I am a good player": it would revolutionise the approach to the game. I do not know why. The code sentence for this is, "I play a great deal." (67)

Holden's essay pretends to give aspiring country-house visitors the code that they think they need to join in the comic "good order" of country house play. Yet Holden's profession of ignorance as to underlying motivation for such codes implicitly suggests that it is not worth the effort of discovery, or even that there may be no underlying meaning or motivation to be got at.

Despite the essay's humorous mockery of bridge-players' obsession, their nonsensical language codes and practice of internal warfare, Holden still is careful to note that her lack of ambition to learn the game "does not mean that I dislike bridge or that I do not enjoy it." This disclaimer about her relation to bridge-playing comes to stand for her relation to the class that knows how to play it so well. In 1934, the same year Holden published *Death in High Society*, she positions herself in the *Harper's Bazaar* essay as existing between classes, enjoying as she mocks the country house people whose complex games she both knows and doesn't know. The trick, in Holden's eyes, for enjoyment and inclusion in country house weekend life, is to be (or pretend to be) a nonplayer, rather than an indifferent one—which many of *Harper's Bazaar*'s socially ambitious readers would have been. For the bad player to gain social acceptance rather than being regarded as "a sort of psychological Aunt Sally" during the entire weekend, Holden wittily advises: "Making a fourth is something to be instinctively avoided; on the other hand making a fifth is to be cultivated. This is done by taking a book and sitting at the farthest end of the room from the game in progress and watching it without seeming to do so" (67). The attractiveness of this position as "fifth" is illustrated later in the sketch through strictly gendered, classed images. Claiming that her complete ignorance arouses the "sporting spirit" of bridge players, Holden describes these players as setting out with a "mixture of determination, self-sacrifice, and chivalry." Their failures make her vulnerable to future confusion "by the next contract bridge crusader who comes along." Chivalry and crusaders in a country house: what more could a graduate of Brown's Paris school of fashion hope for? Holden even dramatizes her competitive sexual advantage as a female nonplayer, describing how

> The third time I was taught this summer it seemed rather unfair, because there was another girl there who really wanted to learn. The first evening at dinner she said to the man on her right:
> "What is the Vanderbilt Convention?"
> He answered: "Oh, no one plays that now."
> She turned to the young man on her left and said:
> "What is the Culbertson Convention?"
> He answered: "There are so many; better call it a system."
> Thinking absent-mindedly of Mr. Justice Darling in court, I said:
> "What is a system?"
> The direct result of this was another lesson on the rules and conventions of the game. (99)

And, one might add, male attention that leaves the eager, novice bridge-player alone and disappointed, the loser in this particular game.

Far from suggesting any hint of leftist sympathies, the humor of this piece disguises its politics of conformity. Holden seems to want to have it both ways, advertising to female readers her value as a nonplayer to presumably rich, bridge-playing gentlemen while professing to prefer the "part of a *précieuse*" who won't play the upper-class game, idling away a solitary afternoon "lying in a hammock reading a novel, dressed perhaps in a rather affected muslin dress" (99). Holden's conclusion to "Country House Bridge" emphasizes the artificiality of the whole country house scene, its function as a set for affectations of varying sorts. The essay is finally about "playing a part." While it may discredit beliefs in the superiority of the "upper" classes, it does not go so far as to upset the patterns of dominance of that class.

In contrast to the nonthreatening, cross-class appeal of "Country House Bridge," Holden's 1935 *Harper's Bazaar* sketch on foxhunting might have been more offensive to any gentrified readers. Claiming that foxhunting is little written about because "the people who write find it difficult to satirise something which already seems such a satire" (94), Holden then embarks on such a project, taking humorous advantage of hunters' reputation for singleminded stupidity. Like the article on the social games of contract bridge, Holden provides evidence of her credentials as an upper-class insider in order to enjoy, like any good satirist, the role of critic of that class. Yet her recounting of her childhood entrée into the fox hunting set emphasizes the cruelty of her induction into the sport: "By my eighth birthday I had been sworn at, shouted at, and even smiled at, by an M.F.H., kicked in two or three gateways, run away with four or five times, and had some forty falls" (94). Holden's veiled bitterness over such treatment may explain why this essay, in contrast to the one on bridge, does not announce its enjoyment in the people or sport that is its ostensible subject. Rather, it gains its energy from attacking the monolith of their elitism and exclusivity. Describing foxhunting as "a colossal organisation, run in a spirit of sportsmanship and snobbery, which localises a lot of people who might be a menace if they were let loose elsewhere," this sketch takes great delight in puncturing the pretensions of the sporting set. Holden's mockery proceeds under the guise of kindly advice to outsiders who are imagined most concretely as American girls. Holden pretends to give such girls access to the foxhunting set through general instructions on correct social ritual: how to buy the right kind of riding boots and hats, take a hunting box, get horses, and contact the appropriate hunt secretary. Acknowledging that some girls arrive from overseas "knowing everything," Holden addresses those others who arrive "full of optimism, enthusiasm and hope, without having much idea of what is in store for them": a season of fear. Holden recommends that outsiders who "have got the right clothes, the right horses and the right place to stay" but are terrorized by the fear of doing or saying something wrong, adopt the strategy of shocking people on their own subject. Only half in jest, Holden claims that if carried to an extreme, this strategy of defying good taste "may gain you a certain amount of respect from hunting people, who will perhaps think you are a genius" (99).

"Foxhunting—Is it Human?," like most of Holden's other 1930s publications in the popular press and all of her stories in Basic, attacks the cultural rituals and social habits of the upper classes into which she was born

without posing any systematic analysis of class oppression or recommendation for social change. While Holden's interest in representing the wealthy
classes to readers of mainstream newspapers and glamor magazines throughout the 1930s contradicts the idea that she "progressed" steadily from capitalist complicity to socialist consciousness, her Basic stories represent on the
level of form her commitment to communicating her social satires to the
broadest audience possible. This commitment is best seen in her wartime
novels, diaries, and newscasts, which allow the working-class people who
exit Esmee Earnshaw's house at the beginning of "Death in High Society" to
claim all of our attention for themselves. More than Holden's witty, satirical
comedies of the 1930s, her working-class, industrial fictions of the 1940s
affirm "the acceptance of diversity, complexity, the incongruous, in a refusal
of finality" in ways that raise the novels and sketches above the sum of their
procedural comic parts (ironic, satiric, witty, burlesque) to what Cavaliero
sees as the final or highest form of comedy: celebration (37).

It Was Different at the Time

"Fellow Travellers in Factory" is an early example of Holden's experiments
with working-class documentary, one that is most revealing of the author's
politics at precisely those points its gaze wanders from its working-class
subjects. The piece appeared in 1941 in Cyril Connolly's *Horizon* under the
heading "War Symposium-I" and uses the techniques that Holden would
effectively utilize in *There's No Story There* to convey the material, psychological, and cultural realities of working-class women in a war factory. The
sketch uses the conversations of working girls to illustrate both their heroism and their boredom, the challenges presented by their economically
stressed positions and the dulled consciousness that results from such challenge. Not a recognizably feminist writer, Holden makes the unfair conditions of and compensation for women's industrial work a prominent theme
in "Fellow Travelers." Her anonymous, outsider narrator introduces a
worker called May and her "silent bodyguard yes-girl" in order to illustrate
the discrimination working-class women could expect to encounter when
attempting to enter the workplace governed by new rules of the war economy. Holden's sketch sympathetically suggests that the first concern of the
war workers must always be money. Conspicuously missing for narrator–
observer and subject–spokeswomen is awareness of the war. The women do
not patriotically sacrifice their labor to employers working on government
contracts. Rather, their consciousness of themselves as workers, their unity
through shared experience of labor, indirectly puts them in opposition to

employers. For example, May's coworkers turn her report of a humiliating job interview experience into a joke that works at the expense of a powerful employer of war workers. Holden, the comedic writer, uses this episode to advocate union among factory women, rendering the exploitative employer into a monolith that is attacked through the laughter of the potentially politically influential audience of *Horizon* readers. When asked what the employer offered her, May responds:

> "Thirty-five shillings a week, and three shillings bonus."
> "That's not very good money for all them long hours, is it?"
> "May was one of the best workers here, you know, she was really."
> The talk went on and around me, the inadequate wage offer was taken as a joke, but May was not taking the job. She was waiting for some better work to come her way. I watched her as she talked, the mobility of expression on her face, the exquisitely timed gestures of her hands. "E says, and I says," backwards and forwards, as if over a net, like a Walt Disney hare playing tennis. ("Fellow" 119)

The impressionistic or sensuous documentary realism of the *Horizon* piece differs from Holden's later representation of the same material in her published wartime diary, *It Was Different at the Time*. In a chapter titled, "1941: February," she explicitly comments on the exploitation of women workers. The factual realism of the diary permits Holden to foreground basic journalistic information that is repressed for the sake of artistry in "Fellow Travellers," addressing with its first words the question of how a middle-class writer found her way into the factory in the first place.

The diary chapter begins, "I am working on an eight weeks' course in a government training centre" and reports flatly, "Women who are finishing their training course often come in and tell us about their interviews with employers and the ridiculously inadequate wages some of these people still dare to offer them. These stories are always received with laughter, because we feel it is the only thing to do" (83). In contrast to this reporting on the social and economic realities of the workplace, May's story in "Fellow Travellers" communicates an emotional, rather than hierarchical, reality. The middle- or upper-class narrator illustrates the distance she must travel to appreciate the meaning of that emotional reality in the following passage:

> " 'er bloke's nice, 'e's a regular gentleman."
> One of the women answered, "I like a bloke like that."
> "Not me, I can't stand them."
> Billie was back in the talk. "You should see 'er bloke when 'e sees me coming to talk to 'er, 'e goes grrrrr—like that—and 'e picks up the bloody spanner. 'e thinks I'm going to waste 'er time with my conversation, see?" (120)

The narrator, like Holden's mostly nonworking-class readers, learns only belatedly that these blokes are not lovers or husbands but rather the "white-coated foremen instructors." The confusion such readers experience over the blokes' roles in the lives of the factory women shows up the conformity of masculine power on personal and professional fronts and the importance of the women's solidarity—their creation of an informal trade union that can resist institutionalized sexism of the employers.[15] In a wartime *Harper's Bazaar* article on "Training for Aircraft Production," Holden describes one aspect of this solidarity with tongue only somewhat in cheek as "new school tie-ism" (60).[16] Aware of the advantages provided by the "Old School Tie," she urges *Harper's* readers to follow her example and take an engineering course in one of the technical institutes because women ex-trainees benefit in the factories from the kinds of networks usually reserved for boys who graduate from, say, St. Cyprian's and Eton.

Surprisingly, it is Holden's essay in *Harper's*, the mass-produced and distributed women's magazine, that emphasizes the possibilities of solidarity between middle- or upper- and working-class women working in the factories rather than her essay on "Fellow Travellers" in the leftist, literary *Horizon*. In the *Horizon* piece, Holden draws attention to her narrator's distance from the workers, her position on the periphery of their conversational, social groups, by a comparison of the meaning of poverty in bourgeois and proletarian lives. The narrator concludes that in relation to their working-class peers, "The two or three bourgeois factory workers suffer in a separate way." They struggle with the grueling hours and harsh soap, but are set apart by their experience in civilian life of a kind of poverty that may entail missed meals and worries about debts, but "passes over" and is accompanied at almost all times by a sense that warmth and cordiality are within reach (121). In contrast, "The proletarian workers' problem is more prolonged, an unending night of never enough money—the horizon they see ahead is probably of the same dreary dust as the semi-quicksand they stand on now. So it seemed to me in the factory" (121).

Holden is careful in this part of "Fellow Workers" to distinguish herself from the other workers: the working-class women are "they." Yet in a previous paragraph she allies herself with the workers in opposition to "everyone who got away into safe or sunny areas." She labels the distance between the people at home and the people far away as "a sort of war" and finds a "second small guerrilla warfare" waging against "the bourgeois pink political talkers who fight armchair class-battles with left wings folded so securely over upholstered plush elbow rests" (121). The intensity of feeling Holden reserves for her criticism of members of the intellectual classes shows off the privileges of eccentric positioning, the pleasures of observing and criticizing without claiming group membership or responsibility. By 1943, in contrast, she is able to make a claim upon group membership without sacrificing the privileges of eccentric perspective, confidently identifying herself with the women workers in the pages of books styled, produced, reviewed, and read predominantly by women and men of the bourgeoisie.

In *It Was Different at the Time*, the war diary, Holden includes herself in the population of women workers who can expect to find sex discrimination in the workplace. Instead of referring to "they" or "them," as she does in the *Horizon* piece, she refers to "we."[17] Readers may regret the diary's omission of the inventive references to possessive blokes and armchair pinks, but they can admire Holden's willingness to risk a more egalitarian politics. Easing the vertical structures of social and narrative hierarchy that characterize her privileged eccentricity in "Fellow Travelers," she begins in *It Was Different* to break down the barriers between self and others, narrating "I" and narrated "they." While she may be most successful as a writer of comedic rather than entirely serious documentary, her attempt in her published war diaries to ground human dialogue upon facts of wages and costs of living shows the changing relations between the materials of her personal history and the more obviously socialist politics of her documentary realism.

By 1944, when Holden published the novel *There's No Story There*, the signs of her struggle with the representation of relations between bourgeois author and working class subjects, overt political content and hollow documentary fact, have disappeared. In this narrative, Holden provides a rich, detailed portrait of working-class life amid the routine and danger of Statedale, a huge munitions factory, in a language of impressionistic, documentary realism that combines the comic sensibility of her 1930s satires with the serious content of war work, violence, social dislocation, and psychological stress. Her anonymous narrator follows a dozen or so men and women out of the 30,000 who keep the factory running, allowing her readers to imagine they know and could befriend the workers. Unlike *Night Shift*, *There's No Story There* does not have a wealthy character like Feather to guide its middle- or upper-class readers into its working-class world. Holden's careful concentration on diverse working-class lives and accomplishments, dialects and characters, represents the last distinctive step in her movement toward writing working-class fiction. Her deployment of the techniques of documentary realism, using the camera eye of her female narrator to implicitly mount a leftist critique of the government while supporting the workers' bravery, contradicts the traditional notion that the war brought an end to 1930s-style political fiction.

Robert Hewison's account of literary life in London during the war uses Cyril Connolly as the mouthpiece for this traditional notion. According to Connolly, by the late 1930s the primary enemy of literary promise was not the threat of bombs or Hitler but rather native politics (127). Connolly's "Ivory Shelter" article in the *New Statesman* of October of 1939 notes that the one advantage for writers working during this time was freedom "from the burden of anti-Fascist activities and the subtler burden of pro-Communist opinions" (qtd. in Hewison 11). According to Hewison, the outbreak of war provided Connolly with "an opportunity, a justification, for the artist to withdraw to his ivory shelter" (11). Holden's engagement in the lives of others, her dedication in *There's No Story There* to earning for workers the understanding of middle-class readers who could advocate on the behalf of factory-bound citizens, contradicts Connolly's isolationist artistic policy. While she struggled as much or more than most writers to find alternative sources of income once paper shortages and bombings of publishing houses made publication very difficult, she did not abandon the political ideals from which Connolly sought freedom.

The limitations of Connolly's view and the critical history that echoes it are apparent as soon as women's and working-class interests are brought into critical conversations. Even if we set aside the political writing of government propaganda, writers' concerns with fair treatment of workers and the poor brought politics to the forefront of home front life and literature.[18] The myth of the blitz unity tends to obscure the history of class conflict early in the 1940s, when people in the East End were paying with their lives for the government's decision to shelter the rich rather than the poor. Journalists and diarists pointed out how quickly public shelters developed their own class systems. The rich or connected headed to steel-frame hotels while the East Enders had to settle for the few squalid, flimsy shelters in their neighborhoods (Hewison 33, 34). These inequities prompted Phil Piratin, future Communist Phil Piratin, future MP, to lead East Enders on 15 September 1940 in a protest march to the Savoy's shelter where they all demanded access. At the climax of the demonstration an all clear sounded and diffused the confrontation, but Piratin's action supports the notion, popular in the early 1940s, that if the raids had concentrated on the East End some workers there would have risen against the government (Hewison 33).[19]

Unfortunately for writers like Holden who perfected their 1930s-style documentary realism upon the subjects of wartime life, critics decided that public opinion was against war books by 1942 or 1943 (Hewison 44). When Kate O'Brien reviewed *There's No Story There* in the 24 November 1944 edition of the *Spectator*, she began with an admission that "it is difficult to guess how much the public wants to read about [the present war] . . . in *imaginative* writing." O'Brien "wonders doubtfully how much appetite can be left for the novelists' view of actualities" since the war "is being so thoroughly reported to us, by straight journalism, by radio, and by pamphlets and volumes of short-range and eye-witness history. . . ." Yet it is Holden's treatment of "actualities" that makes *There's No Story There* memorable and invites critics to reassess the contents of their 1930s and 1940s maps. As O'Brien notes at the end of the review, Holden captures "a very special quality" of lives lived in permanent danger, and if the book "makes sad, cold reading, it is indeed most edifying, too; it has a curious, plain dignity, and leaves many questions in the reader's mind."

In Permanent Danger

According to John Lehmann, the British public was not interested in encountering difficult questions such as those raised by Holden's 1944 industrial novel because "The centre of balance has shifted from a rather extrovert, documentary type of realism to something more introvert" (*New Writing* 14; qtd. in Hewison 89). Yet Pamela Hansford Johnson praised *There's No Story There* in a review in *John O'London's Weekly*, valuing it as "a very English book," timely and important, one that "we should send to America, to let her know what our people, the majority of them, are really like." Johnson's nationalist concerns, as much as Lehmann's literary judgements, are worth noting, even to feminist readers who approach Holden's narratives with the knowledge that during the war, "Women writers were moving in the opposite direction to their male contemporaries. Part of the 'public version' perhaps for the first time, these women were pleased to be participants and co-workers"—in other words, pleased to believe they were "one of 'millions like us' "—even as the "opposite direction" of their literature shows their distance from the male writers who were their allies in the People's War (*Millions* 9).

The words "Search, please," begin *There's No Story There* and immediately place readers on the side of the workers who are submitting to their daily inspection by police before making their way into the secure areas of the factory. The disciplinary context of the inspection emphasizes from the novel's outset the way the state supports class divisions between workers and management. The policy of arbitrary inquisition pursued by inspector Jameson, a character described by Holden in a 1942 diary entry as a "would-be fascist angling for a conviction," represents the dangers authorities may pose to "the People" once class divisions are institutionalized in the name of national security. We first sense the way the factory's structures support Jameson's homebred dictatorial tendencies through the workers who begin to talk about him once they have distanced themselves from the inspection huts.

"Morning, Bill."
"Morning."

"This new inspector Jameson's a bit of a bastard, isn't he?"
"That's right, regular bastard he is."
A man with tattooed arms and a black beret set far on the back of his head
said, "Inspector Jameson, huh!" and spat to the ground. (8)

The alienation of the workers who are contributing to their county's
defense from the security forces of that same country illustrates just one of
the contradictions Holden's workers must negotiate on a regular basis.
More telling are the contradictions faced by the overlooker of Group IV,
Section I, a Jewish man named Gluckstein who is known among the workers for his industrious work habits, health, and good nature.

The potentially tragic implications of the contradictions Gluckstein
faces are most apparent in a scene that describes his reactions to one of
Jameson's arbitrary inquisitions. Gluckstein, like all the workers who
Jameson interviews, mistakenly believes that he has been specially selected
for questioning. Only Jameson and the reader know that selections are
random; Gluckstein, like every two-hundredth worker, is pulled aside
based on his position in the line. The Inspector begins by asking Gluckstein
if he has changed his address and prods him about the performance of two
Irish workers under his supervision. When Gluckstein affirms loudly that
the Irishmen are very good workers, Jameson says, " 'Oh yes . . . I believe
they are good workers; I thought you might have some opinion on these
subjects as you'd be likely to be more observant, wouldn't you, you being a
foreigner?" (126). To Gluckstein's ears, this question must sound like a
combined bribe and threat—a request that he spy on other "foreigners"
precisely because he is regarded by the English policeman as himself a suspicious alien. After exclaiming, "I'm not a foreigner; I'm English" (127),
Gluckstein is dismissed by the inspector, only to feel himself sinking into
back into painful memories of anti-Semitic persecution in London's East
End by the boys of his neighborhood and by Mosley's men.[20]

Even if he could read Gluckstein's thoughts as we can, Jameson certainly
wouldn't understand that his questions fall into a larger pattern of English
governmental activity that has similarities to Nazi intimidation techniques.
However, he would be gratified by the confirmation of his power that
Gluckstein's well-disguised fear attests to:

It was all beginning again, the persecutions which were always in
[Gluckstein's] thoughts. It spread through him like a fever. All his life seemed
to be like that: a recurring fever, an illness that localized itself and came out
in some definite form, and after this he'd be better for a while; but at the
back of his mind he knew that it would be there to happen again. It came
back quite easily into his mind, the day he had asked his brother, "What are
Jews? We are Jews, aren't we? Is everybody a Jew, or is it only us?" (128)

Gluckstein experiences his harassment by Jameson in unique ways because of his individual history, even though the questions that Jameson asks the arbitrarily selected workers are always identical. Jameson is well aware of the more general terrifying effect his questions have on workers; we read that he "always like to see a flicker of fear through men's eyes. You knew you were getting somewhere then" (134). The logic of class division as a governmental policy for home front citizens is simply made more obvious in Gluckstein's case through its intersection with the division he recognizes as racist anti-Semitism.

The reality of England's history of anti-Semitism is emphasized, rather than discounted, by Gluckstein's misreadings of other characters' words and actions. For example, after leaving inspector Jameson, Gluckstein sees a terrifying mark chalked in white on the road that he had seen years earlier in the East End: " 'P.J.'—Perish Judah" (136). The bitter twist to this vision is known only to the reader who has seen another worker, Phyllis Jenkins, scrawl her initials in the road as a sign to her boyfriend that she has passed along that way. What is a joke to Phyllis and her friends is experienced as a vicious assault by Gluckstein. Though an Englishman and patriot, he has been forced to see those two categories as incompatible with his identity as a worker and a Jew. The narrator does not comment on the political lessons provided by the situation she has relayed, but readers are witness to the ways that individual citizens and England as a nation must suffer due to the erection of state-instituted and state-tolerated borders between different classes and ethnicities.

Holden imagines an alternative to such division at the end of *There's No Story There*. When a blizzard hits the factory, the workers who are on shift cannot return to their hostels. A new spirit of cooperation emerges between laborers on different shifts as everyone works together to keep production going. Even the distance between the workers and supervisors breaks down amid the snow. We see this in the last chapter of the novel, which takes the form of a letter that a newly transferred worker writes to her sister. Recalling the effects of the storm, the nineteen-year-old letter writer, Mary Smith, recounts an anecdote that Gluckstein told her about drying off in the boiler room with half a dozen other naked men after shoveling snow for hours. As Mary tells her sister, "He said it seemed like they were all equal and untroubled in their minds at the time, just sitting round the fire talking like kids at bedtime" (183).

Mary's recollection of the blizzard with its moments of laughter and harmony is the closest thing to a workers' utopia that Holden offers. Yet Holden is too much of a documentary realist to pretend such moments can be sustained. She is also too much of a humorist. The blizzard provides her with an opportunity to do what Storm Jameson advised and "get some fun" out of her documentary writing. In this case fun is bought at the expense of Tom Harrison and Charles Madge's Mass Observation movement. Although Mass Observation and Holden's version of documentary realism share common techniques and goals, Holden maliciously represents Mass Observation in the form of the peculiar, horn-rimmed Geoffrey Doran who has been studiously recording the conversations and doings of the workers in a notebook (much the way we imagine Holden doing as she prepared to write *There's No Story There*). Doran loses his precious notebook in the blizzard and as he paws frantically through snowdrifts trying to find it, Holden enjoys a joke at Mass Observation's (and her own) expense when another worker comments, "There was a mass of workers observing him" (184).

In addition to providing Holden with opportunities for humor or for imagining more egalitarian ways of social organization and behavior, the blizzard sets the scene for her most explicit critique of the exclusion of workers' lives from serious literature. In the novel's last paragraphs Mary recreates for her sister another conversation in the factory, in this case with a worker named Nordie who was once a journalist (and comes close to being the author's alter-ego). Mary had asked Nordie why she didn't write about the factory and Nordie had replied, "There's no story there." Mary comments to her sister: "I don't suppose there is, neither. The way you know people at work is different to ordinary life. It is jagged and uneven, not just straightforward like in a storybook" (185). Since Holden has just engrossed her readers with the very story that Mary has been conditioned to believe writers cannot tell, we are able to see the extent to which Holden believes stories themselves have been defined by the exclusion of workers from their pages.

A survey of Holden's fictions written during the 1930s and 1940s allows us to realize how far she had to travel to arrive at this political-literary insight. Holden moves from a prewar humorous cynicism that depends on middle- or upper-class readers' validation of the borders of privilege to a wartime empathetic realism that depends on readers imagining their way across borders of class. The publication of *There's No Story There* in 1944 marks an important event for those who are trying to create an alternative, more inclusive English literary tradition. It proves that readers can be moved by a "jagged and uneven" narrative, a story about workers told by a female narrator, one that unites the two alternative traditions of "red" and "women's" intermodern writing that scholars have recently begun to uncover.

The stakes of recognizing the strength of this kind of understudied fiction can be measured by divergent interpretations of the literary meaning of Labour's sweeping victory in July 1945. Hewison, for example, questions whether books played any part in developing the nation's social conscience or even if a "diffuse" radical feeling was really influential on the election. He seems to suspect the strength of the connection between literature and politics at this point precisely because the "diffusion" of radical feeling makes the boundary between the two realms so hard to discern. For Croft, on the other hand, that election represents the triumph of the socialist ideals that novelists shared with the public in their fictions of the 1930s. He concludes that these ideals were maintained in "serious writing about the war" and that British literary culture was "dominated for nearly a decade by the heirs to the culture of the Popular Front campaigns, by Communists and their allies" (Croft 336).[21] Croft's interpretation of literature's influence on the postwar political and cultural life of England helps us see how Holden's wartime fictions are part of a larger body of literature that breaks down the divide between the decades. *Night Shift* and *There's No Story There* remind us of the importance of seeking and valuing "Thirties novels" written in the 1940s, of looking to women's writing for our war literature.

There are other signs that Holden's dedication to typical 1930s materials of documentary realism, factory work, and women's lives was not out of step with the values of mainstream culture in the later war years. On a page of the *Spectator* immediately following O'Brien's review of *There's No Story There*, an ad in the left-hand corner announces in large type: "The Hand that held the Hoover guides the Barge!" It continues in smaller font,

> A Woman Bargee? That's a man's job, you'd think, if ever there was one. Certainly it's hard work and heavy work. But there are very few men's jobs that the women of wartime Britain haven't learnt to tackle! It's because no job has daunted them, however hard or unusual it might be, that Britain today can claim the highest production per head of population of all the allied countries. (490)

These words are accompanied by an illustration of a woman in ruffled shirt, merrily poling her barge along. The ad concludes with a loud "Salute! from Hoover to the women war-workers of Britain."

The Hoover ad suggests that as late as 1944 manufacturers were still confident that they could sell merchandise by declaring their pride in women who did a "man's job." It represents the way capitalist and national interests commonly joined in a celebration of the woman worker in order to promote consumerism and patriotism. Holden's novel of that same year celebrates workers, both male and female, in order to promote very different ends: the imaginative lives of readers and the interests of the workers themselves. The parallel contents between texts with such different aims suggests that the meaning of labor and the experience of the British working class was still being actively fought over in the popular and serious

literature of the 1940s. While critics are certainly right to argue that the
1930s nurtured the nation's social conscience, they should also note that
the entry of women into the "hard work and heavy work" of wartime
industry sustained that conscience in the literature of the next decade, even
as more dramatic horrors of active combat, fascist terror, and the Holocaust
preoccupied soldier-writers and publishers.

Holden always dedicated herself to entertaining readers with a good
story and interesting language, but her fiction of the intermodern years
often takes on subjects that tie it to the interests of the working class and
simple, documentary forms that ally it with the literature of Mass
Observation and the Popular Front. The freedom of this vision from Party
politics and its accessibility to people of all classes is evident from the end
of *There's No Story There* as the damp, naked workers listen to the man in
charge of the boiler-room telling stories about his youth. This nameless
worker describes his travels to central Europe when he was trying to fulfill
his ambition to be a painter and instead found himself involved in revolutionary workers' movements. After spinning tales about manning barri-
cades, watching his friends die in street fighting, joining the International
Brigade, being thrown in prison and losing his right hand (his painting
hand, we assume) to blood poisoning, he tells the gathered men "I'm not
interested in politics, never have been' " (172).

The man in charge of the boiler room believes that politics are what
overtake people when they are living their lives, but he explains away his
political choices with the words, "I always seem to have been in some place
when there was a flare-up" (172). His comments start Gluckstein thinking
about "his own attempt to get into the fight against everything he hated"—
his attempts to be a hero on the side of the oppressed—and how "each time
it was the same story, somehow he was kept out of it all" (172). Holden's
novel suggests that both these men are blind to the political content of their
lives because they see fragments or a vacant story of exclusion where there
is actually connection, content, and even heroism. Holden did not agonize
in print about the appropriate political role for the leftist artist, but the
ironic reverberations between the title of *There's No Story There* and its contents suggests that she tried to contribute to the decades' long fight for
social justice in England. Her role was to find plot when others saw random
events, see heroes when others saw workers, create stories when others saw
no story there.

Chapter 4

George Orwell's Invention:
The Last Man in Europe

George Orwell achieved what Inez Holden's character Gluckstein could only dream about in *There's No Story There*. Gluckstein, a child-witness to the persecution of Jews in his East End community, grew into a man whose most passionate wish was "to get into the fight against everything he hated" (172). The things he hates include Mosley's anti-Semitic fascists, Hitler's Nazis, English snobs, capitalist exploiters—the list of evils is almost as long as Orwell's. Yet despite Gluckstein's numerous hates and equally numerous good intentions, he feels that each time history has presented him with an opportunity for heroism "he was kept out of it all" (172).

As I argue in chapter 3, Gluckstein's disappointment, his sense of failure in his quest for social justice in England, is in large part a consequence of his limitation of view rather than any lack of possibility for decisive action. Gluckstein can't see heroic contribution or meaningful political intervention in the details of his life because, like many people of his day and ours, he imagines that heroes fight in public spaces, the "man's world" conventionally imagined as some place far outside home, family, and routine. As a writer, Orwell worked for most of his life at home, in a domestic, private "women's" space. But he was not confined or emasculated by his association with such spaces because his writing engaged with key concerns of the public world, emerged from uniquely masculine, public experiences (policing in Burma, tramping in England, mining in Wigan, fighting in Spain), and was published by public men like Victor Gollancz, Cyril Connolly, and Fred Warburg who defined the voice of the Left in literary London. As a result, Orwell's "fight against everything he hated" conforms more easily to popular notions of heroism than the fictional Gluckstein's efforts to advance many of the same leftist causes. Ironically, Orwell was an effective promoter of socialist causes—freedom for India, freedom from poverty, freedom from class oppression, even freedom from anti-Semitism—because he seemed to free himself from the social obligations, social ties, and what I like to call the "social work" that occupied (and exhausted) Gluckstein and the thousands of real men who resembled him.

It would be more accurate to say that Orwell freed his public *image* from his private person's social obligations, ties, and work. In fact, he was as invested in and dependent on the social realm as any political writer of his day. Yet he was adept at hiding these ties, creating the impression that he lived in stoic self-sufficiency, independent of familial, institutional, and more broadly social supports.[1] When the public met Winston Smith in 1949, he fulfilled the heroic fantasy Orwell appeared to pursue in his own life: the image of the decent, common (even unattractive and weak) man fighting alone against overwhelming odds. In the eyes of those readers who could accept the political content and pessimism of Orwell's tale, Winston's nearly absolute isolation, his solitary, individual deviance from the culture, values, and institutions of Oceania, proved he was a true radical. When Orwell died in January 1950, these readers were ready to believe that the famous author was the historical model for his fictional exile, Winston Smith. Orwell was seen as the *real* last man in Europe.[2]

"The Last Man in Europe" was the first projected title Orwell selected for *Nineteen Eighty-Four*.[3] Had Orwell retained it, the evidence of pessimism and despair that many readers discover at the novel's end would have haunted even its opening lines. From the outset, Winston's story would have been read as tragedy, knowledge of his fate as Europe's last man overshadowing the quirky humor of *Nineteen Eighty-Four*'s beginning ("It was a bright cold day in April, and the clocks were striking thirteen. . . ."). By the end of the novel, after Winston has been forced to betray Julia and all the ideas and feelings that have distinguished him from Ingsoc's goons, the title "The Last Man in Europe" would have confirmed the book's status as elegy for liberal (or for that matter, radical or conservative) man. Although the spiritually dead Winston of the novel's end is surrounded by waiters in the café, and presumably somewhere outside, singing prole women, the original title would have squelched any possible hopes that these people might save Winston, let alone inherit his rebellion. It would have been even more difficult to question Winston's status as not only an icon of heroism without socialism, but of heroism without the social.

Many of Orwell's friends and biographers argue that, in contrast to the fictional hero he is confused with, Orwell died a hopeful man. They point out that he was planning another book, had just been married to a beautiful younger woman, was eager to nurture his son Richard, was surrounded by friends, and had achieved fame and financial security. In part because he was seen as being on the side of life, because he did not intend Winston to be his last man, Orwell's funeral at Christ Church near Regent's Park was remembered by Anthony Powell as "one of the most harrowing I have ever attended" (qtd. in Meyers, *Orwell* 311). Friends immortalized him in obituaries: V. S. Pritchett famously described him as "the wintry conscience of a generation," "a kind of saint" (296); Arthur Koestler described him as "the most honest writer alive," "the only writer of genius among the *littérateurs* of social revolt between the two wars" (qtd. in Meyers, *Critical* 296, 297). In 1951 Orwell's friend and patron Richard Rees would write, presumably in an excess of grief, that Orwell was "one of those self-mortifying saints who kissed the sores of lepers" (qtd. in Rodden 325). In *The Politics of Literary Reputation: The Making and Claiming of "St. George" Orwell* John Rodden remarks that "the view of Orwell as 'saint' emerged full-blown soon after his death. . . . By coincidence [the first American editions of *Down and Out, Burmese Days*, and *Coming Up for Air*] were published in the month of Orwell's death. So fresh was the image of the man in critics' minds that reviews of these works more closely resembled new obituary tributes" (46). The praises of prominent men, such as Bertrand Russell and Arthur Schlesinger, Jr., were complemented by those of Stephen Spender, T. R. Fyvel, Julian Symons, E. M. Forster, Edmund Wilson, Rebecca West, Lionel Trilling, Philip Rahv, and Reinhold Niebuhr. Astonishing sales statistics support Rodden's claim that "Orwell's popular reputation soared. . . . The Orwell ascension had become the Orwell cult and, by 1956, the Orwell industry" (46).[4]

Orwell's reputation as "conscience" and "saint," given its impetus by early tributes after his death and the glowing reviews and extraordinary popularity of *Nineteen Eighty-Four*, had the effect of separating Orwell's name and memory further from the social world in which the historical Orwell had been enmeshed. The idea of a man as conscience or saint is the idea of a man apart, superior, perhaps martyred, even Christ-like. He is, in effect, the last man. The myth of Orwell as "the last man in Europe" partakes of and contributes to all of the dominant four myth-types Rodden identifies with Orwell's reputation: the rebel, the common man, the prophet, and the saint. To suggest that Orwell has been mythologized as "the last man in Europe," among other things, is to say that the facts of his extended battle against illness and early death are intertwined in people's notions of what made him great. Inseparable from the mourning that impacted many of those who launched the Orwell myth are the celebratory affirmations: the last man has come to mean not just the tragic, lost man, but the best, strongest, bravest, most honest, most honorable, most prescient living man.[5] Orwell became, after his death, the "good" man's ideal man.

The metonymic substitutions for "last" in this context are endlessly various but the effect in each instance is insidious. Commentators like Pritchett, Koestler, and Fyvel who have contributed to Orwell's posthumous image as the last (lost, best, etc.) man place him in a sacred space separate from, rather than beside, other literary figures, groups, and institutions that history and biography connect him to. Ironically, such politically engaged, socialist-minded commentators have effectively placed Orwell outside of their own society and history. In contrast, this book assumes that Orwell was fully integrated into and dependent on various intermodern social and literary groups, including, importantly, the small group made up of Stevie Smith, Mulk Raj Anand, and Inez Holden. It tries to restore these three figures to studies of intermodernism and English literary history through two related arguments. On the one hand, it argues positively in chapters 1–3 for recognition of Smith's, Anand's, and Holden's contributions to literary London, both as Orwell's friends and as independent, radically eccentric writers. On the other hand, it argues negatively in this chapter that Orwell and his posthumous admirers have erased his relations to these three figures, eliminating several important sources for understanding the contexts of his life and art. Both positive and negative arguments lead to one unsettling conclusion: Orwell was as much a vigorous self-promoter and self-server as he was a humble, self-denying man advocating against all odds for the relief of the oppressed. He systematically if not consciously removed from his "socialist" writing the signs of the social (net)work that was necessary to its production.

In the context of a study on the intermodernists Smith, Anand, and Holden, characterizing Orwell in such an uncomplimentary way creates a thorny problem of critical method. On the one hand, Orwell is a crucial touchstone, the figure whose historical role as BBC boss of Smith, Anand, and Holden justifies or at least consolidates the book's claims for the four writers as a kind of Orwell group. His reputation as the last man in Europe, one who mythically stood apart from mainstream and modernist cultural forces in 1930s and 1940s England, is enough to prove the importance of thinking outside the categories of modernism and postmodernism, of considering the alternative framework provided by my term intermodernism. On other hand, for a socialist (working-class, feminist, and postcolonial) critic, Orwell's claim to fame may seem specious and the need to populate twentieth-century English literary history with alternative working-class, female or feminist, colonial and postcolonial writers acute. To such a critic, Orwell, accompanied by his myth, may pose a threat to intellectual investigation and partnership in the larger community of scholars of intermodernism.[6]

My solution to the Orwell problem is to borrow Orwell's name and stature, his credibility as a prominent, non-modernist presence in English literary history, but to displace discussion of his work to the end of the book, letting the chapters on Smith, Anand, and Holden prove my claims about intermodernism. Reading literature by Smith, Anand, and Holden requires us to engage with subjects that Orwell is famous for confronting: England's history of anti-Semitism and anti-fascism lower-middle-class, little Englander patriotism; Anglo-Indian racism and anti-imperialism; and the labors and lives of working-class men. However, their writings also require us to engage with political materials before which Orwell remained blind or indifferent. Smith and Holden emphasize the politics of sex and gender discrimination in intermodern England, prioritizing and valuing the details of female lives and especially female (though not feminist) rebellion against cultural assumptions of masculine supremacy. Anand emphasizes the political materials of Indian life from the perspective of a colonial subject, representing in fiction group resistance (for example, trades unions, Communist parties, revolutionary gangs) to English and, crucially, Indian caste oppression. Exploring the distinct contents of Smith, Anand's, and Holden's biographies and radically eccentric writings not only improves our understanding of the social contexts that shaped Orwell's career, but also helps us see a diversely peopled, robustly imagined intermodernism.

Orwell's friends, acquaintances, and biographers record the diversity of his social contacts in literary London, but many do so in order to emphasize his solitary status, his image as a man apart who kept his friends apart.[7] Rodden, the expert analyst of contributors to Orwell's reputation, subtitles one chapter-section " 'Permanent Outsider' among Friends: Orwell's Compartmentalized Life." The phrase "permanent outsider" is Julian Symons's. In a 1985 interview with Rodden, he confirmed earlier recorded impressions of Orwell as loner, someone who was never really "inside" social circles, even his circles of friends (134). Rodden cites other friends who were shaken by Orwell's habit of keeping one set of friends from knowing about his contacts with another set; George Woodcock described Orwell's compartmentalization of friends as "almost obsessive" (qtd. in Rodden 135). Woodcock was disconcerted by Orwell's secretive style of managing friendships, but he admired Orwell's ability to "juggle different kinds of relationships, getting everyone [to] accept him on his own eccentric terms" (qtd. in Rodden 135). Woodcock's mention of Orwell's eccentricity makes apparent the assumption underlying many of the descriptions of Orwell's asocial tendencies; that Orwell's penchant for solitude and separation is the defining quality of his eccentricity. Similarly, much of the critical literature promotes Connolly's description of Orwell in "A Georgian Boyhood" as the true (opposed to stage) rebel (163). Connolly's testimony provided early and powerful support for the myth of Orwell the last man. His account of their prep school and Eton days turns

Blair into George Orwell and both into the original English radical, an opposition party of one, doomed since adolescence from ever getting "in."

Of course it is these words, "radical" and "eccentric," that I use to describe Orwell's alliance with Smith, Anand, and Holden And here is a second problem with critical method dogging this study. In the biographical and critical literature about Orwell, the words radical and eccentric are used to describe his position as odd man out, and in some cases, his role as the "real" Winston Smith who has escaped the rules or bonds that govern normal social relations. In contrast, I use the same words to emphasize Orwell's sociability, his debts and gifts to other individuals and groups that contributed to London literary life in the 1930s and 1940s. As I explain in the introduction, my phrase "radical eccentric" is meant to draw attention to Orwell's shifting, unstable position on the peripheries of *multiple* groups and by implication, his expanded possibilities for connection, for social work. This is not to suggest that Orwell felt himself to be socially enmeshed (all evidence points to the opposite conclusion; he seemed to feel much the way Holden's Gluckstein does),[8] but to suggest that we can learn more about intermodern London if we think about the many ways his eccentric social position and his kind of radical politics *guaranteed* social (if not socialist) engagement. Smith, Anand, and Holden are just three of the many eccentric—odd, peripheral, unfashionable—people with whom he became socially engaged. The point of this book is to show that their relatively unknown stories help us read Orwell differently. Orwell is not the last man when he's approached through the writings of Smith, Anand, and Holden. He is one of many intriguing personalities who contributed to a dynamic intermodern literature that was often radical in its commitment to doing social work on behalf of Britain's least privileged citizens.

Unfortunately, no single study can dislodge the myth of Orwell the last man, the best eccentric and most radical writer of mid-century England. However, once scholars produce a critical body of work that can function as a foundation for intermodern studies, the Orwell myth will lose some of its power and appeal. My notion of intermodernism, outlined by stories by and about Smith, Anand, and Holden, will become more meaningful when it is illustrated with studies of other intermodern figures, cultural forms, social and political institutions. Smith, Anand, and Holden may figure in these studies too, but as readers' priorities and purposes change, so will the value of the radical eccentrics for investigations of intermodernism.

In this chapter on Orwell, Mulk Raj Anand is the radical eccentric who is of most value. My attention to Anand is not meant to diminish the more or less explicit relations the previous chapters set up between the lives and literature of Orwell and Smith and Holden, but simply serve my immediate project. Nor is it meant to suggest that Anand was more intimate with

Orwell than either Smith or Holden. In fact, there is little in Anand's literary writings to suggest he is qualified to represent any Orwell group. Unlike Smith, he did not model characters in his novels after Orwell, and unlike Holden, he did not keep a diary that records his relation with Orwell or Orwell's relation to other figures in literary London during the 1930s and 1940s. Even his 1985 memoir of his London days, *Conversations in Bloomsbury*, does not give Orwell any role. Fortunately, Orwell recorded several of his impressions of Anand and Anand's fiction in his writings of the early 1940s. These writings suggest that Orwell relied upon Anand as a colleague but was exasperated with him because of differences in political views about India. Peter Davison cites a brief telegram from Orwell to Anand that hints at other, more mundane workplace issues that may have fueled his irritation. The telegram reads, "MAY WE HAVE YOUR SCRIPT FOR RECORDING TOMORROW IMMEDIATELY. BLAIR" (*CW* 13: 227). Whatever the source of Orwell's disagreements with Anand, the evidence of their political or personal conflicts reminds Orwell fans that he was, like the rest of us, susceptible to various mean-spirited and even prejudiced expressions that challenge his mythical status as the last, best man of Europe.

In the July 1942 issue of *Horizon*, Orwell reviewed *The Sword and the Sickle*, the final novel in Anand's trilogy about an Indian villager turned World War I mercenary, Lal Singh. He had already spoken up on behalf of this novel in the pages of the 23 May 1942 edition of the *TLS*, protesting "some very misleading remarks" in an anonymous review of *The Sword and the Sickle* published earlier in the month (*CW* 13: 337).[9] Orwell's defense might have been inspired by his awareness that Anand was under attack from other quarters too, around this time. On 15 June 1942 Laurence Brander had filed his second, devastating report on the reception in India of Orwell's "Through Eastern Eyes" program. Davison cites J. H. Davenport's summary of that report, including Brander's negative reference to Anand: "Bad voices like Mulk Raj Anand (which does not get over as a voice) . . . must be rejected always" (13: 301). Rushbrook Williams's response to this summary in a letter to Brander of 14 July defends "Through Eastern Eyes" in part by pointing out that "a great deal of care and ingenuity goes to the formation of these programmes; and although some of the broadcasters themselves may not be of the first rank, there is a definite theme and intention about the entire contents." He asks Brander to remember "that English as spoken by Indians is often more intelligible to Indians, however quaint the accent may appear to British listeners, than English spoken by Englishmen" and suggests that any perceived deviation from the standards of the Home Service programming should be measured against the fact that "it has to be done by Indians, for Indians. Hence its defects" (13: 301).

Orwell's public support of Anand stands in sharp contrast to this patronizing defense of the BBC's Indian employees. For example, in a brief introduction to future programming that went over the air before Brander wrote his report, Orwell particularly asks his listeners to tune in to Mulk Raj Anand's talks about the best-known English writers and again mentions Anand in a general puff for his program amid words of praise for the "very varied and very talented body" of Indian's still in England (*CW* 12: 164–65).

Despite Orwell's defense of Anand in the face of public criticism, his *TLS* review of *The Sword and the Sickle* does not focus on the political or dramatic issues taken up by the novel (*CW* 13: 337). Rather, it embarks on a discussion that anticipates some of Anand's concerns in *The King-Emperor's English* by affirming the distinct "dialect" of English in which the novel is written, speculating about the value of Indian English novels to the allied war effort, and projecting their disparagement or disappearance once Indian independence is achieved.[10] This is all interesting and good, but not so good is Orwell's decision to include in his review's last paragraph sweeping generalizations about the political tendencies of the Indian intelligentsia that belittle its members in terms Orwell usually reserved for English "Parlour Anarchists." Orwell claims that "many, perhaps most, Indian intellectuals are emotionally pro-Japanese," not because they want to see Europe a Nazi concentration camp, but because "the nationalism of defeated peoples is necessarily revengeful and short-sighted" (II: 219). The review ends with this sentence:

> Mr. Anand does not like us very much, and some of his colleagues hate us very bitterly; but so long as they voice their hatred in English they are in a species of alliance with us, and an ultimate decent settlement with the Indians, who we have wronged but also helped to awaken remains possible. (219)

We have no record of how Anand reacted to these words. Aside from their failure to encourage readers to buy his book, they suggest that Orwell is not with Anand, but with a different group, "us," with whom Anand and his Indian colleagues are in alliance. But who is "us"? Does "us" refer to *Horizon* readers, a rather select group of Anand's intellectual peers, or to "us English," a much larger and more various group of people? In either case, Orwell's language suggests that he sees himself as a member of a homogeneous group that, in the context of the review, seems unified by race or colour identity as much as shared national identity or imperial responsibility. This impression of English, and more broadly, European racial unity is reinforced by Orwell's use of race to describe the non-Indian characters in Anand's book: "European characters barely appear in the story—a reminder that in India only about one person in a thousand is technically white" (II: 217). Although Orwell's point is to give Anand credit for writing a novel about India that is not really about the Europeans, the English, their race, or race oppression, the terms of his analysis implicitly encourage a race or rather color-based (rather than, say, political or economic-based) understanding of "hatred" between English and Indians.

The last paragraph of the review is inconsistent with Orwell's apparent aim of supporting Anand's novel because it stereotypes intellectual Indians as untrustworthy *anti*-intellectuals, acting according to the whims of emotion rather than political strategy. Orwell even adopts the voice of "an Indian" to illustrate the intensity of hatred and depth of folly that he associates with Indian activist elites: "Half of me is a Socialist but the other half is a Nationalist. I know what Fascism means, I know very well that I ought to be on your side, but I hate your people so much that if we can get rid of them I hardly care what happens afterwards" (II: 219). The embittered Indian voice that Orwell adopts toward the end of the review inevitably strikes the reader as belonging to Anand, even though it is not specifically identified as Anand's. While Anand *was* divided in his loyalties, he was hardly as hate-filled or irrational as the Indian Orwell mimics.[11] We see this division in Anand's response to Sir Malcolm Darling's request that he join the team of English writers working as propagandists at the BBC.[12] Anand's letter communicates no feelings of hatred for the English people but rather some mild criticism of his own confusion and pointed criticism of the English government, which had, in his words, "declared neither its war aims nor its peace aims—and India seems to be its one blind spot" (West 15). Fair enough. But Orwell's review, published one year after Anand's letter was written, is not.

Orwell's disapproval of his Indian BBC colleague is more blatant in his private writings. In his 19 April 1942 diary entry, he wrote

> E[ileen] says that Anand remarked to her yesterday, as though it were a matter of course, that Britain would make a separate peace this year, and seemed surprised when she demurred. Of course all Indians have to say this, and have been saying it ever since 1940, because it furnishes them if necessary with an excuse for being anti-war, and also because if they could allow themselves to think any good of Britain whatever their mental framework would be destroyed. (II: 420)

Orwell's rhetoric about Indians (by which he means educated, politically active "pseudo-Marxist" Indians like Anand) is almost as scathing as anything he published about defenders of the Raj. In this diary entry, *all* Indians believe the worst of England and *all* Indians found their (apparently very vulnerable) mental framework upon their *totally* negative beliefs about Britain.

In the face of such hyperbole and disparagement, it is hard to remember that Orwell is accusing other people of being angry or hateful and is not claiming those emotions as his own. Yet responsible readers cannot ignore the anger and hate in his tone. His contempt for the Indians he alludes to in his review of Anand's novel or his war diary is at least as meaningful as his rational arguments against their nationalist politics. It explains in part why his answer to the problem of "self-pity and race-hatred common among Indians"—simply to point out to Indians that others besides themselves are oppressed and that "The only answer to nationalism is international Socialism" (II: 219)—is so unsatisfying. While at first glance, this may appear to be a solution that shows Orwell's alliance with colonial Indians, upon closer examination Orwell's solution proves false. The socialism he affirms would have been virtually unrecognizable as such to Anand, many Congress Party nationalists, and leftist *Horizon* readers; it complements the Western capitalist democracies' war aims and can best be promoted by "Westernization" (II: 219).

Readers who focus on Orwell's invention of Winston Smith, the last man in Europe, or who are attracted to the image of Orwell as the last man in Europe, usually focus on the way Orwell's last texts accomplish social work, of changing readers, political cultures, even the English language itself, through satire. Another way of putting this is to point out that Orwells' texts accomplish their social work by depicting societal failure, the betrayal of individuals by cultural, familial, and political groups. His major works represent decent, ordinary individuals working, perhaps, but no decent, ordinary working society. *Wigan Pier* is the best example of the invented character of Orwell's textual visions because it is easy to find examples of his deliberate exclusion of evidence he collected of Wigan's working-class society working for itself.[13] The socialist causes and goals that motivated *Wigan* and much of Orwell's writing compete for attention with the antisocial images and arguments those writings put into public circulation. Perhaps this gap between social intention and reception and antisocial representation explains why thinkers on the right and left of the political spectrum still argue over who can claim Orwell as their spokesman.[14]

Of course many leftists gave up on Orwell long ago and regard him as an elitist fake or hopeless reactionary. They interpret his tendency to stereotype and insult other people whose causes he supported as evidence of his antisocial experience and impact. But to grant Orwell the anti- or asocial qualities of his representations is to further separate him from the society that sustained and concerned him. Ironically, leftists who conflate Orwell with his antisocial images (of himself, of others) only contribute to the Orwell myth they find so irritating. This is not to suggest that leftist critics should ignore patterns of rhetoric that turn the social(ist) Orwell into an antisocial(ist) force, but rather urge them to demonstrate how that rhetoric disguises Orwell's real involvement in the characteristic social and cultural work (discourses, projects, relationships) of his time. For example, we learn something about the structure of Orwell's antisocial disguises by observing similarities between his denigration of nationalist Indians in his review of *The Sword and the Sickle* and his denigration of the anti-imperialist English author Lionel Fielden, whose book advocating Indian independence, *Beggar My Neighbour*, Orwell reviewed for *Horizon* in 1943. Deploying a favored rhetorical strategy, Orwell tries to gain mastery over his political opponent by describing his own opinions as "facts." To discredit Fielden's support for Gandhi's three-part program of Indian independence, neutrality, and nonindustrialization, Orwell confronts his readers with the "fact" that "India is very unlikely ever to be independent in the sense in which Britain or Germany is now independent" (II: 309). The review's scornful rhetoric appears to divide Orwell from someone with whom he had much in common, and then tries to conquer him with contempt, leaving Orwell the victor, the last man in Europe to declare the truth of India.

Seldom cited, Orwell's review of Fielden's book is worth reading if only for the extraordinary range and color of his denunciations. Having compared Fielden to the "worst of the appeasers" and declared him an irritant to possible friends of India, Orwell finally explodes into what sounds like Marxist metaphor: "We live in a lunatic world in which opposites are constantly changing into one another, in which pacifists find themselves worshipping Hitler, Socialists become nationalists, patriots become quislings, Buddhists pray for the success of the Japanese army, and the Stock Market takes an upward turn when the Russians stage an offensive" (II: 314).[15] Unable to contain his incredulity and disgust, Orwell denounces in the strongest terms possible a reality where "all that is solid melts into air, all that is holy is profaned" (Marx 338). Under Orwell's rough gaze, the slippage of contrary positions, identities, and moral codes into one another shows up the utter betrayal possible or perhaps inevitable in modern life.

I assume it is for this reason, Orwell's wartime political imaginings of total betrayal by modernity and of modernity, that scholars have invoked his name as they struggle to understand the fate of another oppressed group at the center of intermodern discourse, the European Jews. The Jews' persecution by Hitler, culminating in the Holocaust, is both a typical and an extreme instance of the kind of conflict between powerful and oppressed groups that involved Orwell in fights for social justice. It is possible to describe the Holocaust, the Nazi destruction of the bodies, identities, homes, and communities of six million European Jews, as the most horrible example of modern transformation, the grossest of betrayals, the most terrifying meltings of solids into air. As such, it seems to meet the criteria necessary to gain Orwell's attention; certainly Orwell has gained the attention of scholars of the Holocaust.

One of the best examples of a scholarly text that uses Orwell to influence understanding of the Holocaust is *Modernity and the Holocaust* by sociologist and theorist Zygmunt Bauman. The book begins with three epigraphs, one of which is by Orwell:

> As I write, highly civilized human beings are flying overhead, trying to kill me. They do not feel any enmity against me as an individual, nor I against them. They are "only doing their duty," as the saying goes. Most of them, I have no doubt, are kind-hearted law-abiding men who would never dream of committing murder in private life. On the other hand, if one of them succeeds in blowing me to pieces with a well-placed bomb, he will never sleep any the worse for it. He is serving his country, which has the power to absolve him from evil.[16]

These sentences come from the beginning of Orwell's most radical and radically optimistic book, *The Lion and the Unicorn*. They were written during the summer of 1941 at the height of the German bombardment, when Orwell was working as Talks Producer for the BBC's Indian Service during the day, watching for fires during the nights, and spending weekends in the country visiting T. R. Fyvel, his Jewish, pro-Zionist friend, and his Jewish publisher, Fred Warburg. Fyvel's 1982 memoir of Orwell suggests that it was at Fyvel and Warburg's country home, Scarlett Farm, that Orwell wrote the detached, memorable lines that Bauman cites. Paradoxically, Fyvel describes this time with Orwell, dodging death from German bombs, as a "golden tableau," an exhilarating period filled with utopian talk about a postwar Socialist Britain. Fyvel's representation of modernity embraces the extremes of fear and hope, of the extraordinary possibilities for a civilization that can produce German air raids, lush English farms, and the vision of *The Lion and the Unicorn*.

Unlike Fyvel, Zygmunt Bauman doesn't comment on what Orwell's words about highly civilized bombers mean to him, but we can assume that Orwell gives Bauman images that help him frame an approach to the Holocaust as "a characteristically modern phenomenon that cannot be understood out of the context of cultural tendencies and technical achievements of modernity" (xiii). Put simply, for sociologist Bauman writing about modernity must mean writing about the Holocaust. In the following case study, I adopt Bauman's core assumption in order to understand something more about Orwell's intermodern literature and his posthumous reputation. "Orwell and the Holocaust" functions as a challenge to readers who, consciously or not, support Orwell's reputation as the last man in

Europe, the intermodern spokesman who best represents those qualities of Englishness that history and Hitler threatened to wipe out.

My investigation of Orwell and the Holocaust, as much as any other subject, requires readers to confront Orwell's weaknesses of logic, imagination, compassion, and moral vision in his published and private writings. Many, many others have testified to those writings' strengths—moral, literary, intellectual, political—and I assume that readers are familiar with these accounts and that there is no need for me to repeat them here. My case study emphasizes Orwell's contradictions and blindnesses not in order to posthumously humiliate him, but in order to humanize him and socialize him—to show that Orwell is more like than unlike other intermodern writers who have no claim upon the moral high ground, the public imagination, or critical attention.[17] Only this kind of analysis can do justice to the complexities of Orwell's literature and the intermodern society that shaped and received it. In the long run, the production of more balanced, critical examinations of Orwell in studies of intermodern literature and culture will facilitate the investigation of other literary and cultural figures who can help us navigate, in their own brilliant and flawed fashions, the devastating, astonishing extremes of modernity.

Orwell and the Holocaust: A Case Study

Two rather curious facts determine the shape of this case study. The first is that Orwell himself did not write about the Holocaust.[18] The second is that Bauman, the theorist who best exemplifies contemporary responses to Orwell, seizes on the phrase from the *Communist Manifesto* that haunts Orwell's review of Fielden's *Beggar My Neighbor*. Bauman writes, "Truly, the fate of the Jews epitomized the awesome scope of social upheaval and served as a vivid, obtrusive reminder of erosion of old certainties, of melting and evaporating of everything once deemed solid and lasting" (45). He repeats Marx's image of disappearing solids five pages further on, writing: "Jews were perceived as a sinister and destructive force, as agents of chaos and disorder; typically as that glutinous substance which blurs the boundary between things which ought to be kept apart, which renders all hierarchical ladders slippery, melts all solids and profanes everything sacred" (50). In Bauman's terms, the Jew isn't providing a merely symbolic body that absorbs and reflects the world's deeply negative feelings about modernity. Rather, the Jew is perceived as the very agent or catalyst of destruction, a figure that has the power to dissolve material reality, profaning all that is blessed. This is a powerful and powerfully disturbing interpretation but one that could explain further the relation of modernity and the Holocaust if Bauman emphasized the more deeply ambivalent, rather than simply negative, meanings provided by Marx's language of melting and profaning. Marx's melting metaphor should help us see the Jew as a key substance of modernity that produces not simply fear, but fear and fascination: not just horror, but horror and attraction: not merely degeneration, but degeneration and development.[19]

Emphasizing the ambivalent extremes, the positive and negative terms of a modernist time and place where "all that is solid melts into air" allows us to better understand Orwell's relation to the Holocaust and his relation to the connected, but by no means identical issue of anti-Semitism.[20] For as the most careful commentators on this subject have pointed out, Orwell himself was ambivalent about Jews. David Walton's 1982 essay "George Orwell and Antisemitism" concludes that Orwell began to question the habitual anti-Semitism of his childhood environment as he realized some of the physical horrors it was leading to abroad and the psychological distortions at home (34). Walton admits that "[Orwell's] efforts at self-awareness were not altogether successful" but seems to validate scholarly uses of Orwell as a touchstone for investigations into English anti-Semitism because he "tried to clarify his own thoughts[,] [. . .] encouraged others to do likewise" and continued to act "decently" despite lingering negative feelings about Jews as Jews (34).[21] In a more recent essay, Andrea Freud Loewenstein pursues the bolder argument that Orwell projected his "fear and loathing of the female" onto Jewish, and especially male Jewish characters (146). It is important to note that the Holocaust enters only indirectly into these scholars' considerations of Orwell's anti-Semitism, presumably because Orwell himself had so little to say about it.[22]

This last point about the absence of the Holocaust from Orwell's publications would not be especially meaningful to the study of Orwell or his texts' social work were it not for two things: first, the number of Jewish men, Fyvel and Warburg among them, who were important to Orwell personally and professionally and who cared deeply about the fate of Europe's Jews and second, the number of scholars who have sought out Orwell's authority in the course of developing their own arguments about the role of "the Jew" in the history and literature of English modernity. Understanding Orwell's relation to the Holocaust demands consideration of texts by both groups of people; however I focus on the words of Orwell's Jewish, pro-Zionist friends in order to promote understanding of Orwell's relation to the Holocaust.

Among Orwell's Jewish friends, Fyvel tries the hardest to confront the implications of Orwell's silence about the Holocaust for himself and his country.[23] In his book-length memoir, Fyvel's explanations follow two paths: first, the path of understanding the shifting forms of Orwell's anti-Semitism and second, the path of understanding the causes of Orwell's unwavering hostility to Zionism and the establishment of the state of Israel. This essay attempts to further the discussion on Orwell and anti-Semitism begun by Walton, Loewenstein, and Fyvel by pursuing one undeveloped strand of Fyvel's argument: the idea that Orwell's inability to write in any detail about the implications of the Holocaust was due to his crude analogies between Palestine and India, Arabs and coolies, Jews and the kinds of Anglo-Indian rulers and businessmen that made up his own family.

During the 1930s, while Orwell was washing dishes in Paris, tramping in England, and talking to miners in Wigan, Fyvel was in the Middle East, writing a book on the triangular Zionist–Arab–British conflict over Palestine (92). Fyvel and Orwell met in January 1940 through the efforts of their publisher, Warburg, and together they founded Searchlight Books in an effort to advance progressive war aims (Fyvel 98).[24] Orwell's *Lion and the Unicorn* (the source for Bauman's epigraph), was published as the first contribution to the series. Commenting on Orwell's journalism preceding his Searchlight book, Fyvel notes, "Since [Orwell] placed so much stress on the precise use of words, one should mention again that quite remarkably not once in his writing of these two years [1938–1939] did he refer to Nazism or Nazi Germany. Instead he spoke only in the I.L.P. [International Labour Party] revolutionary language of 'Fascist Germany,' thereby turning Hitler into an abstraction" (86–87).

Fyvel's remarks on Orwell's avoidance of the terms Nazi and Nazi Germany appear in his analysis of Orwell's essay, "Not Counting Niggers." Published with its shocking title and equally shocking argument in 1939 in the leftist magazine *Adelphi*, the essay argues that for Westerners who congratulate themselves on their progressive tolerance and difference from Hitler, "the unspoken clause is always 'not counting niggers' " (I: 397). Orwell chides, "For how can we make a 'firm stand' against Hitler if we are simultaneously weakening ourselves at home? In other words, how can we 'fight Fascism' except by bolstering up a far vaster injustice? For of course it *is* vaster. What we always forget is that the overwhelming bulk of the British proletariat does not live in Britain, but in Asia and Africa" (I: 397).[25]

Anticipating his description in *Nineteen Eighty-Four* of the corrupt system whereby dominant nations reaped economic benefits from "scores or hundreds of millions of ill-paid and hard-working coolies" (188), Orwell wants readers of his 1939 essay to confront the contradiction between their desire for a world free of racism and their support for a government that would not relinquish its claim to a distant, highly profitable, rebellious colony. In his memoir, Fyvel recalls telling Orwell that he agreed with his anti-imperialism but could never agree that a final phase of British rule in

India was "just as bad" as Hitler (86). This comment is in itself interesting because Orwell did not actually proclaim in "Not Counting Niggers" that British rule in India was "just as bad" as Hitler; he said it was *worse* than Hitler. In contrast, Fyvel believed that "[R]esistance to Hitler came first and foremost, while freedom for India was somehow an abstract idea for the future." He notes, "In Orwell's conscience, on the other hand, the two themes were indissolubly linked; indeed, new progress towards Indian freedom might be the more urgent need" (101). Although Orwell's views of the relative evils of British imperialism modified to the extent that he could write in 1944 in a private letter, "I know enough of British imperialism not to like it, but I would support it against Nazism or Japanese imperialism, as the lesser evil" (III: 150), the link in his mind between the defeat of Hitler and freeing of India becomes an even more pressing theme in his writings of the final years of the war.[26] The subject of anti-Semitism enters awkwardly into this equation, telling us much about Orwell's changing views toward Jews and Indians, and the inadequacy of his traditional pattern of finding his politics and morality through identification with "symbolic" victims and traditionally socialist positions (Rai 76).

In a July 1944 *Tribune* essay on freedom of the press in wartime, Orwell insists that even during war, literature must be evaluated as literature rather than propaganda, although "of course, no paper will give space to direct attacks on the things it stands for" (III: 199). His example of acceptable censorship for the socialist *Tribune* is suppression of "an article in praise of anti-Semitism" (III: 199). Without being clear about his definitions, Orwell suggests that a "necessary minimum of agreement" between a publication's political policy and its literature is consistent with the goals of democracy. Never comfortable with the idea of censorship, however, Orwell in the next sentence seems to ease his troubled conscience, caught in the act of an antilibertarian sentiment, with a reminder that "if this war is about anything at all, it is a war in favour of freedom of thought" (III: 199). Orwell is assuring Britons that short-term intensifications of censorship will insure freedom of thought in the long term.

The difficulties evident in Orwell's attempts to reconcile his radical belief in absolute freedom of speech with the demands of wartime defense and patriotism point to his continued use of a "formula of accommodation with his 'given society'" that Alok Rai associates with *The Lion and the Unicorn* (101–02). Rai argues persuasively that *The Lion and the Unicorn* is simply the first text in which we see Orwell effectively manoeuvring his way out of contradictory ideological positions by transferring "the feeling that properly belongs to the alternative community of socialist aspiration towards the available community of patriotic Englishmen" through an asserted compatibility between socialism and the English genius (101).

By 1944, after Orwell had abandoned his faith in a socialist English revolution, he could still deploy his formula of accommodation to reconcile contradictory ideological positions and thus advance powerful, seemingly plainspoken, honest arguments. To return to his *Tribune* article on self-censorship in the wartime press, there are signs of such contradiction in a comment he makes about the relative claims of British and German morality. Immediately after he states that the war is being fought "in favour of freedom of thought," we read:

> I should be the last to claim that we are morally superior to our enemies, and there is quite a strong case for saying that British imperialism is actually worse than Nazism. But there does remain the difference [. . .] that in Britain you are relatively free to say and print what you like. Even in the blackest patches of the British Empire, in India, say, there is very much more freedom of expression than in a totalitarian country. (III: 199)

In what seems to be an unconscious association, Orwell turns from mention of anti-Semitism and the voluntary censorship it inspires in the British press during wartime to censorship in India under British imperialist rule. Yet this association has the unusual effect of turning Orwell into a defender of the two subjects he spent much of his time denouncing: censorship and British India.[27] To get to such unusual endorsements, Orwell distances himself from the "strong case" of finding British imperialism worse than Nazism and pursues a logic that leads him to exactly the claim that he says he'd be the last to make: that Britain is morally superior to its opponent. My point isn't that Orwell was wrong to condemn the Nazis for being morally worse than British imperialists; the cousin in Smith's story, "To School in Germany," was right to protest, "But we ARE holier than him [the Nazi war criminal]" (*MA* 38). Rather, I am critical of Orwell's inability to do so without tying himself in logical knots. Analysis of his inconsistencies says as much about his critics' fantasies of Orwell as the man of plain, clear writing as it does about the history or forms of Orwell's ideas themselves.

My focus on Orwell's status as moralist brings us back to the core question of this paper: Why doesn't George Orwell, Pritchett's "kind of saint," consider the example of the Holocaust to measure (as he was wont) the relative goodness or badness of British imperialism and Nazism or at least to answer the question "Why?," which he increasingly posed to readers in an attempt to substitute analysis for propaganda (Zwerdling 184). Reverberations of this missed opportunity for significant intervention in a key debate about modernity and more specifically, for development of his investigations into totalitarianism, are evident in two essays he published in the first half of 1945. The first, "Antisemitism in Britain," was written in February 1945 and appeared in the *Contemporary Jewish Record* in April

1945. The second, "Notes on Nationalism," was written May and published in October 1945 in Humphrey Slater's *Polemic*. Read in terms of each other, the essays go a long way toward explaining why Orwell's pattern of seeing Jews as sahibs and Palestinians as coolies could be blinding rather than progressive, illuminating, or prescient.

In "Antisemitism in Britain," Orwell claims Hitler has not diminished English prejudices against Jews, but has only caused people of "political conscience" to disguise that prejudice because the "Jews were in trouble and it was felt that one must not criticise them. Thanks to Hitler, therefore, you had a situation in which the press was in effect censored in favour of the Jews while in private antisemitism was on the up-grade" (III: 336).[28] Orwell is not especially occupied by the danger anti-Semitism might pose to Jews, but rather the danger voluntary censorship poses to a free press and the integrity of British democracy. He worries that the true nature of anti-Semitism cannot be investigated because private prejudices are not publicly aired. Although Orwell's stated aim in this essay is to encourage processes that will root out anti-Semitism, his implied means of doing so are questionable on practical and moral grounds. In effect, he is encouraging people to publicly voice their prejudices toward Jews in the name of "truth" *without consideration of the contents, contexts, or effects of such comments.*[29] Even with his limited knowledge of European Jewish persecution, it seems odd that Orwell doesn't expand upon the meanings of Hitler's ability to silence altogether the speech of thousands of Jews rather than Hitler's ability to censor certain kinds of negative speech of English intellectuals.

The case for reading "Antisemitism in Britain" as an introduction to "Notes on Nationalism" is supported in part by Orwell's insistence in the final paragraphs of the earlier essay that

> the disease loosely called nationalism is now almost universal. Antisemitism is only one manifestation of nationalism, and not everyone will have the disease in that particular form. A Jew, for example, would not be antisemitic: but then many Zionist Jews seem to me to be merely antisemites turned upside-down, just as many Indians and Negroes display the normal [*sic*] colour prejudices in an inverted form. The point is that something, some psychological vitamin, is lacking in modern civilisation, and as a result we are all more or less subject to this lunacy of believing that whole races or nations are mysteriously good or mysteriously evil. [. . .] [T]hat antisemitism will be definitively cured, without curing the larger disease of nationalism, I do not believe. (III: 340–41)

These sentences compel close examination for several reasons (not all of them complimentary to Orwell), but analysis of only two will serve my purposes. First, it is important to note that Orwell is treating anti-Semitism as a species of a larger problem of nationalism, but that he has not yet clarified what he means by "the disease loosely called nationalism." It is hard to judge whether Orwell's thesis about anti-Semitism is valuable without comparing it to "Notes on Nationalism," which no reader of the *Contemporary Jewish Record* could have done. Second, Orwell's characterization of anti-Semitism as "disease" and "lunacy" may be rhetorically effective, but the terms lead him to a moral, rather than political, explanation of the problem. While Orwell is certainly right that Zionists (or Indian nationalists and African-American activists) believed in the moral claims of their causes, his argument here minimizes or even eliminates the language of politics from discussion of anti-Semitism. As a result, we are left with an exhortation to use reason to understand or cure the "lunacy" or "mystery" of nationalism, but no way of seeing the *un*mysterious, discernable historical causes of anti-Semitism or understanding any aspects of nationalist movements as legitimate, reasonable, responses to political realities.

The troubles caused by Orwell's transformation of political movements into irrational moral contests are only exacerbated in his "Notes on Nationalism," which is virtually incoherent if read as a theoretical declaration or analysis of a major "ailment" of modernity. His essay only makes sense if it is interpreted as part of an ongoing attack on English "russophile" intellectuals and as an initial working through in print of the theory of totalitarianism that was so important to the success of *Nineteen Eighty-Four*.[30] Orwell's core distinction between nationalism and patriotism lies at the heart of his troubles. He defines nationalism as an "emotion" and as bad habits, the "habit of assuming that human beings can be classified like insects" and more importantly "the habit of identifying oneself with a single nation or other unit, placing it beyond good and evil and recognising no other duty than that of advancing its interests" (III: 362). Orwell's examples of nationalism seem to include every potential political or religious group; among other practices or ideologies, he condemns anti-Semitism, Zionism, and Indian nationalism. As protection against nationalism Orwell recommends patriotism, which he defines as "devotion to a particular place and a particular way of life" (362). He admits the vague nature of these definitions and tries to clarify further by defining patriotism as "defensive" and nationalism as "as inseparable from the desire for power" (362). As John Gross points out, Orwell's "confident distinction" between patriotism and nationalism "comes more easily to an Englishman than it would to someone who had been on the receiving end of imperialism" (38). More pointedly, Rai comments "[It] is surely not that difficult to see that the patriotism of violated peoples must inevitably be aggressive, as they seek to recapture their sense of their identity from the perceptions and distortions of others" (110).

For Orwell, consumed at this time with a Cassandra-like fear that his warnings about Soviet-style totalitarianism would go unnoticed, it was impossible to see the nationalism of violated peoples as aggressive patriotism. Even his explicit reference to the structures of the Holocaust in "Notes on Nationalism" is intended to illustrate the danger Stalin poses to England.[31] After commenting on the English admirers of Hitler who contrived not to learn of Dachau and Buchenwald, he notes, "And those who are loudest in denouncing the German concentration camps are often quite unaware, or only very dimly aware, that there are also concentration camps in Russia. Huge events like the Ukraine famine of 1933, involving the deaths of millions of people, have actually escaped the attention of the majority of English russophiles" (III: 370). To his credit it should be noted that Orwell also records his incredulity over the fact that "Many English people have heard almost nothing about the extermination of German and Polish Jews during the present war" because their "antisemitism has caused this vast crime to bounce off their consciousness." His outrage undermines his logic, however, because he fails to make any connection between this example of anti-Semitic English "nationalism" and his discussion elsewhere of a supposedly equally dangerous Zionist "nationalism" (III: 370). The irony of all this confusion is that Orwell's most explicit denunciation of English blindness to the Holocaust does not appear in "Antisemitism in Britain," but rather in "Notes on Nationalism" where it is lost among paragraphs that testify to Orwell's own version of "negative nationalism," his obsession with the evil empire of the USSR.[32] In a final paragraph that is as contradictory as anything else in the essay, Orwell asserts his faith in an objective truth that allows people to make judgements about the competing claims of various causes, admits that nationalistic loves and hatreds are "part of the make-up of most of us," and then makes another declaration of faith: "Whether it is possible to get rid of them [nationalist loves and hates] I do not know, but I do know that it is possible to struggle against them, and that this is essentially a *moral* effort" (III: 380). Torn between his belief in the possibility of objective political thought and the inevitability of infection by the emotions of nationalism, Orwell again seeks reconciliation through a formula of accommodation, in this case through affirmation of a kind of patriotism only available to citizens of established or imperial nations—a patriotism that is finally equated with moral goodness.

We can begin to measure the extent of Orwell's trouble with the role of political moralist if we compare his contributions to Semitic discourse in the mid-1940s with those of Fyvel, who took over Orwell's job at *Tribune* in early 1945. Recalling those years, Fyvel writes, "As far as I could do so while slowly taking in the full details of Hitler's Holocaust, I liked my first two years on *Tribune*. [. . .] I contributed editorials and notes criticizing British policy in the Palestine conflict in which I felt deeply involved" (142). Like historian Bernard Wasserstein, who argues that "the question of immigration to Palestine is of crucial importance to the discussion [of England and the fate of Europe's Jews] because it was here that the British Government was most directly and continuously involved in the problem" (v), Fyvel believed British policy was carried out at the expense of the Jews attempting to escape to Palestine. He also knew that Orwell couldn't have disagreed with him more. At one point, Orwell's solution to the crisis of European Jewry was to send Holocaust survivors back to their homelands in Central Europe (Fyvel 178).[33] Fyvel notes that the origins of Orwell's astonishing solution originated in his belief that "the Palestine Arabs were coloured Asians, the Palestine Jews the equivalent of the white rulers in India and Burma."[34] Calling this "an over-simplification from which he would not be budged," Fyvel still defends Orwell against critics, forgiving him all his rigidity and insensitivity (142).

In the face of Orwell's stubborn negation—his rejection of his friends' logic, evidence, and feelings about the meaning of the destruction of European Jews and its implications for British policy in Palestine—it is important to ask what Orwell *gained* from resisting moral thinking about the Holocaust. I propose two answers to this question. The first answer, more general in scope, is that he gained strength to face modernity's other horrors by affirming a position outside the "politically correct" positions friends like Fyvel, Warburg, and Koestler adopted. Here we see him acting as though he is Winston Smith, the last man in Europe. Refusing to adopt the arguments of his pro-Zionist Jewish friends and the mainstream Left, he gained confirmation of his status as a socialist freethinker who could measure his claim to a unique and heroic moral rebellion against the pressures of identity and power politics, which he believed fostered "nationalism." It also may have gained him a sense of freedom from groups, which he believed inherently demanded conformity and thus enforced nationalistic emotions or nationalistic-type loyalties. This fear of groups is apparent in political writings published long before Orwell began to draft "Notes on Nationalism" or *Nineteen Eighty-Four*. For example, his wartime diary entry of 27 April 1942 records a kind of despair over duplicity that is stunning in its universal condemnation of groups.

> We are all drowning in filth. When I talk to anyone or read the writings of anyone who has any axe to grind, I feel that intellectual honesty and balanced judgement have simply disappeared from the face of the earth. [. . .] The Indian nationalist is sunken in self pity and hatred of Britain and utterly indifferent to the miseries of China, the English pacifist works himself up

into frenzies about concentration camps in the Isle of Man and forgets about
those in Germany etc etc. [. . .] Everyone is dishonest, and everyone is utterly
heartless towards people who are outside the immediate range of his own
interests and sympathies. [. . .] All the pinks, or most of them, who flung
themselves to and fro in their rage against Nazi atrocities before the war, for-
got all about these atrocities and obviously lost their sympathy with the Jews
etc as soon as the war began to bore them. Ditto with people who hated
Russia like poison up to 22 June 1941. [. . .] But is there no one who has
both firm opinions and a balanced outlook? Actually there are plenty, but
they are powerless. All power is in the hands of paranoiacs. (II: 423)

Here is the same vocabulary, the same disgust and despair, even the same
examples of corrupted groups that Orwell would, by 1945, describe as
nationalist lunatics: Indian nationalists, English pacifists, the pinks, anti-
pinks, and worse yet for poor Orwell, "everyone who has definite opinions"
(423). In other words, people very much like himself, perhaps even friends
like Fyvel and Koestler.

My second answer to the question of what Orwell gained from resisting
moral thinking about the Holocaust has more important implications for
Orwell studies. If Fyvel is right that Orwell's views of Jews as sahibs blinded
him to the Nazi responsibility for Holocaust atrocities and the rationale for
establishing a Jewish national homeland, the terms through which he established his position on British "despotism" in India gained or at least preserved for him a particular notion of race as "colour" that was crucial to his
understanding of human identity, social organization, and imperialism.
One of the many problems with this notion is that Orwell's protest against
imperialist oppression of colonized populations depended for its coherence
on the language of race and color utilized by his colonizing, often racist,
opponents.[35]

Orwell's debt to a discomforting color-thinking is evident in his first
novel, *Burmese Days*, a protest novel against British imperialism and racism.
The most effective agents for showing off British color-hatred in *Burmese
Days* are the assistant timber merchant, Ellis, and Elizabeth, the memsahib-
in-the-making with whom the hero John Flory has the misfortune to fall in
love. In each case, the characters' despicable prejudices are linked to their
hatred of black skin.[36] Orwell's exposure of extremist color prejudice is
unsettling, but also unsettling is the narrator's seemingly unironic use of
adjectives of blackness. The kindly Dr. Veraswami is described as "a little
black and white figure" (36), a "small, plump, black man" (36), who would
"nip his black thumb and forefinger together" while searching for a word
(38), or would come home from witnessing a hanging "with his black face
faded grey" (40).[37]

In *Burmese Days* and elsewhere, race emerges as an ancient, essential category synonymous with color, and thus visible and containable, subject to surveillance and policing. Orwell's ideas about race are most self-consciously explored in his antiexploitation documentary-cum-autobiography, *The Road to Wigan Pier*. If we accept Orwell's representation in *The Road to Wigan Pier* of his path toward identification with "the symbolic victims of justice," race understood as color is at the base of all his subsequent campaigns on behalf of the oppressed (148). In the notorious second half of *Wigan* Orwell writes, "When I was not yet twenty I went to Burma, in the Indian Imperial Police. In an 'outpost of Empire' like Burma the class-question appeared at first sight to have been shelved. There was no obvious class-friction here, because the all-important thing was not whether you had been to one of the right schools but whether your skin was technically white" (141). Privileged in terms of his skin color and his education, Orwell came to hate the "evil despotism" of British imperialism, his job, and even himself. ("At that time failure seemed to me the only virtue" (*Wigan* 148).) The wiser, older Orwell of *Wigan* looks back on his thinking at the time and describes it as "quite simple." Depending on color hierarchies for his rebellion, he decided that since "The whites were up and the blacks were down [. . .] as a matter of course one's sympathy was with the blacks" (148).[38] This sympathy for "blacks" led to another simple theory of Orwell's, "that the oppressed are always right and the oppressors are always wrong" (148). Thus out of a reaction of disgust and withdrawal from the political conditions of race-structured Burma, Orwell discovered in the 1930s an interest in the English working class, which provided him with a "local analogy" for the color hierarchy he had observed in Burma.[39]

Fyvel's anecdotal accounts of Orwell's vision of Jews as sahibs who achieved their identity in Palestine not through Hitler's hierarchies of gentile, Jew, German, alien, but rather in opposition to "black" Palestinian coolies, allows us to recognize the importance of what might otherwise appear transient, superficial, or eccentric in Orwell's journalism of the war years: the influence of his notions of race as color upon his writings about Jews.[40] A telling example that Fyvel recounts is Orwell's belief that "In the twenties, anti-Jewish references were not out of order. They were only on a par with the automatic sneers people cast at Anglo-Indian colonels in boarding houses" (Fyvel 181). Orwell's equation of Jews and sahibs (sahibs who he imagines have wandered, like Jews fleeing Hitler, from the East to England) endured long after he had written his essays of 1945 exposing anti-Semitism in Britain and calling for its investigation and elimination. More discomforting than this careless defense of anti-Jewish speech is Orwell's more familiar position that anti-Semitism in mainstream English literature only counts as anti-Semitism in a post-Hitler world. In his 29 October 1948 letter to Julian Symons he describes how he held as "nonsense" Fyvel's opinion that T. S. Eliot's early poems are anti-Semitic. He explains to Symons,

> Of course you can find what would now be called antisemitic remarks in his early work, but who didn't say such things at that time? One has to draw a distinction between what was said before and what after 1934. In the early 'twenties, Eliot's antisemitic remarks were about on a par with the automatic sneer one casts at Anglo-Indian colonels in boarding houses. On the other hand if they had been written after the persecutions began they would have meant something quite different. (IV: 450)[41]

Fyvel's defense of his position, impassioned and informed, bears repeating, especially since Orwell repeated in print his idea that hostile representations of Jews in literature written before 1934 would only constitute anti-Semitism if published after Hitler came to power.[42] Although Orwell's letter to Symons leaves out this piece of the story, Fyvel reports that he pointed out "the cases [of Jews and sahibs in boarding houses] were not at all on a par and that to draw an arbitrary dividing line between anti-Semitism permitted and not permitted in the year 1934 was to take a very parochial English view of the matter" (181). He recalls that he gave Orwell a bit of a history lesson in pre-Hitler European Jewish persecution, including that in Vienna, countering that Eliot's famous "ironical definition of the cultural enemy as 'Chicago Semite Viennese' " showed his political naivete and his association with the "wrong camp" (181).

Orwell may have persisted in his unfortunate habit of classifying Jews as sahibs because it brought him the unintended political advantage of preserving or reconciling the two models of protest he was, in the late 1940s, committed to. It sustains his anti-imperialist protest against the oppression of the "weak" coolie, the silenced "black" man, and it permits him to continue his belief in the universal totalitarian tendencies of all nationalisms, including Zionism. Put differently, this interpretation of Jewish identity in terms of color doesn't require him to modify his absolute stance against nationalism as totalitarianism (for example, Zionism) when he was enjoying the success of *Animal Farm* and beginning *Nineteen Eighty-Four* and his commitment to this theory was at its most intense. One of the most obvious problems with this model is that it hides from him the realities of the Holocaust and the political and moral complexities of Jewish settlement in Palestine. While Orwell certainly understood that Jews seeking to enter the British mandate of Palestine were victims of the Nazi imperialist-like expansion, his vision of them as white sahibs meant that he did not have to revise or jettison his race-inflected model of anti-imperialist protest. Jews (real and symbolic) threatened Orwell in precisely Bauman's terms, as the "glutinous substance which blurs the boundary between things which ought to be kept apart, which renders all hierarchical ladders slippery, melts all solids and profanes everything sacred."

Arthur Koestler, like Fyvel, tried to persuade Orwell that the specific kind of devastation wrought by the Holocaust required Britain to expand opportunities for Jewish immigration to Palestine. As always, Orwell was "immovably opposed" to such action. Fyvel reports that during the 1945 Christmas holidays, which Orwell spent in North Wales with Koestler, Koestler's wife Mamaine, and Mamaine's twin, Celia Kirwan (Celia Goodman), Koestler and Orwell went for a walk and began arguing so vigorously about the establishment of a Jewish state that Koestler decided to drop the subject rather than lose a valued friend. At that point, Orwell shifted the topic of conversation to India, complaining that the Labour government had not yet unconditionally pulled out of India. When Koestler objected that if the British went, there would be 100,000 dead in Calcutta and a million elsewhere, Orwell replied, " 'Let them kill if they want to. [. . .] It's their business.' " Koestler told Fyvel that Orwell then added, " 'At least there won't be a white man's burden any more' " (Fyvel 146). In the context of a conversation haunted by the deaths of millions of Jews, how can we make sense of Orwell's apparent indifference toward the idea of a million dead in India? What is the significance of Orwell's eagerness to shed the Kiplingesque burden of whiteness at such a cost?

We needn't trust the accuracy of Fyvel's or Koestler's memory about Orwell's contributions to a distant conversation to see the relevance of these questions for understanding Orwell's approach to the Holocaust. As I hope I've demonstrated, there is evidence in Orwell's writings up through the war years to support the idea that his comments about Jews, anti-Semitism, and Palestine were repeatedly constrained by his impulse to make political, racial injustice in India the fundamental question for leftists interested in addressing modern European oppressions. His "London Letters" to the *Partisan Review* repeatedly prioritize the question of a decent settlement with India; in his letters of 1942, he consistently reports on and interprets the meaning of the failed Cripps mission to India; in his letters of 1945 he is still telling his American readers that among the problems any new government will face, "above all there is India" (III: 381) and insisting that a Labour government that really meant business would, among other things, "offer India immediate Dominion Status (this is a minimum)" (III: 396). To argue that imperialism and racism in India remained a fundamental question for Orwell runs counter to the popular vision of Orwell as the English writer whose imagination was consumed by the horrifying vision of England as Air Strip One and thus a man who was primarily concerned with the evils of totalitarianism in a Europe imagined as white. Yet it is unlikely that the world of *Nineteen Eighty-Four* that is known to every teenager around the English-speaking world could not have emerged without Orwell's youthful immersion in the apartheid society of colonial Burma and, crucially, his equally passionate immersion in the poetic and fictional world of Kipling's fictional India. While the errors of memory and biography make any close reading of Orwell's or Koestler's language as recorded in Fyvel's memoir into a speculative exercise, it is appropriate to subject Orwell's writings on "the white man's burden" to such analysis. A key statement in this regard is Orwell's almost off-hand comment in his essay "Rudyard Kipling" (1942): " 'White man's burden' instantly conjures up a real problem, even if one feels that it ought to be altered to 'black man's burden' " (II: 193).[43]

Those Indians in London who sympathized with the Indian independence movement and many of those who worked with Orwell at the BBC would have been more confident than Orwell that "black man's burden" accurately conjured up in a few words one of the real problems in India.[44] Yet their answer to this problem, Indian nationalism, repelled Orwell. As much as he might have respected and enjoyed the conversation and professional skills of Mulk Raj Anand, for example, his correspondence, war-diary, and journalism all suggest that Anand's political arguments could not sway Orwell from his distrust of group practice and ideology, even if that group was composed of "black men" who were working to overthrow the British Government of India.[45] Whether nonviolent and reformist or violent and revolutionary, Orwell saw Indian nationalism as a terrible political solution to Britain's prior terrible political injustice. In that conversation with Koestler during his Christmas trip to Wales, Orwell's seemingly callous regard for Indian lives (presumably all "black"), reveals a bitterness that probably grew out of his despair that those "coloured" people whose claims to equality he had always supported were now fighting for a cause that by 1945 he regarded as a form of totalitarianism that was no better, and perhaps worse, than British imperialism.

Anand might have recommended to Orwell that he look to Gandhi for an example of a nonviolent, non-Western mode of defense against both English and Japanese imperialism, but Orwell at this time regarded Gandhi as yet another "superhuman fuehrer," a charismatic leader able to sway millions of Indians, the majority of whom who were either power hungry nationalists or duped victims (III: 149). The contempt for Indians implicit in Orwell's belief in their sheeplike devotion to Gandhi is made explicit in his diary entry of 18 April 1942 where he speculates that if the USSR took over India, the Russians would be tempted to treat Indians as "natives," because "It's very hard not to, seeing that in practice the majority of Indians are inferior to Europeans and one can't help feeling this and, after a little while, acting accordingly" (II: 419). Even though Orwell was at this time in regular contact with highly educated, English-speaking, Westernized Indians, was repeatedly reminding his readers that "It is of the highest importance that Socialists should have no truck with colour prejudice," was regularly recording in his diary testaments of his despair over the Government's lack of progress toward settlement with India, he still seemed to believe at some level that the problems in India were a sign of the superior "white man's burden," rather than the "black" man's (III: 305).[46]

He criticizes the two most prominent Indian men to claim responsibility for this burden, catching Nehru in a moment of nationalist fervor quoting, of all people, Kipling—"Who dies if India live?" (II: 310)—and exposing the conflicting, and therefore to his mind useless and profascist recommendations of Gandhi: "at one moment he thinks it best to come to terms with the Japanese, at another he wishes to oppose them by non-violent means— at the cost, he thinks, of several million lives—at another he urges Britain to give battle in the West and leave India to be invaded, at another he 'has no wish to harm the Allied cause' and declares that he does not want the Allied troops to leave India" (II: 312). Orwell's frustrations with Gandhi's tactics were compounded by his belief that the British had, long before the war, been using Gandhi as a tool for their own imperial ends.[47]

Orwell was writing about Gandhi in very different terms after the war ended, India had achieved independence, and Gandhi had been assassinated. In his January 1949 review of *The Story of My Experiment with Truth*, Orwell exhibits a better-informed appreciation for Gandhi's non-Western attitudes and techniques, evincing newfound respect for the man who he now understands to teach resistance as "a sort of non-violent warfare, a way of defeating the enemy without hurting him and without feeling or arousing hatred" (IV: 467). No longer confusing Gandhi with the English "pansy left" pacifists whom he loathed, Orwell praises "masculine" qualities he now sees in Gandhi and that he always valued in himself: the ability to see that in war it is usually necessary to choose sides and to face awkward questions.[48] Orwell's mention of Gandhi's willingness to sacrifice millions of Indian lives in the face of Japan's Fascist threat, presented in his review of Fielden's book as evidence of Gandhi's equivocal position in the war, reappears in his later positive assessment of Gandhi as evidence of his bravery and honesty. While this detail of Gandhi's life has new meaning for Orwell, it is somewhat unsettling to see a familiar train of thought directing his comments; as in his argument with Koestler during the Christmas holidays of 1945, Orwell presents the horrifying picture of millions of dead Indians as a departure from or substitution for discussion about the Holocaust and its relation to a Jewish state.

"Reflections on Gandhi" is distinguished from virtually any other major work by Orwell by its explicit reference to Hitler's final solution. Orwell raises the specter of the Holocaust in a paragraph that begins with analysis of Gandhi's pacifism and moves to the questions that Orwell (at least retrospectively) considers it the duty of every pacifist in the last war to answer; "What about the Jews? Are you prepared to see them exterminated? If not, how do you propose to save them without resorting to war?" (IV: 468). Orwell cites Gandhi's answer to a similar question posed to him in 1938 and recorded in Louis Fischer's *Gandhi and Stalin*. Fischer reports that Gandhi said that all the German Jews should commit collective suicide in order to arouse the world to Hitler's violence. Apparently Gandhi justified himself after the war by pointing out that the Jews had died anyway and they might as well have died significantly. Orwell does not make any direct moral or political judgments about Gandhi's recommendation that German Jews seek out a self-imposed Holocaust; he notes somewhat wryly that "This attitude staggered even so warm an admirer as Mr. Fischer," but then suggests,

> Gandhi was merely being honest. If you are not prepared to take life, you must often be prepared for lives to be lost in some other way. When, in 1942, he urged non-violent resistance against a Japanese invasion, he was ready to admit that it might cost several million deaths. (IV: 468)

There is a disturbing admiration evident in Orwell's citation of Gandhi's extremist position that recalls his fierce comment to Koestler that the English must get out of India at any cost. By 1949 Orwell could represent Gandhi's willingness to shed millions of ("black") lives in confrontations between unarmed Indians and the Japanese army much as Koestler represented Orwell's willingness in 1945 to shed a million ("black") lives in confrontations between Muslim and Hindu Indians. This parallel breaks down when it comes to tone, however. Orwell seems a bit bemused by Gandhi's attitude, but obviously respects his logical consistency and adherence to principle. Koestler, on the other hand, seems rattled by Orwell's attitude. "[S]omething in the grimness of Orwell's tone" about the prospect of massive deaths in India "made him look up sharply at him" and report the confrontational, upsetting conversation to their mutual friend T. R. Fyvel (Fyvel 146).

Yet it was Koestler who praised Orwell after his death for *his* "uncompromising intellectual honesty" that "made him appear almost inhuman at times" (Koestler, qtd. in Meyers 296). Perhaps it is no coincidence that Orwell's first sentence in his essay "Reflections on Gandhi" seems, in retrospect, to be written about himself: "Saints should always be judged guilty until they are proven innocent, but the tests that have to be applied to them are not, of course, the same in all cases" (IV: 463). Orwell's posthumous elevation to saint through the efforts of Koestler, Fyvel, Pritchett, and other friends, suggests that the tests for sainthood might not be as different as Orwell had once assumed.

In "Reflections on Gandhi" Orwell admits "I have never been able to feel much liking for Gandhi" (IV: 469), in part because Orwell sees an incompatibility between his choice for the humanistic ideal of Man rather than Gandhi's otherworldly choice of nonattachment or "God" (IV: 467). Describing Gandhi's attitude as "a noble one but [. . .] inhuman," Orwell defines the "essence of being human" in terms that are could very well describe his vision for his own ideal self as a radical writer:

> The essence of being human is that one does not seek perfection, that one is sometimes willing to commit sins for the sake of loyalty, that one does not push asceticism to the point where it makes friendly intercourse impossible, and that one is prepared in the end to be defeated and broken up by life, which is the inevitable price of fastening one's love upon other human individuals. No doubt alcohol, tobacco, and so forth are things that a saint must avoid, but sainthood is also a thing that human beings must avoid. (IV: 467)

One of the last, long essays Orwell wrote before he died, "Reflections on Gandhi" can also be read as "Reflections on Orwell." Broken up by disease, some would say depressed and defeated by a world where solids melt all too readily into air, the suddenly world-famous, wealthy author affirms in this essay his loyalty to the job of making "life worth living on this earth, which is the only earth we have" (IV: 466). His expression of humanist ideals is as generous and courageous as anything we might find in *The Lion and the Unicorn*.

While Orwell's engagement with the specific realities and consequences of the Holocaust never extend beyond the comments he makes in "Reflections on Gandhi," his changing attitude toward Gandhi indicates that had he lived, he might have achieved a more nuanced understanding of nationalist politics and thus the politics of Jewish settlement in Palestine. While Orwell may not have shed completely the racial thinking or "colour feeling" that shaped his youthful imagination and limited his political thinking about nation-building for Jews in a post-Holocaust world, he could write about Gandhi's color blindness with sincere admiration: "Even when he was fighting what was in effect a colour war he did not think of people in terms of race or status" (IV: 464). Such comments can lead us to write of Orwell as Orwell wrote of Gandhi, "One feels of him that there was much that he did not understand, but not that there was anything that he was frightened of saying or thinking" (IV: 469). Certainly, it was Orwell's fearless contemplation of so many frightening, overwhelming aspects of modernity that led his pro-Zionist friends to remember him so fondly.

Fyvel told Koestler, "I could always agree with Orwell about the injustice of British rule in India and the injustices under Stalin's Communism, but that when I talked about the Jewish fate in Europe I found him curiously distant." In response, Fyvel records that "Koestler made what I thought was an apt remark. 'Probably Orwell's imagination was limited,' he said 'as the imagination of each of us is limited. We can all produce only a limited amount of calories of indignation' " (Fyvel 182). For Fyvel, "That was really the point," but for those of us who do not have a personal friendship at stake, Koestler's summation may not be a sharp enough point to explain how Orwell could, in Fyvel's words, "set himself to write of the limitless immorality of totalitarianism without having any close knowledge of, or even as it could seem a special interest in, Hitler and Hitlerism and Nazi Germany—the supreme revolutionary force for evil active in his lifetime" (177).

The contradictory intellectual and emotional responses that we see in Orwell's writing about Indians, Englishmen, and Jews testify to the deeply personal, psychological level at which he can be described as a important writer of twentieth-century modernity. Not only did Orwell diagnose many of the signs, causes, and effects of a violent world where "all that is solid melts into air," but his writing demonstrates that he also lived, thought, and felt those same kinds of conflicts. These internal conflicts, extreme and unresolved, require us to name the political, moral costs, as well as benefits, of accepting him as a guide through the crises of mid-century modernity. Near-blindness to the Holocaust is one of the costs; bold criticism of racial injustice in India is one of the benefits. In this light, it is ironic that Orwell has attracted attention from scholars of modernity for his journalism on anti-Semitism, while his journalism on India goes relatively unexamined.

My case study of Orwell and the Holocaust assumes that Orwell will continue to be important for studies of modernity, modern history, modernism, and postmodernism, but not for the usual reasons. Orwell has achieved fame for his satirical wit, powerful rhetoric, uncompromising honesty, bravery, nonconformity (eccentricity), and compassion. But many writers of the 1930s and 1940s can be described as being witty, rhetorically powerful, honest, brave, eccentric, and compassionate. What sets George Orwell apart from all these others? One answer is that Orwell has achieved in the public imagination a position of radical, nearly inhuman, isolation. The fantastic social context in which Winston Smith undertakes his stand against Big Brother has been mistakenly projected onto the social materials of Orwell's life, transforming both men into martyrs, into heroic last men. Accepting this mythology, we lose sight of what Winston Smith needed and

George Orwell actually enjoyed: society, sociability, and socialism. We also lose sight of the "ordinary," "decent" people whose lives and literature provide the context and support for Orwell's last and most influential (anti)social work.

My effort to humanize and socialize Orwell begins and ends with attention to the work of three other intermodernists Smith, Anand, and Holden. These three writers' relations to Orwell show that he is not some kind of last man in twentieth-century English literature, but one of many literary men and women who committed their writing to advancing social justice, and often socialist, goals in intermodern England. Giving Smith, Anand, and Holden the collective identity of radical eccentrics makes good rhetorical, as well as historical, sense; it implicitly justifies my analysis of their extensive biographical and textual connections to the most famous radical eccentric of all, George Orwell. Without such justification, the literary interventions of Smith, Anand, and Holden would most likely remain unimportant, and nearly invisible, within scholarship on Orwell. Even worse, their interventions might be excluded from literary criticism on the whole period of the 1930s and 1940s. Exclusion of such eccentric figures from accounts of intermodern literature and culture has, in the past, been virtually insured by scholars' dependence on opposed or dualistic critical categories: modernism and postmodernism; modernism and female modernism; Thirties and Forties; home front and war writing. This book advocates adoption of a new vocabulary of intermodernism in order to disrupt the bad habits and intellectually limiting frameworks that have blinded us to the diversity and dynamism of literature connecting the 1930s and 1940s. Discovering the intermodernists and inventing intermodernism will not require us to abandon the vocabulary, contents, and literary history provided by more familiar categories, but it will encourage us to think more creatively: to look for our subjects in the spaces between modernisms, in the fringes of literary London, in the literary and social work of Britain's radical eccentrics.

Epilogue

In England, the Orwell centenary was celebrated in 2003 with conferences, exhibits, television specials, newspaper articles, and much correspondence to editors about the meaning of Orwell's life and writings (especially "the list") for twenty-first-century politics. Most significantly, 2003 also saw the publication of new books on Orwell including rival biographies by Gordon Bowker and D. J. Taylor. The year before, 2002, marked the centenary of Stevie Smith's birth, and there were significant though less-frequent and less-publicized efforts made to celebrate her contributions to English literary culture. In 2005, Mulk Raj Anand's centenary will undoubtedly be observed with proper pomp and honor, at least in India, where he may still be alive to join in the festivities. It is almost equally certain that 2004 will come and go without anyone else remarking upon the centenary of Inez Holden. She remains an unknown figure, even among scholars of 1930s and 1940s literature, her cultural legacy still measured most easily through footnotes in the biographies of more famous and successful writers rather than through critical or popular appreciations of her own literary efforts or their meaning for English cultural history. This epilogue is devoted to her, the most fascinating if least famous of the radical eccentrics, because so few people have had any opportunity to read her novels and stories and because we still have much to learn from her writings about English intermodernism.

Holden's neglect by today's readers and scholars is not nearly as astonishing as that of her parents, who reportedly failed to register her birth. Perhaps it is fitting that someone who lived with such careless disregard for the burdensome formalities of life can invite only an approximate centenary celebration; we simply do not know for certain the year Holden was born. Library records list her birth year as 1906, while Anthony Powell claimed in his obituary tribute in the *London Magazine* that she was born 21 November 1903. Holden's family tree, kept in her private papers, ends with the names "Wilfred Herbert Holden, born 1902," and "Elisabet Inez Holden 1904?–1974." Celia Goodman, Holden's cousin, has recorded that

Holden was born in 1903 ("Inez" 29) and Orwell's biographer Bernard Crick lists her birth year as 1904 (264).

We know more about Holden's ending than her beginning because there are people alive today who knew her and cared for her and recorded their impressions of her last months. She died on 30 May 1974 in the care of Celia Goodman, who notes in her memoir of Holden that she bore her final illness with "extraordinary courage and without a word of complaint; and as her mind remained lucid she continued to be as amusing as ever right up to the time of her death" (35). Goodman also notes that the years leading up to Holden's fatal illness were happy and serene, in large part because she had found a firm and appreciative friend in Lord Shackleton, who was at one point during their friendship Lord Privy Seal in a Labour government. Lord Shackleton became the permanent tenant of the lower floor of Holden's two-floor flat in Lower Belgrave Street, the lease of which she had purchased (somehow) in the mid-1960s. She lived above him on the upper floor. Lord Shackleton himself wrote a brief posthumous appreciation of Holden, which appeared in the 9 August 1974 *Times*. He comments on her qualities of courage and hopefulness during her last illness, notes the highlights of her career, including her coverage of the Nuremberg Trials as a special correspondent, and concludes, "She was a brilliant creator of short stories—she could always invent a plot for a story at a moment's notice—and similarly, even a casual conversation could spark some characteristic Inez-style anecdote" (18).

Holden outlived George Orwell by twenty-four years and Stevie Smith by three years. Mulk Raj Anand, extraordinary man, has outlived just about everyone of his generation, Indian or English. Holden's diary indicates that she had very limited contact with Anand after he returned to India, but as late as 13 June 1959 she could write in her diary, "Mulk Raj Anand rang up and turned up here. Full of talk about the village of untouchables in which he lives. I enjoyed the evening with him." She remained very close to Orwell until his death, visiting him on Jura several times, commenting on these visits in her diary. Her diary entry of 22 January 1950 shows how upset she was upon learning from a radio announcement that he had died. She admits that when she had seen him three weeks previously, she had not believed there was much chance of him recovering from his illness, but death itself came as a shock. She writes that it stirred up old memories of their lives during the war, of conversations and old places, of Orwell's heroic attitude toward life. In contrast, we do not know how Holden reacted to news of Stevie Smith's death in 1971 because the surviving volumes of her diary do not continue beyond 1960.

In one of the last entries of Holden's diary, that of 25 August 1960, Holden records her adventures with a gallant, lost dog named Pim Hummel. Written long after the end of intermodernism, this entry serves as a tragi-comic meditation upon her own efforts to write, live, and love amid immense challenges family and history threw her way.

> Just near the gate into the Park I saw a dog coming slowly towards me, he was walking very slowly and I thought was in danger of being run over. I caught him and looking at his collar saw his name Pim Hummel and also the name of his owners Hummel of Springfield Road and a telephone number. I got a piece of string from the Newspaper man at the corner and put it round his collar and then I rang up from the telephone box. Pim came into the box with me and then he became quite cheerful. I got through to a woman who said that she had been planning to take the dog to the vet that day and somehow he must have guessed it because he had wandered away and they were desparately sad as they thought he would get run over and die a miserable death. I was surprised to hear this as Pim now seemd quite cheerful and ready to follow me. Mrs Hummel said that he had not had anything to eat for a fortnight and that he could hardly move and she couldn't think how he had got up there by himself. He was bleeding a bit from a sore near his mouth but I wiped that with my handkerchief and it seemd alright. I took him up by taxi, as soon as I took him inside the house he lay down on the floor, colapsed and shivering and yet he had been all right apparently, before. . . . This was a most extra ordinary thing about the old dog Pim because when I took him by taxi he seemed quite cheerful and happy yet once back in his own home with his devoted owners he colapsed, yet he had travelled at least eight miles . . . Mrs Hummel said she would ring me up to night and let me know what had happened about the dog.
>
> I can't settle down to any work. I feel restless and a feeling of anxiety, insecurity and failure—rather like the dog Pim Hummel.

This is not by any means the last word by or about Holden, but a parable that reminds us of the hidden costs and lost gifts that Holden's private writings record. This small tale, with its unlikely canine hero, its spelling errors, and idiosyncratic punctuation, captures Holden's qualities as a writer—observant, unsentimental, humorous, and compassionate. It hints at the more complex story that emerges once Holden's public, published writings are read against her private, unpublished diaries. Although this story cannot be fully told, it holds special value for literary historians and scholars interested in raw historical materials that can support a theoretical category of intermodernism. It also holds value for biographers interested in the creative processes of writers, of the way private experience and reflection become public performance. But we also find something in this story that is hidden from every successful writer's public performances: the signs of all the work and worry that goes into finding a publisher and audience. For Holden, this meant endless attempts to persuade influential male publishers or BBC producers to print or broadcast her work. Although Holden is memorialized as an astonishingly witty woman who could make a party out of a lamp shade and a box of Spam, her diary suggests that she also deserves to be remembered as a serious, ambitious, pragmatic worker who yearned, as all writers yearn, for more quiet, more solitude, more peace of mind, more publication. In the early 1940s Holden was in close and regular contact with men who could model the kind of discipline necessary for literary success; the names of Wells, Orwell, Powell, Koestler, Anand, and Empson repeatedly appear on the pages of her diary. These authors, like Holden, had to figure out how to survive and write amid a threadbare, bombed out, clothes-rationed, nearly revolutionary London, in which everyone was scrambling for jobs, flats, money, and paper. But these men also had women helping them out at home, doing the job of being "a sort of psychological shock-absorber, to comfort and help the weak-hearted" (or, one might add, the weak-lunged) that F. E. Baily describes in a *Woman's Home Journal* article of the mid-1930s, "Can a Woman Serve Two Masters?" Philippa Polson cites Baily's article in her 1935 *Left Review* essay "Feminists and the Woman Question." Polson's essay, an attack on comfortable conclusions about feminist progress published by the middle-class writer Winifred Holtby, argues that the feminist movement has failed because it ignores the continuing struggles of working women. She speaks directly to the concerns Holden raises in her writings of the 1940s about finding factory work for women that pays a living wage. Polson links the problem of women's depressed wages to the problem of their invisible primary jobs as caretakers. She writes:

> If part of the price a woman has to pay for the privilege of being the receptacle of a man's sexual attentions is this function of buffer, then without a doubt, this slavery to one master is a full time job. But why this conception of service? Why, if woman is emancipated and the theoretical equal of man, must she serve the man with whom she sleeps? The answer is obvious.
> She is fettered, by the level of wages for women, to an economic unit, the family. . . . Because of this series of social relationships that we call capitalism, the relationship of marriage cannot be free from the "shock-absorber" element, or from other inequalities. (qtd. in Deane 262–63)

Holden did not marry and she did not tie herself to the economic unit of the family, but she suffered as a single person from the same low wages that negatively affected the lives of the married working women Polson discusses. And Holden's devotion to her inconstant lover, Humphrey Slater, brought her the unpaid service job of "a sort of psychological shock-absorber" that Baily and Polson describe. At no point in Holden's intermodern working life did Slater or any other man (excepting perhaps H. G. Wells) serve her usefully and reliably; there was no one she could count on to do the shopping, make dinner, contribute to the household budget, buy her stockings. Nor was there anyone apart from her cousin and close friends who she could count on to buffer her from the unwelcome contingencies of life. No wonder she occasionally fantasized about becoming the companion of a great and successful writer. Unlike Sonia Brownell, who futilely tried to live out such fantasies by marrying the dying Orwell, Holden never gave them much serious consideration. She was too aware of the absurdities of sexual relations to fall under the spell of the romantic fable of masculine rescue. No, Holden is the type who would have cackled with naughty delight over Stevie Smith's send up of a lower-middle-class version of the same feminine dream. It is in *Novel on Yellow Paper* that we read about the "silly fatheads" who believe that from the "matrimony of their dreams will flow all blessings and benefits," about the "half wits" who buy twopenny weeklies and believe that marriage is the "*fons et origo*" (150). Holden's job as Slater's psychological shock-absorber was, after all, a big enough undertaking without the burdens of marriage that Smith parodies. It was complicated by the demands of her other fulltime job of earning a living and by widespread practices of economic and sexual discrimination. Holden was astute enough to perceive the signs and consequences of this discrimination, but could not combat it with anything other than her documentary publications. She, like the disenfranchised factory women she writes about, could only laugh and try again.

Holden's diary does not have the penetrating political observation or analysis typical of Orwell's wartime diary or even Polson's short essay, but it is valuable for containing a different kind of serious material: compelling evidence about the peculiar struggles faced by women from different classes who were serving "two masters." As a drop out from the gentry class who worked as both factory hand and intellectual, Holden offers feminist scholars interested in intermodern work and the politics of sex and class an unusual subject for investigation. Chapter 3 in this book begins this work of investigation, focusing on her alliances with and representations of working-class women. This epilogue urges readers to consider the implications for literary history of her membership in the smaller, more elite group of women writers and intellectuals who got onto publishers' lists or the airwaves. Unlike Smith, Holden did not portray literary women—radical eccentrics among them—in her novels or stories, but the history of her career told by her private and public writings suggests ways she can serve as a representative of this understudied group.

Documenting the peculiar challenges facing women of Holden's generation who wanted to break into London's literary establishment should motivate literary scholars to seek out their stories in the spaces between modernisms. Those spaces undoubtedly contain accounts of unknown radicals, women like Holden who responded to the conditions of wartime London with outright glee because of the healthy leveling of social classes and who felt compelled to share their sociopolitical hopes with audiences in literary forms. In Holden's case, the signs of revolution that she detected in wartime London inspired and energized her documentary literary efforts, her radical war literature. While Orwell wrote his best documentaries in the 1930s, his ideas about the relation between world war and revolution appear in Holden's writings of the early 1940s. Perhaps writing under Orwell's influence—passages of the diary seem to echo arguments of *The Lion and the Unicorn*—Holden adopted the Thirties form of documentary to the Forties contents of war.

It would be inaccurate to imply that Holden's life in the early to mid-1940s was totally consumed by details of manual labor, exploitative employers, and possible revolution, making her one with the mythical people of "the People's War." She enjoyed P.E.N. dinners, comfortable evenings with wealthy, intelligent, and sometimes influential friends, and weekend escapes from London. Chronically broke, she still had the social and cultural resources that brought occasional respite from the strains of London life, respite that would have been unavailable to the working-class women she met in the factories and represented in her fiction. At the time she was seeking a publisher for *Night Shift*, Wells's affection and hospitality provided her with a sense of respite even within blitzed London. Holden returned Wells's affection, her interest in and nurturing of the often tired, sometimes defeated elderly man suggesting that her work of psychological shock-absorber extended well beyond her care for Slater. At least in the case of Wells, she was rewarded for her work with lovely meals, fascinating company, and until Wells's break with Orwell, sincere and steady regard. Her repeated expressions of sympathy for Wells represent her unusual, even unique generosity of spirit as well as her representative status as female caretaker.

We can imagine that in Wells's eyes, Holden was a near-perfect companion: young, vibrant, suitably socialist, endearingly attentive. Holden's months in his mews are the closest she ever came to being the companion of masculine genius. When Wells broke with Orwell and required Holden to leave his property, Holden never complained of this unfair treatment or held this action against her one-time friend and mentor. Given the special needs of writers for protection from noise and interruption—their need, whether male or female, for a sort of psychological shock absorber—we can only imagine what it might have meant for Holden's writing and career had Wells kept her beside him in Hanover Terrace. Such speculation is not very productive, of course. The fact is that Holden carried on in characteristic fashion, presenting a sparkling face to the world no matter what her emotional disappointments or material struggles. Like all born survivors, she was an expert at adapting to the exigencies of dislocation. All through the period she was removing herself from Wells's flat, she kept writing. Her diary is filled with pages of acute observation and precisely remembered conversations, some of which she transformed into her most important published work, *There's No Story There*. Her most important unpublished work, the diary, is characterized by the same kinds of telling and incongruous details of person and place that make her published literature distinctive. It is a valuable record of the experiences of a single, unattached woman working her way through war, writing her way into the racial literature of the 1940s. The names of famous writers that jump out from the pages of the diary sixty or more years later are not there for effect, but represent an experience, impression, or interaction that might become the basis of a story destined for *Harper's* or *Horizon*. These famous, public personalities are not any more important to the flow of this private narrative than the hundreds of unknown characters—friends, workers, landladies, supervisors, eccentrics like Holden herself—who wander in and out of the diary's pages.

Telling stories as habit, as profession, as self-defense, Holden entertained workers, writers, lovers, and lords with her wit and sophisticated sense of the absurd. This epilogue seeks to gain new readers for her rare literary forms, although it cannot convey the qualities of voice and character that so amused the other radical eccentrics during conversations at the Café Royal or Orwell's flat. Unable to reproduce Holden's inimitable social style, this study makes its case for her inclusion in English literary history through the scholar's tools of citation, analysis, and footnotes. This book's concluding argument is that Holden, an intelligent, attractive, uneducated woman with no assured means of support and no instinct or ambition for marriage, is worth remembering and, one hundred years after her birth, celebrating, despite a career that produced no best sellers and earned no literary awards. If for no other reason, she deserves our respect for her ability to compose a life out of the colorful scraps of material others left behind and weave from them stories that represent a uniquely radical and eccentric contribution to intermodernism in literary London.

Notes

Introduction   In the Space between Modernisms: George Orwell and the Radical Eccentrics

1. Throughout this study I refer to historical periods, usually the years between 1930 and 1949, with dates rather than words: the 1930s or the 1940s. When referring to the more limited literary-historical periods constructed by classic anthologies or accounts of these periods such as Robin Skelton's *Poetry of the Thirties*, Samuel Hynes's *The Auden Generation*, or Valentine Cunningham's *British Writers of the Thirties*, I use words rather than dates: the Thirties or the Forties.

2. Orwell himself contributed to the critical bias against English prose written after the height of modernism with his influential essay, "Inside the Whale," which contains the oft-cited pronouncement: "No decade in the past hundred and fifty years has been so barren of imaginative prose as the nineteen-thirties. There have been good poems, good sociological works, brilliant pamphlets, but practically no fiction of any value at all" (*CEJL* I: 518). Until recently, most scholars of modern British literature have come to the same conclusion as Orwell, although they tend to single out the 1940s rather than the 1930s as especially barren of literary accomplishment. See for example, Michael North's *Henry Green and His Generation*. Although North is interested in promoting Green's reputation in large part through appreciation of his publications of the 1940s, he echoes the received wisdom of previous critics that "The Second World War lacks a literature of its own. The common journalistic cry during the second world war was, 'Where are the war poets?' " He supports the wartime journalists' worries about weak war poetry with citations of Anthony Burgess's and P. H. Newby's studies on the novel without challenging the problematic assumptions about genre and form (not to mention gender) that structure the majority of postwar surveys that "agree that the later war, unlike the first, failed to become a literary event" (North 101).

3. Aside from the explicitly biographical discussions of this study (such as the next section of the introduction or the book's epilogue) my subject throughout this book is almost without exception "Orwell," the figure represented in writings by George Orwell and constructed by those who have reflected on and written about the man and his writing, not George Orwell (or Eric Blair), the actual person who is the subject of biographies. Similarly, I am most interested in "Smith,"

"Anand," or "Holden," the subjects of discourse rather than "true" historical personages. Indicating this distinction between Orwell and "Orwell," or Smith and "Smith" with insertion of quotation marks around proper names would be ridiculously irritating, so I ask readers to remember that I do not write biography, but textual criticism informed by biographical frameworks.

It is possible, if slightly dangerous, to make judgments about the personal, historical Orwell of biographies because of the tremendous number of documents—public and private—that record his thinking. I admit to assuming this risk in chapter 4, "George Orwell's Invention: The Last Man in Europe." However, I try to limit personal judgments in my discussions of Smith, Anand, and to a lesser extent Holden, because there is not enough documentation available to support sure knowledge about their inner lives and private thoughts. Anand certainly has published innumerable pages recording and analyzing his own emotional, intellectual history, but as I explain elsewhere, he is an unreliable witness about his own past. Holden is unusual in having written extensive diaries throughout (and beyond) the years Orwell was alive, but these are full of gaps and are not publicly available. Our knowledge of Smith, the historical person, is greater than most scholars' knowledge of the "real" Anand or "real" Holden, but even with two good biographies and public collections of Smith's manuscripts, letters, and other writings, it is difficult to determine how closely Smith modeled the opinions of her fictional alter egos upon herself. My focus in these chapters on issues like racism, anti-Semitism, and sexism makes it especially important that I make my claims and judgments about the things a critic can discuss with confidence: representations, characters, narrators, styles, languages, metaphors, fictions.

4. In *Reading the Thirties*, Bernard Bergonzi insists that "a group need not necessarily imply a circle of writers sitting round a café table composing a joint manifesto. A group can still be recognisable as such, even if the separate members rarely meet or do not know each other personally at all" (7). The group I am calling the radical eccentrics did gather round café tables but they did not recognize themselves as a group, let alone define their group relationship by signing manifestos. While there may be other candidates for membership in the radical eccentrics (Anthony Powell comes to mind) and while there are many radical and eccentric artists at work in London contributing to intermodernist movement, I am not aware of anyone whose writings to or about Orwell bring them into regular dialogue with the other members of the group.

5. Bernard Crick's biography of Orwell does a better job than other biographies or memoirs of conveying the sense of the Orwell–Smith–Anand–Holden alliance, in part because he cites Holden's diaries so extensively. Frances Spalding's biography of Smith also tells the story of the writers' friendships, though her footnotes are not as helpful as Crick's. Other than John Rodden's critical study on the history of Orwell's reputation, which foregrounds the constructed or invented nature of his reputation as a lone, eccentric warrior or saint for truth and justice, there are no studies that explicitly set out to understand Orwell's politics or art as an extension of his social relationships and experiences.

6. Margery Sabin's problem is the inverse of my own. Instead of defending cultural values before readers who are likely to be most invested in literary studies, she must defend literary and aesthetic values before readers who are likely to be most invested in cultural and postcolonial studies.

7. This study is most indebted to the discussions of literary scholars working in feminist, postcolonial, working-class, or cultural studies who have already begun this work of discovery. Andy Croft's *Red Letter Days: British Fiction in the 1930s* (1990) and Alison Light's *Forever England: Femininity, Literature, and Conservatism between the Wars* (1991) are two early examples of such revisionary literature; Michael T. Saler's *The Avant-Garde in Interwar England: Medieval Modernism and the London Underground* (1999); Tyrus Miller's *Late Modernism: Politics, Fiction, and the Arts between the Wars* (1999); and Janet Montefiore's *Men and Women Writers of the 1930s* (1996) are later important additions. Also of note are Jane Dowson's *Women, Modernism, and British Poetry 1910–1939: Resisting Femininity* (2002); Elizabeth Maslen's *Political and Social Issues in British Women's Fiction* (2001); Margaret Stetz's *British Women's Comic Fiction, 1890–1990: Not Drowning, But Laughing* (2001); Lynne Hapgood and Nancy Paxton's *Outside Modernism: In Pursuit of the English Novel 1900–30* (2000); Maroula Joannou's *Women Writers of the 1930s: Gender, Politics and History* (1999); Keith Williams and Steven Matthews's *Rewriting the Thirties: Modernism and After* (1997); Patrick Quinn's *Recharting the Thirties* (1996); and John Carey's *The Intellectuals and the Masses: Pride and Prejudice among the Literary Intelligentsia, 1880–1939* (1992). The introduction to Patrick Deane's *History in Our Hands: A Critical Anthology of Writings on Literature, Culture and Politics from the 1930s* (1998) provides a concise defense of the movement to revise "the Thirties," and an invaluable selection of primary materials written by figures who could represent both a "classic" and "revisionary" 1930s.

Revisionary work on the 1940s has also prepared the way for this book. Phyllis Lassner's *British Women Writers of World War II* (1998); Karen Schneider's *Loving Arms: British Women Writing the Second World War* (1997); Jenny Hartley's *Millions Like Us: British Women's Fiction of the Second World War* (1997); and Gill Plain's *Women's Fiction of the Second World War* (1996) have been especially important. See also several revisionary studies of combatants' writing, exemplified by Mark Rawlinson's *British Writing of the Second World War* (2000); Adam Piette's *Imagination at War: British Fiction and Poetry 1939–1945* (1995); and Alan Munton's *English Fiction of the Second World War* (1989), which argue for a new appreciation of British war literature of World War II.

8. My proposal of a new category of intermodernism should be seen as part of the widespread project to rethink mid-century English literary history. Signs of this project include a number of sessions on "new" or alternate modernisms proposed for the annual conferences of the Modernist Studies Association, a stream of conferences on topics like "British Women in the Thirties" (held at CUNY's Graduate School in September 2000), "Retrieving the 1940s" (held at the University of Leeds in April 2002), and "The Noise of History" (held at the Dylan Thomas Centre in Swansea in November 2003), and special issues of

journals on topics like "Gender and Modernism between the Wars, 1918–1939" (*NWSA Journal*'s 2003 issue) and "The Thirties Now!" (Sheffield Hallam University's *Working Papers on the Web* 2004 issue).

Another encouraging sign of scholars' commitment to exploring the new subjects and histories supported by the types of panels and special journal issues mentioned above is the existence of a group called The Space Between. Dedicated to the study of literature and culture between 1914 and 1945, the society's annual conferences have provided stimulating contexts for my efforts and those of other younger scholars to reconsider modernism and its relation to the 1930s and 1940s. Two volumes of collected essays have emerged to date from The Space Between conferences, Stella Deen's *Challenging Modernism: New Readings in Literature and Culture, 1914–1945* (2002) and Antony Shuttleworth's *And in Our Time: Vision, Revision, and British Writing of the 1930s* (2003). These books extend the discussions of The Space Between conferences into print and so provide a relevant textual backdrop for this study.

9. A cursory glance at any of the bibliographies of the revisionary studies mentioned here will demonstrate that scholars are already navigating the gaps between modernism, postmodernism, the 1930s, the 1940s, but they have to rely on old maps with fading signs—fading labels—to do so.

10. The need for the tool of intermodernism is implied by the number of scholarly books that are devoted to defining and redefining relations within and between modernisms. In one of the best of these books, *The Concept of Modernism*, Astradur Eysteinsson rejects all the most familiar descriptions of post-modernism's relation to modernism, finally leaving readers with the idea that "while [. . .] there may be no postmodernism" there is a modernism whose major achievement may have been "its subversion of the *authority* of tradition" (emphasis in original; 136–37). Modernism understood in this way invites us to add the names of the radical eccentrics to those of other, earlier antitraditionalists who populate books like *The Pound Era* or *The Genealogy of Modernism*. But such an expansive modernism asks us to settle for a category with periodizing meanings and effects without attending to the problems with history and value that typically accompany the very concept of period. The tenuous connections between literary period and historical narratives in Eysteinsson's chapter point to the differences between our approaches to the modernism/postmodernism problem.

11. Exploring the uneasy relations between modernism and writing of the 1930s, Shuttleworth, like many other 1930s scholars, assumes that the period has been "overshadowed by the achievements of classic modernism" (11). He suggests that the essays in his collection indicate that the period is "both more and less modernist than critics have supposed, more and less postmodernist" (13). Alan Munton makes a similar argument about the relation of World War II literature to modernist categories. He criticizes David Lodge's conventional "tripartite system" of dividing the twentieth century into a modernist period, antimodernist period, and postwar period of the Angry Young Men, concluding that "In its literary aspect the war has disappeared into an Orwellian memory hole" (3).

12. The last of these terms, "interwar," "war," and "postwar," avoid the problems with periodization encouraged by the modernism and postmodernism pairing, but the constant term within each category of the interwar-war-postwar spectrum, "war," evokes for most readers "the myth that war compels men to go forth and fight in order to protect their women, who remain passive and secure at home with the children" (Higonnet et al. 1). The masculine bias of this myth is evident even in revisionary studies such as Rawlinson's *British Writing of the Second World War* and Piette's *Imagination at War*. These scholars usefully interrogate the values that have elevated the combatants' literature of World War I at the expense of the combatants' literature of Word War II, but do little to help us conceptualize a robust interwar or intermodern literature created by men and women. In contrast, Lassner's *British Women Writers of World War II*, Plain's *Women's Fiction of the Second World War*, Hartley's *Millions Like Us*, and Karen Schneider's *Loving Arms* construct, in effect if not intent, a critical space that links interwar, war, and postwar writings through their focus on women's texts. See also Montefiore (120–25) for a discussion of "women's war poetry" of the 1930s.

While many wartime and immediately postwar studies of war writing support the bias that characterizes more recent critical studies of World War II literature, it is worth noting that Denys Val Baker's 1947 anthology, *Modern British Writing*, offered readers an impressive array of poems, stories, and essays, many by women, that were first published in British little reviews during 1939–1945. Of special note is Baker's inclusion of Patricia Johnson's essay, "The Younger British Women Writers." Johnson singles out Inez Holden for special mention, praising her documentary style as "peculiarly suited to describe aspects of modern war, when we were on such tragic terms with calamity that we could only bear to personalize it in an impersonal way" (180).

13. See Maria DiBattista and Lucy McDiarmid's *High and Low Moderns*, Light's *Forever England*, and Hapgood and Paxton's *Outside Modernism* for feminist studies of the popular culture of modernity that have made identification of an intermodern literature possible. Hapgood and Paxton locate the origins of their study in the words of cultural studies icon Raymond Williams, citing the conclusion of his lecture "When Was Modernism?" (reconstructed by Fred Inglis from notes he took as Williams spoke to students at the University of Bristol on 17 March 1987), which calls for scholars to "search out and counterpose an alternative tradition taken from the neglected works left in the wide margin of the century" (qtd. in Hapgood and Paxton 3; Williams, *Politics* 35). One of Williams's last public lectures, "When Was Modernism?" shows how strongly he objected to the modernism-postmodernism trap, decrying a " 'Modernism' [. . .] confined to [a] highly elective field and denied to everything else in an act of pure ideology, whose first, unconscious irony is that, absurdly, it stops history dead. Modernism being the terminus, everything afterwards is counted out of development. It is *after*; stuck in the post" (emphasis in original; Williams 34–35).

14. Caution must accompany celebration; Light warns in "Outside History?" that "to be marginal, is never just oppositional, it is also heartbreaking and

demoralising" (251). Her comments about reading poetry by women, that it "cannot easily be reconciled to that search for a liberated, fully achieving self-hood," apply equally well to the experience of reading fiction by outsiders Inez Holden and Mulk Raj Anand.

15. Rushdie's 1984 essay "Outside the Whale" passionately opposes Orwell's recommendation in 1940 that writers hide in the belly of the whale until "the world has shaken itself into its new shape" because "passivity always serves the interests of the status quo, of the people already at the top of the heap." He argues that "the Orwell of 'Inside the Whale' and *Nineteen Eighty-Four* is advocating ideas that can only be of service to our masters. If resistance is useless, those whom one might otherwise resist become omnipotent" (97). In contrast, the writings of Smith, Anand, and Holden urge us to resist our masters in their various guises.

16. As many have noted, Smith's politics are hard to pin down. Her refusal to ally her artistic practice with either Tory, Labour, or Catholic ideologies during these most political of decades has certainly contributed to her marginal position within standard accounts of Thirties or Forties literature. So have her generic practices. She was publishing prose in the 1930s when poetry and drama were the fashionable forms for elite writers and she was trying to publish poetry in the 1940s when everyone else was publishing their war novels and memoirs. She is missing from Hynes's *The Auden Generation* and even Valentine Cunningham's monumental *British Writers of the Thirties* does not treat her work in any depth. It took the feminist critical studies of the 1990s to really bring Smith into literary-critical discussion.

17. Smith seems to be remembering a passage late in the novel when Celia is on her holiday in Lincolnshire with her beloved Uncle Heber. She tells him, "Basil Tait is rather a fool, you know Uncle. . . . He is like a fourteen-year-old clever boy, with his Lord Rivaulx and this and that. You would say: He is promising, he is like a fourteen-year-old boy you know, he thinks girls can't play" (145).

18. I want to distinguish my notion of radical eccentricity from any simple, unmotivated, or purposeless display of unconventionality. Smith shared with Irish playwright Denis Johnston her impatience with those who took up unconventional behaviors in the name of unconventionality. Her satire of Kay Boyle, who she anticipated visiting in 1938 with her friend Nina Condron, is quite funny about this: "[I]t's all very odd, weird somehow, I mean Kay . . . seems to spend her whole time Being Unconventional, this sort of thing, Why put cups on the table, why not on the floor, the English are so conventional, if you want to throw somebody out of the window, why not do it, the English are so conventional . . . " (*MA* 268).

19. Asa Briggs's third volume, *The War of Words*, in his authoritative, four-volume history of the BBC, sets up the context for understanding the roles of Orwell, Smith, Anand, and Holden at the BBC. For a study that emphasizes the BBC's propagandistic role during war, see Sian Nicholas's *The Echo of War*. T. O. Beachcroft's early history, *British Broadcasting*, represents the BBC as the "authentic voice of truth in a world bewildered by propaganda," providing a heartwarming, even romantic contrast to Nicholas's more recent scholarly study.

20. There is some confusion over the time and place of the first meeting between Anand and Orwell. W. J. West mentions in *The War Broadcasts* that Anand was "a veteran of the struggle against Franco in Spain (where he had been a close friend of Orwell's)" and cites other memories Anand shared with him of contacts with Orwell (14). Yet these memories are just that: memories. Bernard Crick recalls that one of his Ph.D. advisees returned from a research trip to India with notebooks full of Anand's "long, detailed and well remembered conversations with Orwell in Madrid. Only one snag, Orwell was never in Madrid and almost certainly did not meet Mulk until after he came back from Spain" (personal correspondence, 17 June 1998). Peter Davison's footnote description of Anand in *The Complete Works* claims that Anand fought for the Republicans in the Spanish Civil War but did not meet Orwell there (*CW* 13: 100).

21. Personal correspondence, 5 October 2003.

22. Holden anticipates Orwell in her attempt to define the young men of the 1930s in terms of their ambivalent longing for inclusion in World War I. Orwell wrote in 1940 in "My Country Right or Left" that "[M]y particular generation, those who had been 'just too young', became conscious of the vastness of the experience they had missed. You [*sic*] felt yourself a little less than a man, because you had missed it" (*CEJL* I: 537–38). Samuel Hynes echoes Orwell, suggesting in *The Auden Generation* that the sense of having failed a test without even taking it is "an important factor in the collective consciousness of the whole generation of young men who came of age between the wars" (21). Holden's 1932 novel is refreshingly funny, even naughty, in its satiric send up of the specifically gendered and decidedly neurotic character of the longing Orwell ascribed to his generation. Anand's intermodern trilogy about World War I, *The Village, Across the Black Waters,* and *Sword and the Sickle,* which traces the disillusioning, though not fatal journey of the runaway youth Lal Singh from a rural village in India to the British trenches in World War I and back home to a band of Marxist revolutionaries, provides a very different kind of satiric commentary on the longings of Hynes's "whole generation of young men."

23. Personal correspondence, 5 October 2003.

24. Reports of Holden's youthful pleasure in social gatherings should be weighed against her own memories of her bohemian days. In her diary entry of 22 August 1948 on her experience of the 1920s, Holden reflects, "I read *Brideshead Revisited* by Evelyn Waugh which gave me, still more, a feeling of nostalgic depression with all those stories of High Life of the Twenties which everyone seemed to have enjoyed but I never did" (22 August 1948).

25. Personal correspondence, 5 October 2003.

26. See chapter 1 in this book, "Hurrah to Be a Goy!" for a more in-depth analysis of the story and its disastrous impact on Smith's relations with another couple, the Hemmings. Holden, like Lopez, seems to emerge unscathed from the sad affair.

27. I have not found confirmation in sources other than Spalding of Anand's membership in the Communist Party, although such membership would have been consistent with his passion for Marx in the 1930s and 1940s.

28. Anand has recorded different versions of this incident. In Spalding's biography of Smith, Anand remembers Sackville-West saying, "no writer could deal with the working class without making a joke of them" (157).
29. BBCWA correspondence, 22 March 1941.
30. Personal correspondence, 25 October 2003. Helen Fowler shared her memories of Smith with me during conversations in her home on 11 April 2002 and a more extensive interview on 26 July 1998.

CHAPTER 1   "HURRAH TO BE A GOY!":
STEVIE SMITH AND SUBURBAN SATIRE

1. I adopt Tony Kushner's definition of anti-Semitism as "a hostility to Jews as Jews" (7) and assume, with him, that the two "clearest features" of modern British anti-Semitism are (1) Jews are perceived as a foreign group and (2) Jews are perceived as a malevolent power in society. Kushner argues that both features have their roots in a medieval view of Jewry, though he insists that anti-Semitism is not an "unvarying force" and that its "dynamic character needs examination" (9).
2. Several of Orwell's friends and a number of his critics have argued that he was emotionally conflicted about Jews or even harbored anti-Semitic attitudes. For fuller treatment of this subject, see chapter 4 in this book, "George Orwell's Invention," in particular my case study of Orwell and the Holocaust.
3. Between 1933 and 1939, about 50,000 European Jews emigrated to England. Bernard Wasserstein judges Britain's prewar record of popular treatment toward Jews as relatively generous (9). He cites A. J. P. Taylor's conclusion that Nazi treatment of the Jews before the outbreak of war "did more than anything else to turn English moral feeling against Germany, and this moral feeling in turn made English people less reluctant to go to war" (Taylor 420). Yet Kushner comes to the depressing conclusion that "Deportations, pogroms or death camps were seen as unacceptable solutions by the vast majority of the [British] population, but it seems doubtful whether there would have been mass protests had the Nazis implemented such a policy on British soil. . . . Jews who were prepared to use cyanide capsules in the event of a Nazi invasion of Britain were not necessarily suffering from paranoia" (191). Complementing Wasserstein's conclusions about the causes of official Britain's shameful response to the crisis of European Jewry during the war, Kushner shows that domestic antipathy to Jews permitted a mass diversion of popular awareness of the scale of Jewish suffering in Europe and at home (191).
4. See for example Jameson's *Europe to Let* (1940), Bottome's *The Mortal Storm* (1937) and *Within the Cup* (1943), and Miller's *Farewell, Leicester Square* (1941; written 1935).
5. See Lassner's essay, "A Cry for Life: Storm Jameson, Stevie Smith, and the Fate of Europe's Jews" and " 'The Milk of Our Mother's Kindness Has Ceased to Flow': Virginia Woolf, Stevie Smith, and the Representation of the Jew." The evidence from these essays enters into and supports the more ambitious argument made in her 1998 book *British Women Writers of World War II*.

6. Smith's poetry does not fit any more easily than her fiction into the readymade categories and characterizations critics favor. Frances Spalding, a biographer of Smith and one of her most sympathetic readers, resolves the problem of how to place Smith in this way: "[Smith's] work was and is difficult to pigeon-hole. Her play with a small range of ideas, often repeated, introduces a philosophical element that makes her a kind of lower highbrow, halfway between a solid middlebrow such as Rosamond Lehmann and the sparkling philosophy of Iris Murdoch" (224). Other critics have tried more or less successfully to ally Smith with modernism or postmodernism. Certainly any of these classifications, suggestive as they are of some kind of historical connection between Smith, other English writers, and English literary culture, are preferable to the decision by the *Norton Anthology of English Literature* editors to describe Smith as "one of the absolute originals of English literature, whose work fits into no category and shows none of the characteristic influences of the age" (2221).

7. Smith's concentration on ethnic and national politics in her novels is not evident in her poems. As a result, outside of feminist analyses, her poems were for many years regarded as apolitical, despite their exposition of discrepancies of power in domestic and religious contexts. Representations of Jews are equally absent from the poems, with the bizarre, perhaps hysterical exception of "A Jew is Angry with his Friend who does not Believe in Circumcision."

8. In her "Introduction" to *Over the Frontier*, Janet Watts demonstrates her understanding of the significance of Pompey's comment, "Hurrah to be a goy!" in the context of Pompey's inspection of "the blackest specks in her soul": "In *Novel on Yellow Paper* there was something—not anti-semitism, no—but something that felt elation at a Jewish party [. . .] and that later felt the tweak of a link between that and the horrors of Germany, 'as if that thought alone might swell the mass of cruelty working up against them [the Jews]' " (7). Gill Plain does not examine in depth the "extremely discomforting opening of *Novel on Yellow Paper*" (69), but her comments are suggestive and stand in contrast to the silence of many of Smith's critics on the subject of Smith and Jews.

9. Pompey's refusal or inability to see herself as a "shiksa," the more specific and thus more insiderly term that distinguishes itself from goy along the lines of gender, heightens the ambiguities of Pompey's membership claims. It thus helps set the stage for her later exposure of the inherent cruelties that come with attempts to define membership by more public, powerful groups signified by words like "German" or "English." I am indebted to Karen Karl for pointing out the implied "insider" status indicated by Pompey's use for the word goy and to Jacqueline Schweitzer for asking me how the use of shiksa might have changed the meaning of the text.

10. See chapter 3 of Andrea Freud Loewenstein's *Loathsome Jews* for a concise history of Anglo Jewry.

11. Sander Gilman's *The Jew's Body* documents the long history in Europe of regarding Jews as having a diseased interior (morality, psychology) that was reflected in external differences (skin, hair, nose, penis). In the early twentieth century the demand among Jews for blond hair and bobbed noses was actually meant to "cure" the disease of Jewishness, the anxiety of being seen as a Jew (171, 191).

12. While the term "complicity" may seem too strong to describe Britain's relation to the Nazi attack upon the Jews, Smith's inquiry encourages us to entertain this possibility. Historical research suggests that, at least on the level of policy, Smith was right to find support in Britain for Nazi persecutions abroad. Wasserstein draws the "unavoidable" conclusion that, when set in the context of total war and of British policy toward Allied nations in general, "the Jews received peculiarly ungenerous treatment [from Britain]. Far from shedding a more favourable light on Britain's Jewish policy, an examination of it within the broader context merely highlights its deficiencies" (353). See Yahuda Bauer for discussion of the lengths to which Allied leaders went to avoid saving Jews, even in the face of "a mutinous British public that wanted the government to help the Jews" (222).

13. See Severin 37 and Jack Barbera and William McBrien's *Stevie* 112–15 for summaries of critics' disappointed reactions to *Over the Frontier*'s ending.

14. Pompey is faithful to the crude facts of Georg Grosz's life. Born in Germany in 1893, Grosz left Europe and became an American citizen in 1938.

15. Plain explains in similar terms the way Pompey's confidences in *Over the Frontier* create a moral dilemma for readers who watch her transformation into a practical, ruthless, uniformed spy: "The reader becomes a witness to the conversion of the sceptical observer [Pompey] into the most fervent disciple. To see this happen to a close confiding 'friend,' the narrator, is an attack on the complacency of the reader" (70).

16. Spalding bases her judgment about the difference between Smith's and Pompey's sentiments about Jews on interpretation of Smith's fiction and assumptions about the behaviors of "truly anti-Semitic" writers. She does not point to other, nonliterary documents to support her interpretation, although her research shows that none of Smith's gentile friends regarded her as harboring anti-Semitic feelings and that Smith never displayed signs of overt anti-Semitism by doing things like writing anti-Semitic tracts or refusing to initiate friendships with Jews. It is likely that Smith, like Orwell, had different feelings about Jews at different times in her life but again, such judgments are more the concern of biographers than critics. Critics should note that as late as 1955 Smith published a story called "To School in Germany" that features a narrator who falls in love with a German boy named Maxi who is constantly irritating her with his "hackneyed exascerbating (*sic*) and wicked sentiments vis-à-vis the Jews, the English or any other persons, institutions or opinions" (*MA* 36). Here Jews and English are allied as the butts of Maxi's ideologically motivated contempt. At the end of the story, the narrator, much older, recognizes Maxi as he is arrested by her cousin as a Nazi war criminal. The narrator complains to her cousin, "I hate this 'holier than thou' situation we are all in now." And the cousin replies, "We ARE holier than him" (*MA* 38).

17. "Enemy Action" was finally published with the new title "Sunday at Home" in *The New Savoy* in 1949, three years after its composition. This was followed by its BBC broadcast on 20 April 1949, which Smith earned through entry in a short story competition. The story had originally been accepted for publication

.946 by the editor of an anthology called *The Holiday Book*, but was quickly
urned when fears of libel arose. See Barbera and McBrien 152, 164–65.

　　palding includes more details about the Millers's lives than Barbera and
McBrien, thus providing a better social context in which to understand the dis-
solution of Smith's friendship with Miller. She cites a paragraph from the letter
Miller sent Smith following her initial telephone response to "Beside the
Seaside." See Spalding 186–88.

19. By 1949 when Smith's story appeared, many British Jews feared outbreaks of
violence against them. These fears were inspired in part by English reactions to
the UN's partition of Palestine into Jewish and Arab states in 1947 and the
1948–1949 Israeli War of Independence. Two years before Smith's story
appeared and one year before her holiday with the Millers, there was anti-
Jewish rioting in Jewish neighborhoods all over Britain, precipitated by the
hanging of two British sergeants by the Irgun in Haifa.

20. In reality the English did set up internment camps in September 1939, to
which a large number of Nazi sympathizers, some left-wing refuges, and some
Jews were sent. Several months later, on 12 May 1940, 2,000 male enemy
aliens living in coastal areas were rounded up and interned. Then on May 16
and 17, all "B" class aliens were rounded up in great haste and secrecy, with
some refugees committing suicide at the idea of internment. The press flamed
the hysteria, and "INTERN THE LOT" was the slogan of the day. It created
"something unpleasantly close to 'pogrom-mindedness' " among sections of the
population. See Calder, *People's War* 130–33. Many writers, including most
vocally Storm Jameson, protested the incarceration of harmless and often
homeless interned refugees, some of whom were Jewish.

21. Smith makes Pompey participate in the popular, futile endeavor of trying to
define Jews as a race. While understanding of Smith's fiction depends, in part, on
interpretation of her narrator's efforts at racial definition, it is important to keep
in mind that, in sociologist D. Van Arkel's words, "the race concept is meaningless" (20). It is a "hodgepodge of linguistic, arbitrarily chosen somatic and cultural traits, usually ill-defined or not at all defined, without serious efforts to
come to a consensus, and above all serving social needs as they might arise" (12).

22. See the January 2003 special issue of *Modernism/Modernity* on T. S. Eliot and
anti-Semitism for defenses of Eliot couched in the terms that Pompey sees
through: "Some of his best friends were Jews."

23. The distinction Pompey makes between English battle cruelty and other kinds
of cruelties (Spanish, Nazi), is more clearly made in *The Holiday*. Celia uses the
contrast between suffering in Tennyson's *Maud* and in her own story, "Over-
Dew," to illustrate a difference not just between English and Nazi cruelties, but
between Victorian and intermodern sensibilities. Tennyson "gave his creatures
dignity in suffering," but her story, like the life that she knows, "seems like the
Nazis to give always the maximum of pain with the maximum of indignity"
(181). The result is that postwar English "cannot believe a word of the *Maud*
situation" (181). Nazi-style cruelty of dealing death without dignity has
become the norm for intermodern and postwar readers.

24. Alan Jackson describes the late Victorian "fertile ground" that paved the way for the development of semi-detached London in the early decades of the twentieth century. He chooses Smith's hometown of Palmers Green, among others, to represent one of three kinds of typical London suburbs (22).

25. See John Carey's wonderfully tendentious study *The Intellectuals and the Masses* for extensive documentation of early- and mid-twentieth-century anti-suburban sentiment in the chapter "The Suburbs and the Clerks." Recalling in some ways Andreas Huyssen's thesis in the third chapter of *After the Great Divide*, "Mass Culture as Woman: Modernism's Other," Carey's larger argument is that modernist writing was designed to turn newly educated (or "semi-educated") readers created by late-nineteenth-century educational reforms into the metaphor of "the mass" in order to defeat their power, remove their literacy, deny their humanity, and so preserve the intellectual's privilege (21). Those intellectuals who Carey attacks include the usual suspects of Nietzsche, Hamsun, Hardy, Lawrence, Yeats, Eliot, Lewis, Waugh, Huxley, Greene, and Conrad, and the not-so-usual suspects of Shaw, Wells, Gissing, Priestley, Woolf, and Forster. Arthur Conan Doyle and to a certain extent, James Joyce, are among the astonishingly few writers who emerge from Carey's study with their reputations intact.

26. According to geographer Richard Harris and urban planning historian Peter J. Larkham, "When writers have used 'culture' and 'suburb' in the same sentence, they have usually done so with one of two purposes in mind. Those who use 'culture' in the 'high' sense have usually deplored its virtual absence in bland, middlebrow suburbs. . . . Those who use culture in a broader, more anthropological sense have discussed the culture of the suburbs. . . . Typically, they have seen this as a private culture, focused upon domesticity and family pursuits, reinforced by home ownership, and increasingly associated with mass consumption" (15–16).

27. Having cited hilariously incriminating passages from a wide array of books (high- and lowbrow) in order to show the pervasive, anti-suburban horror evident in intellectual's writings, Carey reminds his readers that "Like 'masses,' the wor[d] 'suburban' is a sign for the unknowable. But 'suburban' is distinctive in combining topographical with intellectual disdain. It relates human worth to habitat. This history of the word shows how a development in human geography that caused widespread dismay came to dictate the intellectuals' reading of twentieth-century culture" (53). For a refreshing break from such intellectual dismay, see J. M. Richard's classic intermodern study *Castles on the Ground*, which defends the suburb as "our own contemporary vernacular" (19), worthy of serious analysis due to the puzzle it poses about society; how could something known for deficient taste represent an ideal home for ninety out of one hundred Englishmen (17)?

28. Carey identifies Smith and John Betjeman as two writers who, "intent on finding an eccentric voice could do so by colonizing this abandoned [suburban] territory" (66). Although the ominous imperialist metaphor that shapes this statement about Smith might lead one to suspect Carey will trounce her too, in fact he treats her poetry with sympathy, recognizing that "her taste for

suburban sensations is keen and immediate" (67). Having identified a
tendency among intellectuals to treat the suburb as a site of a specifically female
triviality, Carey draws a parallel between suburban experience and the features
that distinguish Smith's poetic voice. Seeming to anticipate Light's feminist
argument in "Outside History? Stevie Smith, Women Poets and the National
Voice," he notes that Smith "evolved a model of female writing that avoids and
undercuts the kinds of dignity and authority that males have appropriated"
(69). However Carey then places Smith outside literary history, calling her
"uncategorizable," and throwing into question her connections to other
intellectuals by claiming her poems "achieve cultural significance because they
are entirely careless of cultural significance" (69).

29. See Gordon Maxwell's *The Fringe of London* and Walter George Bell's, *Where
London Sleeps*. The only one of these ramble books readers would be likely to
recognize today is J. B. Priestley's *English Journey*, which carries the astonishing
subtitle *Being a Rambling but Truthful Account of What One Man Saw and
Heard and Felt and Thought during a Journey through England during the
Autumn of the Year 1933*. Priestley famously described the outer suburb as the
site that came closest to representing the "Third" or modern England. Other,
more typical titles and texts include Moyra Fox-Davies's *Eighty Miles around
London*, Henry Bridges Fearon's *Tramping around London*, and "Pathfinder's"
The Footpath Way around London.

30. See Jackson 74–89 for a case study of Golders Green. He describes Ernest
Owers (1860–1938) as "an almost legendary figure in the world of estate
agents," a man who started out as a solicitor's clerk and grew to be one of the
most successful developers during the Golders Green bonanza (74). Jackson
does not explain when or how the Golders Green of Owers's pamphlet became
known as one of London's Jewish areas.

31. For an innocent contribution to the dialectic of development and nostalgia
nurtured by the literature of the suburbs, see Clive Smith's 1974 book *Golders
Green as It Was*, which consists of reproduced photographs from the years of
Golders Green's most ferocious, and in some minds, tragic development.

32. Carey reads Waugh's verdict on suburbia as a reaction to the consumption of
his childhood home on the edge of Hampstead Heath by—what else?—
Golders Green (48).

33. See Carey 198–208. Like the geographers and historians of suburbia that I cite,
Carey does not discuss Jews or anti-Semitism—even when alluding to *Mein
Kampf*. He notes in his postscript how the population explosion of the last half
of the twentieth century has inspired academic predictions of massive numbers
of human deaths with conclusions that "agree broadly with Hitler's warning in
Mein Kampf" (213). Carey reminds readers, "we are just as responsible for [the
frightening figures of population explosion] as anyone else" and suggests that
our own impulse to see the problem elsewhere should "make us sympathize
more with the intellectuals' predicament in the early twentieth-century], however repellent we may find the cultural attitudes they favoured and the reme-
dies they proposed" (213). It is worth noting that outside of this sentence,
Carey himself does not extend or encourage sympathy for the intellectuals' fear

of the masses. Waugh or Woolf, Lewis or Wells, gentile or Jew—all end up looking like monsters.

34. See *Collected Poems* 81–82.

35. Barbera and McBrien cite the "mandarin approval" Smith's first novel earned from literary heavy weights Noel Coward, Raymond Mortimer, and John Hayward, and record her invitation from Hayward to lunch with Eddy Sackville-West, Rosamond Lehmann, and Joe Ackerley. Yet many of Smith's best friends came from the ranks of London's lesser-known women writers and editors, including Sally Chilver, Olivia Manning, Helen Fowler, Cecily Mackworth, Alice "Liz" Ritchie, Narcisse Crowe-Wood, Betty Miller, and, of course, Inez Holden.

36. In 1956 Smith could write to an editor, "Very few in this suburb know me as Stevie Smith & I should like it to stay that way" (*MA* 301). She had been in Palmers Green for fifty years at this point.

37. See Simon Dentith for a reading of "The Suburban Classes" that is less confident about Smith's distance from the speaking voice. He suggests that Smith's ironies are, as in "Suburb," self-consuming ones that "suggest no outside perspective on the topic of the poem, unless it be the complexities of the performance itself" (121).

38. One of Mamaine Koestler's letters to her twin sister, Celia (Kirwan) Goodman, written upon learning of the engagement of Sonia Brownell to George Orwell, sheds anecdotal historical light on *The Holiday*'s words about spinsterhood. In contrast to those friends of Orwell's who saw Brownell as a gold digger and regarded the marriage as a farce, Mamaine thought news of the alliance "splendid." She continues, "I am most impressed by Sonia's courage in making what must have been a very difficult decision. It will of course be wonderful for George, and may save him; in any case I think it can only be good for Sonia to be released from the crushing difficulties of life as a single woman, of finance, or dreary work and solitude" (111). Ironically, when Goodman received this letter she had already turned down an offer of marriage from Orwell to continue the "crushing difficulties of life as a single woman."

39. Barbera and McBrien propose tentatively that Smith is referring in these comments to her relationship with Frederick "Eric" Hyde Armitage, the neighbor in Palmers Green immortalized as the hapless Freddy in *Novel on Yellow Paper, Over the Frontier,* and the poem "Freddy" (*CP* 65). See Barbera and McBrien 58–62. Spalding is more confident that Smith became engaged to and then disengaged from Armitage and that Pompey's romantic misadventures with Freddy, embarked upon amid the structures and according to the strictures of their shared suburban community, are based on Smith's. She notes, "By her late twenties and early thirties Stevie had reached a critical age form the point of view of marriage, on which the suburbs placed much emphasis. She would have been exposed to this pressure which occasional invitations underlined. 'Would you maybe be thinking of a walk at all?' reads one postcard she received from an H. G. Hilton who lived at New Barnet" (94–95).

40. My valorization of Smith as radical eccentric, spokesperson for a new nationalism based on the qualities of ordinary (that is, lower-middle-class or what I

prefer to call working-middle-class) Englishness, should be read alongside of Rita Felski's exploration of relations between identity, shame, and the lower middle class. Finding the petite bourgeoisie "peculiarly resistant to the romance of marginality," Felski suggests provocatively that "there are genuine, perhaps irresolvable antagonisms between the cultural values of the intelligentsia and those of the traditional lower middle class" (44). My portrayal of Smith as an intellectual who shows us the possibility of a much happier, downright fruitful relationship between her lower-middle-class structures of feeling and her status as a writer and intellectual does not necessarily contradict Felski's conclusions but rather shows how important it is for scholars to listen to Smith's unusual, eccentric, voice.

CHAPTER 2   MULK RAJ ANAND'S PASSAGE THROUGH BLOOMSBURY

1. *Conversations in Bloomsbury* was first published in 1981, approximately sixty years after the conversations it claims to record took place. In her 1992 essay on Anand and autobiography, Marlene Fisher notes, "the distance between Anand the author and Mulk the subject in *Conversations* compared with the relative lack of distance between Anand as both author and subject in *Apology* [*for Heroism*] is autobiographically telling. It represents, in part at least, the difference between autobiography as fiction [*Conversations*] and autobiography as history [*Apology*], primarily in this instance as re-created self-history" (199). Fisher's phrase "autobiography as fiction" provides a useful lens through which to regard all Anand's more recent autobiographical writings. Until we have a carefully documented biography, it will be difficult to know what is fact and what fiction in many stories Anand has told about his relations with English writers. For example, in a letter to Saros Cowasjee of 10 January 1970, printed in *Author to Critic* and reprinted in *So Many Freedoms*, Anand tells the story of a "frightful scene" between Orwell and H. G. Wells during a dinner Wells had set up with Eileen Orwell to complain about her husband's treatment of him in some essay (it was *Horizon* and the essay "Wells, Hitler and the World State") (*So Many* 28). Anand's letter records his late arrival at the dinner with Orwell, both having left the BBC together, and describes how Wells hurled a copy of the offending journal at Orwell and cried, "Burn it!" Anand tells the story well, including details of how he tried to sooth "the old man" by offering to cook him a curry (*So Many* 28). The problem with this story, which is well known to all Orwell biographers, is that it gets several details wrong, including the detail of Anand's and Inez Holden's roles in the episode. It was Holden who had, prior to the evening of the frightful scene, first brought Wells and Orwell together over a dinner at her flat in the mews of Wells's Hanover Terrace home and Holden who, in August 1941, persuaded Wells to go to dinner at Eileen's in Langford Court, having forgotten about Orwell's criticism of Wells in the just-published *Horizon* essay. While Holden publicized the story of the second, unfortunate dinner late in *her*

life (in "Orwell or Wells?" *Listener*, 24 February 1972) her article is based on her diary entries made at the time of the altercation. At least three of Orwell's biographers, Crick, Bowker, and Taylor, cite Holden's diary entry of 30 August 1941, Crick citing it at the greatest length (including its descriptions of the drunken contributions of BBC employee, William Empson). Anand is never mentioned in Holden's diary and was probably not at that particular gathering (Crick 293–94; Bowker 288–89; Taylor 305). Orwell's biographers also tell about Orwell's second attack on Wells in the spring of 1942, this time in a broadcast called "The Re-discovery of Europe," later published in the *Listener*. Orwell's diary entry of 27 March 1942 records, "Abusive letter from H. G. Wells, who addresses me as 'you shit' among other things" (Crick 291). Wells broke entirely with Orwell and "forbade Orwell to set foot on his property again" (Bowker 293). Holden, who had brought Orwell and Wells together, is the one who suffered most from Wells's fury, the older man associating her with the younger's insults and demanding she, too, leave his property. Though she never expressed bitterness toward Wells's treatment of her, she lost her precious flat and her precious friendship with Wells. Her unpublished diary includes a copy of her 23 April letter to Wells, which reads "I am already planning my departure, of course, but am slightly inhibited because I am supposed to be ill. [W]ould it be an intolerable bore to you if I was not completely gone before about this time next week? . . . I am very happy to hear you are really a bit better. Thank you so much for letting me be here so often. I have loved it. Shall you stroll over and see me before I am gone." It is signed, "With much love from Inez." It turns out that the figure who Anand eliminates from the story is exactly the one who had the most at stake.

2. In 1978 when Anand was in his early seventies, he wrote to his infinitely patient correspondent and researcher Atma Ram, "About a literary biography of Mulk Raj Anand the difficulty will be the English part of my background, which was decisive for my writing" (47). Without archives containing independent accounts of Anand's activities abroad, that "English part" remains "difficult." Anand must have realized this because in 1988 he wrote another letter to Atma in which he again urged his correspondent to write a literary biography "in about 250 pages." In addition to directing Atma to the resources of his confessional novels he helpfully offers to "give you tapes of the UK period of the thirties." In this same letter he says that this literary biography would have to include material on his relations with Gandhi, Bertrand Russell, Wittgenstein, the 1930s intelligentsia, Aragon, Malraux, Picasso, Ehrenburg, Ralph Fox, John Cornford, Christopher Caudwell, John Strachey, Forster, Leonard and Virginia Woolf, Bonamy Dobree, George Orwell, Bernal, Haldane, and others without which "the record of my growth and fulfilment will not be complete" (107). It is not clear from the context whether all these relations were personal or if some were simply intellectual.

3. Frances Spalding writes that Anand was a member of the Communist Party, and while he was certainly sympathetic to Soviet Communism and must have visited the Soviet Union a score of times since his first visit in October 1948 (Cowasjee, *So Many* 32), I have found no other sources verifying Spalding's claim. Few of

Anand's critics have analyzed the relationships between Anand's and Orwell's socialist fiction and journalism, and only Spalding has explored the personal and literary relationships between Anand and Smith. See Graham Parry's "Anand, Orwell and the War," or, for more general accounts of Anand's role in 1930s London, Gillian Packham's "Mulk Raj Anand and the Thirties Movement," Shyam M. Asnani's "The Socio-Political Scene of the 1930s: Its Impact on the Indo-English Novel," and R. K. Dhawan's "The Thirties Movement and *Coolie*."

4. In addition to Anand's writings, see Cowasjee's *So Many Freedoms* 27 and his edition of Anand's letters, *Author to Critic*, for references to Anand's diverse London associates in the 1930s.

5. Iyengar's study had its beginnings in the war years when he published a pamphlet, *Indo-Anglian Literature*, for the P.E.N. All-India Centre's fifteen-book series on "The Indian Literatures." This pamphlet became, in 1945, the complete book, *The Indian Contribution to English Literature*. All of these studies discuss Anand's early novels and describe him as one of the originators of Indian literature in English.

6. The first "New Modernisms" conference was held in 1999 at Pennsylvania State University. The sponsoring Modernist Studies Association has since that date held annual conferences on "new modernisms" in the United States and, in 2003, in England, and is affiliated with the highly regarded journal, *Modernism/Modernity*.

7. In *So Many Freedoms*, Cowasjee includes an impressive list of thirty-four writers who Anand was friendly with in the early 1930s, "not to cast reflected glory on Anand but rather to emphasize that of this impressive list only a few remained close friends" (27). He assumes that Anand's politics lost him the friendships in the early 1940s of all but seven: Orwell and Read, who as "Anarchists" did not object to Anand's "passion for Indian freedom and his attack on Britain"; Forster, Dobree, and Henry Miller, who "valued personal friendship above state and politics"; and Edgell Rickword and Jack Lindsay, who were "arch-enemies of Imperialism under all circumstances" (30).

8. See Andrew Davies's essay on Jack Lindsay in *Jack Lindsay: The Thirties and Forties* and his study, *Where Did the Forties Go?*, for a rare account of the radical culture of the 1940s.

9. Anand's heroes in his 1940s novels are more resistant than his 1930s heroes and, in the case of Lalu in *The Village*, *Across the Black Waters*, and *The Sword and the Sickle*, more resilient (Ananta the union-organizing coppersmith protagonist of *The Big Heart*, is heroically, if somewhat pedantically, resistant, but he dies at the end of his novel, his skull split on a transparently symbolic machine part). Cowasjee has observed that in Anand's first nine novels there is a "gradual progression in the caste and social standing of his hero" ("Anand's Literary Creed" 17). I focus on Anand's 1930s novels in part because they feature the most humble and despised kinds of people—untouchables, coolies, near-slaves on an Assam tea plantation—while his 1940s novels increasingly look to higher class and caste sections of India's population for their characters—from peasants to coppersmiths, machine-hands, members of the petite bourgeoisie, and in 1953, a prince.

10. See Urmila Seshagiri's "Misogyny and Anti-Imperialism in George Orwell's *Burmese Days*" for a trenchant critique of Orwell's representations of women in *Burmese Days* with parallels to my argument about the function of Anand's images of women in his 1930s novels: "The life narratives of women in *Burmese Days* demonstrate that Orwell not only naturalizes but actively deploys misogyny to intensify his critique of imperialism" (Seshagiri 111).

11. See for example his speculations about Indian women in *Author to Critic* in which we read that they are doomed to suffer and "seek awareness always in their last moments. That is the reason why I say I adore women" (109).

12. See Meena Shirwadkar's chapter, "Woman in the Family," for a sympathetic interpretation of Anand's female characters as "very much alive" (26), and essays by Jasbir Chaudhury and O. P. Mathur for interpretations of Anand's 1960 heroine Gauri as a revolutionary New Woman born out of the ancient Sita myth. Anand does indeed seem to possess a progressive imagination when his fictional women are read in terms of the dominant cultural ideal for Indian women that twentieth-century Indian writers inherited; in Chaudhury's words, "Indian literature and mythology are full of . . . women whose imposed dumbness, blind devotion and physical fragility is extolled as their best virtue" (47). But when read in terms of the English literary and political context that shaped and received Anand's first nine novels, his women characters no longer seem revolutionary or "new."

    Anand himself urged study of his fictional women, writing in a letter of 30 August 1978 to Atma Ram that "the most rewarding subject for possible study will be the women in Anand's novels and a study of the short stories" (47). It doesn't seem to occur to him that such a study might be somewhat critical instead of purely celebratory.

13. *The Bride's Book of Beauty* was republished in 1981 as *The Book of Indian Beauty*. Unless noted otherwise, all in-text citations are to the 1947 edition. In his preface to the new edition, Anand describes the changes as slight except for a "re-edited" initial essay on the bride, cleansed of its more "didactic" materials, and a substitution of reproductions of paintings from the National Museum of India, New Delhi, for the main illustrations in the 1947 and 1949 editions (*Indian Beauty* 13). Another significant change is the appearance of the full name of Krishna Nehru Hutheesing on the title page, and shortly thereafter, Anand's dedicatory letter to his late coauthor. This letter describes the roles the two authors played in the book's creation, and if Anand's memory is accurate, suggests that he can take credit for most of the research and writing. Anand recalls that he had collected most of the formulas for beauty aids from the old Hindu and Buddhist texts and that he had asked Hutheesing, a friend who had been active in the freedom movement, to edit the manuscript and add whatever she thought necessary. He urged her to add her name to the book in order to "save me from the objections of our womenfolk to my knowledge of their secret lives" (*Indian Beauty* 15).

14. Anand's concern with the devastating symptoms of Indian women's social inferiority continues late into the twentieth century. His 1989 edition of *Sati: A Write-Up of Raja Ram Mohan Roy about Burning of Widows Alive* is dedicated

to the memory of Ram Mohan Roy and Lord William Bentinck, "two dynamic pioneers of the struggle for equal human rights for men and women." Anand praises the "utilitarian radicalism" of this nineteenth-century Indian scholar and describes this collection of Roy's protest writings as "a gift of conscience from the acknowledged 'great' initiator of the modern Indian renaissance, to our people, who still persist, in traditional India, on perpetuating the inhuman rite of *Suttee*" (Preface).

15. Curiously, Anand altered this sentence in the 1981 edition of the book, substituting "plaything" for "doll." The paragraphs on "primitive communism" following his "doll" metaphor are entirely missing from the 1981 edition. These must have been among the "didactic" parts that Anand admits to changing.

16. Notable exceptions include Christopher Isherwood's Sally Bowles, Storm Jameson's Hervey Russell, Virginia Woolf's Orlando, and last but not least, Inez Holden's Rose Leaf.

17. This argument echoes Daphne Patai's claim that Orwell "invites the reader to view Julia in a largely negative way and to contrast her lack of seriousness with Winston's heroic attempt to understand his society" (243). See Patai 243–48.

18. Maya continues to be a vehicle for Lalu's education even when he has abandoned her to work full time for the Revolution. At the end of the novel Lalu is in prison when an assistant jailer tells him that Maya has given birth to their son. It all ends happily enough with Lalu's affirmation of his connection to family in addition to the Cause. However, the purely symbolic, rather than real, nature of Maya's maternity is represented by Anand's cavalier aside that the baby was born "a little prematurely, for it was not due for two months yet" (377). If Maya were real for Anand, the book could not have its hopeful ending since any baby born at 32 weeks gestation would be in grave danger—or could not be the progeny of Sardar Lal Singh.

19. See feminist critic Jane Marcus's discussion of Anand in *Hearts of Parkness: White Women Writing Race* for a less critical reading of Anand's sexual-textual politics.

20. My debts in this chapter to Daphne Patai's analysis in *The Orwell Mystique* of the sexual dynamics of reading Orwell's texts will be most obvious at this point of my argument. Patai theorizes that "At the base of [Orwell's] apparent challenges lay the reassurances of perceived similarity" between the (masculine and often misogynistic) perspective of author/narrator and reader (16). She theorizes that Orwell's disdain for deviations from traditional masculinity must have "soothed and calmed many of his readers, who sorely needed this reassurance as they read through his angry and pessimistic texts" (16). While not suggesting that Anand suffered like Orwell from anxieties about deviations from traditional masculinity, I argue that his fictional women could function in a similarly soothing and calming way for his English and Anglo-Indian readers, "who sorely needed this reassurance as they read through his angry . . . texts."

John Rodden in *The Politics of Literary Reputation* is critical of exactly that part of Patai's analysis that I find so persuasive; it is thus important to take on his objections here because they will certainly be shared by many of my readers. While agreeing that feminist critics have "accurately" pointed out that "Orwell's writings consistently reflect the sexist assumption that the male is the human norm" (212), and even conceding that Patai's book "often [provides] acute insight into Orwell's—and our culture's—patriarchal values" (214), Rodden criticizes Patai for failing to provide in her book "biographical or historical evidence linking Orwell's alleged misogyny to his reception," for failing to "distinguish clearly, let alone show the interaction, between what *Orwell* did and what others have done *to* him" (215). This is not fair criticism on two accounts. In the first place, her argument assumes that it is precisely the *unrecorded, invisible* history of masculine self-creation and affirmation through textual feminine objectification that needs analysis. In the second place, she does investigate what Orwell did in his writing and what others have done to him in theirs. Her introduction, "The Orwell Myth," takes up this very point, which is why its title shares one of the key terms of the title of Rodden's book on Orwell's reputation.

Rodden's emphasis on historical, biographical research may tempt him to repeat in his criticism of Patai Orwell's errors of judgment when it comes to the subject of women. First, Rodden innocently reveals his tendency to think of men when generalizing about the agents of literature and history. For example, he writes, "Fairly or not, feminists have expected more of Orwell than of his contemporaries" (224). Here, "contemporaries" takes on a specifically gendered meaning. In the context of Rodden's argument, it is clear that he assumes the people who Orwell should be compared to, the contemporaries who count, are not women like Stevie Smith (a friend critical of Orwell's sexual politics), Virginia Woolf, Nancy Cunard, Rebecca West, or any number of writers who provide the foundations for latter-day Anglo-American feminism, but contemporary male writers who (presumably) shared the dominant culture's beliefs about women's inferiority. Rodden is also like Orwell in his effort to excuse irrational bias because it is "conventional" for the period. See Rodden 218 and 313–21.

21. Anand used the word "revolutionary" to describe his artistic ideals in *Apology for Heroism*, but the separation of these ideals from history makes them seem more indebted to Shelley than Marx. Anand declares that the artist is revolutionary to the extent that he (*sic*) is capable of communicating "the most intense vision of life" through a "new myth" (133). Because of "his addiction to truth," the writer can help educate humanity to "recognize the fundamental principles of human living and exercise vigilance in regard to the real enemies of freedom and socialism" (134–35). Sounding more like a real socialist, Anand continues: "The revolutionary writer can help thus not only in the development of the individual, but in conjunction with his brother (*sic*) artists, also take forward the history of the human race from the elementary struggles of the present to the more complex and subtle realizations which denote real cultural development" (135–36).

22. Anand was still paying a high price for his literary rebellion when Cowasjee evaluated his situation in 1977: "Today, Mulk Raj Anand is an angry old man. Though his books have won him world acclaim, they have not transformed society as he had hoped. The Imperialists consider his writings seditious, and the underdogs of society about whom he writes cannot read them. The

government of his native state, Punjab, has already banned two of his novels—
The Village and *Across the Black Waters*—and he is frequently attacked in the
press by the Sikh fanatics who feel he has maligned them" (*So Many* 34).

23. Anand includes a chapter on "Tea and Empathy with Virginia Woolf" in
Conversations in Bloomsbury, but more than other Bloomsbury portraits in that
volume, this one seems to depend on public images of Woolf than any intimate
memory of her reception of him or his work.

24. In the 1960s, Cowasjee urged Anand to revise *Coolie*'s ending because of its
offensive treatment of May Mainwaring ("a bitch to all the dogs who prowled
around her bungalow"). In a letter dated 18 January 1968, Anand wrote:

> I am amenable to your advice about Mrs. Mainwaring. If her disease is too
> obvious it could be toned down. I never though of her as an Anglo-Indian
> woman, but merely a nymphomaniac; it is important to keep her sexual-
> ity well in the picture. Also, the revision of novels in too drastic a manner
> after publication would give the impression as though one is responding
> to advice after the event. One would like to revise one's novels all the time,
> to rid them of the many weaknesses which go into books from impetuos-
> ity, impulsiveness and the first on-rush. Though in this case, Herbert Read
> went through it, Philip Henderson with a red pencil and Marion Evans
> with a blue pencil—the last angel sat patiently going through Coolie, line
> by line with me to cut out everything redundant, verbose and inessential.
> And then Celia Strachey as well as Amabel Williams Ellis read the proofs
> as well as William Ellis, who was also a writer.
> Anyway, please send me the revised and emended text as against the
> original . . . (21)

> Although I am uncomfortable with the sexist ideology that shapes Anand's
> representation of Mrs. Mainwaring, I understand why he ultimately
> rejected Cowasjee's advice. Anand explained in another letter to Cowasjee
> of 15 October 1971 that he had left Mrs. Mainwaring as she was because
> he wanted to show the "death of innocence by contrast with the refulgence
> of vulgarity. There was no racial attack intended. Mrs. Mainwaring was to
> be a symbol of 'vanities' of British rule." He continues, "I may have failed.
> Do send me a two-page summary of how you would do it . . . " (*Author to
> Critic* 119). It is interesting that in the 1970s Anand thought readers
> might accuse him of offensive racial, rather than sexual, stereotypes.

25. Orwell's *Burmese Days* also ends with an attack on a hateful woman, the "burra
memsahib" Elizabeth Lackersteen. As Seshagiri points out, "Orwell's final
invectives against Empire and its agents take the form of an anti-woman diatribe" (118). *Coolie* and *Burmese Days* were published within two years of each
other but before Anand and Orwell had met.

26. Cowasjee also points out that Orwell, to his credit, was alone in publicly
defending Anand, using his 19 March 1943 *Tribune* review of *Letters on India*
to explain (one assumes needlessly) to Anand ("you") that "we [London
Socialists] are all nearer to the blimp than we are to the Indian peasant" and

tend to expect and accept Indian criticism of British colonialism only if it mirrors "our" own criticism of British colonialism (*So Many* 30).

27. Dropped by his English friends in the early 1940s, Anand was, illogically, kept out of their memoirs of the 1930s that they wrote in the 1950s and 1960s (Cowasjee, *So Many* 27). Louis MacNeice's unfinished memoir, *The Strings Are False*, provides an exception to this rule. He remembers Anand from the 1930s as "a crusader for the Indian Left" (209). Jack Lindsay's testimony of respect is evident in his extended analysis of Anand's novels in *The Elephant and the Lotus* (1965).

28. For alternate interpretations of Anand's radicalism, see Gita Bamezi's *Mulk Raj Anand: The Journalist* and Rozina Visram's *Asians in Britain*. Bamezai places Anand's literary activities in the context of Indian revolutionary politics. She believes that "anti-untouchability movements and caste mobilisation during [the early 1930s] greatly influenced Anand's decision [to write about untouchables]." But she notes, "Anand's own experience of casteism was restricted to Punjab which had not witnessed any radical movement against untouchability" (56). Visram's chapter on radical Indians in Britain mentions Anand's activism on behalf of the India League, which, under the leadership of V. K. Krishna Menon, devoted itself in England "To support the claim of India for Swaraj" in line with the 1929 Congress resolution (321). Cowasjee believes that once Anand joined his publicity skills to Menon's, "the two did more to influence British public opinion in India's favour than any other Indian residing in Britain" (*So Many* 21).

29. The personal history recounted in *Apology* is retrospectively shaped to reveal the origins of Anand's acceptance of two such comprehensive theories, Marxism and humanism. There is a literal rebirth in *Apology* at the point Anand describes his Marxist conversion; the narrative unconsciously begins again with a return to the materials of its earliest pages: "I was, then, an Indian, a British subject by birth, born of a father who had broken away from the hereditary professions of artisanship and joined the mercenary British-Indian army, and of a peasant mother. . . . " (103). The story of Anand's embrace of humanism is less dramatic, but informs his statements of belief at the end of *Apology* and is the subject of Anand's comments in the prefaces to the various editions of this memoir. Literary criticism on Anand's fiction that appeared during the Cold War decades of the 1960s and 1970s is largely taken up with arguments about whether his humanism is sufficiently purged of his Marxism.

30. In defense of Anand's English writer-friends who do not earn favorable mention in *Apology*, Anand's standards for the committed artist are almost impossible to meet, in part because he keeps changing them. One of his more sensible declarations is, "[Precisely] because modern commercial society had forced the writer into isolation, it was necessary for him to link himself with the disinherited, the weak and the dispossessed, as a human being and as an artist with special talents, to help transform society" (*Apology* 122). While it is not clear what form of heroism the writer should adopt to fulfill such a goal, at least readers can imagine the heroism taking place in a mortal realm. Anand later compares the writer to God in language that recalls the American Boy Scout manual or maybe the immature ambitions of Stephen Dedalus in Joyce's *Portrait*: "For the writer alone, if he is honest and brave, is in a position

to . . . perceive the most delicate processes of the human sensibility, on the aesthetic as well as the cognitive and conative planes. And, if he is possessed of true creative ability, he can transform his knowledge into a vision such as can claim the loyalty of men in his own locality, and across national frontiers, and lead them to a universal awareness of life, thereby possessing them with the will to renew it and to change it. The writer is like God who realises his own many freedoms and confers them on others" (130–31).

31. Although Anand never changed the title of *Apology*, he regularly gave it new subtitles. When the book first appeared in 1946 it carried the subtitle "An Essay in Search of Faith." It went through numerous editions, including the second 1957 edition with its new, one-paragraph preface and the third 1975 edition with its new nineteen-page preface and new subtitle, "A Brief Autobiography of Ideas." The changing subtitles may tell us something about Anand's vision of the book's place in his oeuvre or in Indian intellectual discourse, but does not address the bad fit between the *Apology* of the book's title and its unapologetic contents.

32. Raymond William's distinction in "The Bloomsbury Faction" of Bloomsbury's "social conscience" from "the *social consciousness* of a self-organizing subordinate class" or subject people may point to the source of Woolf's antagonism toward Anand in the introduction of *Letters on India* (165). See Sumit Sarkar's discussion of Leonard Woolf, Raymond Williams, and interwar Bloomsbury in his afterward to *The Other Side of the Medal* (116–17).

33. Secretary of State L. S. Amery was despised by Indian National Congress Party members for his conservative stance toward Indian independence and his receptivity to the divisionist appeals of Jinnah's Muslim League.

34. Gauri Viswanathan's *Masks of Conquest* is the most influential of the postcolonial studies of the politics of English education in India. Viswanathan argues that the British colonials "masked" their true intentions for institutionalizing English studies in India, which "in the long run served to strengthen Western cultural hegemony in enormously complex ways" (2). For a study that considers what Viswanathan ignores, the implications of Indians' response to British literature and especially the popular British novel, see Priya Joshi's *In Another Country: Colonialism, Culture, and the English Novel in India*. Chapter 5 of her study, "The Exile at Home," is most closely tied to the concerns Anand voices in *The King-Emperor's English*. Joshi states that "Anand's role in Indian letters is an important one," but like Anand's Cold War critics, overestimates his literary submission to the Communist Party, concluding "Anand's stories are interesting, useful, even vital social documents, but less notable for groundbreaking literary merit" (210–11). See Cowasjee, *So Many Freedoms* 32 for evidence and discussion of Anand's independence from Moscow.

35. Other than Lawrence, Anand does not mention any English working-class writers in this pamphlet.

36. Anand's statement of faith in man as shaper of his destiny is consistent with his more explicit definition of his humanism in the contemporary text, *Apology for Heroism*. In contrast to the "mystical humanism" of Gandhi and Tagore, which rests on "Divine Sanction," Anand says his humanism "puts its faith in the

creative imagination of man, in his capacity to transform himself, in the tire-less mental and physical energy with which he can, often in the face of great odds, raise himself to tremendous heights of dignity and redeem the world from its misery and pain" (141). Anand's humanism offers "this reverence" to man not because "he belongs to some superior race, religion or colour, but because he is man (never mind how degraded at present) and therefore poten-tially creative, howsoever low in the hierarchy of the conventional structure of society" (141). See chapter 4 for discussion of Orwell's affirmation of a more modest, and correspondingly more convincing, humanism in his 1949 "Reflections on Gandhi."

37. Orwell's changing relation to Basic English is best summarized in Howard Fink's essay, "Newspeak: The Epitome of Parody Techniques in 1984." Fink argues that Orwell's positive predisposition toward Basic in the early 1940s, recorded in his *Tribune* columns and BBC correspondence with Basic's inven-tor, C. K. Ogden, shifted once he began to suspect Winston Churchill was appropriating Basic for imperialist purposes. See chapter 3 in this book for analysis of Inez Holden's Basic writings.

38. Anand's presence in Sabin's book is implicit in her extended discussion of his 1989 edition of Edward Thompson's *The Other Side of the Medal*, first pub-lished by the Hogarth Press in 1925, and its concluding "Afterword," a long essay by Sumit Sarkar on Thompson's life and his role in British Indian historiography. Nirad C. Chaudhuri was born in East Bengal in 1897. This chapter's title and opening sentence allude to the titles of two of his best-known books, *Autobiography of an Unknown Indian* (1951) and *A Passage to England* (1959).

Chapter 3   Inez Holden: "Adventuress" to Socialist

1. See Pamela Fox's *Class Fictions* for an important exception to this general rule. Hartley's *Hearts Undefeated* includes a chapter on "Other War Work" that pro-vides one of the most easily accessible collections of original writings by women about war work, including industrial work. In the "Introduction" to *Millions Like Us*, Harley identifies Holden as one of the only women to be published in the exclusive *Horizon*. Interestingly, Hartley describes Holden as the "man's woman writer" because her work is "detached and dislocated." Harley surmises that this "alienated stance . . . which Hewison and Piette identify in the male writers of the time" earned her the respect of the *Horizon* crowd (8). Heather Ingram and Daphne Patai's collection *Forgotten Radicals* brings questions about relations of women writers to analysis of working-class writing. The most pro-lific editor and writer of books on British working-class literature is H. Gustav Klaus, whose volumes include several essays on writing by working-class women or gender's impact on working-class and industrial fiction. See Klaus

and Stephen Knight's *British Industrial Fictions*, especially Knight's essay on Welsh industrial fictions by women, in which he claims:

> [I]n Welsh industrial women's writing, as elsewhere in the world, what is most marked is that, while women's voices are to a considerable extent consistent with the social politics of male industrial writing, and have clearly recognized the patterns developed by male writers, they also redevelop those formations: there are quite striking differences of formations, evaluation, tone and—most notable of all—genre to be found when women create industrial fictions (164).

Ian Haywood's survey provides a useful, classroom-friendly intervention in this debate, and he is careful to discuss interwar novels by working-class women (for example, Ellen Wilkinson's *The Clash* (1929) and Ethel Carnie Holdsworth's *This Slavery* (1925)); he also explores the implications of gender for discussion of male-authored class writings. Croft provides one of the best examples general studies on radical, and often working-class, writing that is sensitive to the importance of women. His chapters "Class War Across the Diner Table: Tales of Middle-Class Life" and "A Long and Draughty Sermon: Documentary Novels" are especially important for study of Holden's 1940s fictions.

Other studies that treat working-class or industrial fiction and provide useful though almost exclusively masculine contexts for understanding Holden's documentaries include Jeremy Hawthorne's *The British Working-Class Novel in the Twentieth Century*, North's *Henry Green and the Writings of His Generation*, Raymond Williams's *The Long Revolution* and "Working-Class, Proletarian, Socialist: Problems in some Welsh Novels," Carol Snee's "Working-Class Literature or Proletarian Writing?" in *Culture and Crisis in Britain*, and Roy Johnson's "The Proletarian Novel." See also Charles Madge and Tom Harrison's *Britain by Mass Observation*. Especially intrepid readers should consult Peter Hitchcock's publications on theories of working-class fiction.

Studies on comedy, like studies on class, are most persistent in their investigations of implications of sex and gender for their subject when they are authored by feminists. Regina Barreca is the most famous contributor to a feminist literature on comedy. See first *Untamed and Unabashed: Essays on Women and Humor in British Literature*. A sense of Holden's place in a tradition of funny writing by women emerges from study of Audrey Bilger's *Laughing Feminism*, which looks at subversive comedy in novels by three eighteenth-century women, Eileen Gillooly's *Smile of Discontent*, which examines humor and gender in nineteenth-century British fiction, and Margaret Stetz's *Not Drowning but Laughing*, which examines British women's comic fiction during the last hundred years. Lisa Colletta's study on dark humor in twentieth-century British fiction is an especially helpful context in which to read Holden's (and Smith's and Orwell's novels) since she makes consideration of women's interwar comedic fiction integral to her more general theorizing about modernist dark humor.

2. Holden's diary entries of October–December 1942 record impressions about her earliest experiments writing documentary film treatments for the M.O.I.

(Ministry of Information). He first film, "Danger Area," was successful but she had to rely on Montagu Slater to bring her additional M.O.I. film jobs. Her 4 January 1943 diary entry speculates, "Montie will give me some more [film treatments] to do" and then provides the following anecdote that sheds humorous light on the potential hazards for leftist writers seeking government employment in wartime: "[Montagu] told me that the Min. of Labour had said 'you know we can't send Inez Holden down to do this Essential Work Orders film she's a raging communist'—Montagu thought this very funny that they should cho[o]se to say this to him as he is a doctrinaire party member himself. However he went round to see the min. of inf. explained that I was persona grata at the Min. of Supply and asked home security to check up on me, this was done and an O.K. came back— I would like to have asked Monty just when they came out with this startling pronouncement but I was afraid of asking him too many questions."

Her diary entries of February 1944 record her work as a Marks and Spencer clerk for a Paul Rotha film and she continued to write of her hopes for more documentary film jobs. Frances Spalding notes in her biography of Smith that Holden eventually allowed film script writing for J. Arthur Rank take over her literary career.

3. Of these terms, Holden would have found all but "writer" inaccurate or incomplete. While she might have described herself in the 1940s as a nondoctrinaire socialist, fellow traveller, or occasional factory worker, it is doubtful that she would have accepted the terms that I've used to name her social position in the 1920s and early 1930s—party girl, adventuress, society beauty, bohemian, Bright Young Person. All of these fall short of describing her life on the peripheries of various social groups. Although she wrote about debutantes, film stars, chorus girls, bohemians, and millionaires, her journalism of the 1930s makes it clear that she considered herself an outsider rather than member of London's high life. An editor at the *Evening News* described Holden to readers of her 30 August 1932 article, "Farewell to the Bright Young People," as a writer who "knows London's fashionable Bohemia well," but Holden herself ends the piece with the sentence, "Personally I don't mind who gets labelled a Bright Young Person as long as it isn't me!" Her 20 July 1932 article "The Adventuress To-Day" paints a sympathetic portrait of the modern adventuress who resembles, in some ways, others' portraits of Holden: "The modern adventuress . . . cannot work or scheme or even save money. She is the sort of person who 'simply can't do anything about anything.' To some people she seems appealingly helpless, and to others, just appallingly hopeless; finally, they are either moved, or irritated, into helping her. And that is how she lives."

4. The vision promoted by Orwell's "Inside the Whale" found its strongest support in the recantings of one-time Communists who contributed to Richard Crossman's influential *The God that Failed*: Arthur Koestler, Richard Wright, Louis Fischer, Ignazio Silone, Andre Gide, and Stephen Spender.

5. Of course there are many who would disagree with my choice of adverb— "convincingly"—to describe Orwell's, Isherwood's, Green's, and Holden's contributions to working-class literature. There is a long history of debate about who can write authentically about workers. Valentine Cunningham cites

ex-miner James Barke's questioning of the working-class credentials of his
Scottish, working-class rival author, Lewis Grassic Gibbons (309). Haywood
says Barke wrote his epic *The Land of the Leal* (1939) to solve the problem he
saw of inauthenticity in Gibbons's novel. One of the more memorable, recent
challenges to Orwell's claim to represent the working class is Beatrix Campbell's
Wigan Pier Revisited: Poverty and Politics in the 80s.

6. One of these novels, *Friend of the Family* (1933), does not receive treatment in
   this chapter simply because it fails to instruct or amuse. It was Holden's last
   intermodern novel to examine the lives and mores of wealthy Englishfolk.

7. Orwell's early novels, like Holden's, earned respectful, but often superficial,
   attention of reviewers and did not sell very well. For selected reviews of Orwell's
   1930s writing, see Jeffrey Meyers's *George Orwell: The Critical Heritage.*

8. More contemporary praise of Holden is equally generous, but hard to find. The
   Centre for Metropolitan History website refers to *Night Shift* as a classic
   (http://www.history.ac.uk/cmh/arpt94.html), Mark Rawlinson mentions
   Holden in *British Writing of the Second World War*, and Angus Calder cites her
   in *The People's War.*

9. Among Holden's papers is a copy of a typed, undated letter written by Gene
   Jolas from 69 Warrington Crescent that describes *Night Shift* as "a wonderful
   and remarkable book. . . . a cameo, a human documentaire of this epoch."
   Jolas also compares the novel to camera work, claiming, "One can see a certain
   cinematographic training in your style. You have fine powers of observation
   and an acoustic and visual sense."

10. Holden can be situated among the many contemporary writers, including Mulk
    Raj Anand, who used the form of the novel, largely developed and read by mem-
    bers of the bourgeoisie who peopled its pages, to promote a vision of working-
    class heroism. Aside from its inattention to Anand and other colonial writers in
    Britain, Haywood provides a good bibliography of intermodern working-class
    novels and critical summary of the tradition that they uphold. He identifies the
    following working-class writers as those who committed their fictions of the
    1920s and 1930s to the political project of arousing Socialist or Communist
    consciousness: Harold Heslop, James Welsh, Ethel Carnie Holdsworth, Ellen
    Wilkinson, Lewis Jones, Frederick Boden, Lewis Grassic Gibbons, James Barke,
    Simon Blumenfeld, John Sommerfield. He does not discuss working-class or
    industrial fictions of the 1940s, moving from a chapter on the "Black Earth" of
    the interwar period to "The Influence of Affluence: The Road to 1979." The
    gap in his survey is a symptom of the larger critical problem this study attempts
    to address through its construction of an intermodernism that makes visible the
    continuities, rather than divisions, of 1930s and 1940s writing.

11. Holden's Wildean novels of the 1920s and early 1930s are complemented by a
    serious, ambitious piece of literary criticism that she wrote on Wilde's friend, the
    writer Ada Leverson, in the late 1940s. This critical essay demonstrates Holden's
    impressive breadth of novel reading, fine critical sensibility, and real sympathy for
    the literary accomplishments of this Edwardian woman writer of light, satirical
    novels. The following sentences reveal much about Holden's literary ideals; with
    a few changes of reference and name, they could almost be read as commentary

upon the critical dilemmas of her own career: "Perhaps Ada Leverson's two greatest qualities—readability and lightness of touch—somehow had the effect of hoodwinking reviewers into under-rating her as a novelist. Wilde, Wells, E. M. Forster, Hardy, Bennett, G. K. Chesterton, Bernard Shaw and Conrad were all writing at this time, and minor writers of the period may well have been overlooked. But Ada Leverson's *The Limit* strikes me as more witty than Anthony Hope's *Dolly Dialogues*; and I find her novels funnier than Saki's short stories which have been reprinted seventeen times since 1930" (433).

12. Holden admired Ada Leverson's decision to leave "social consciousness" out of her novels: "Yet Ada Leverson did not write, as both the literary giants and the prolific dwarfs were then doing, of current political trends. It would be possible to read all her novels without becoming aware that the Fabians were already on the footpath, that Woman's Suffrage was a subject of violent controversy or that the 'New Woman' was forever putting on her bloomers for the next spin on her bicycle" (430). Evidence of the political character of Holden's radical vision comes most directly from biographical, rather than fictional, sources. For example, her cousin Celia Goodman characterized Holden's and her own politics this way: "We were opposite of Communist—Socialist socialists. . . . I think you are one by nature" (personal interview, 26 July 1998).

13. See Patrick O'Neill's *The Comedy of Entropy* and the essays in Alan Pratt's collection, *Black Humor*, for further discussion of the subject.

14. "Death in High Society" was reprinted in Holden's wartime story collection *To the Boating*. Holden saved clippings of three standard English versions of the story that were published under the story's original title "Death of a Hostess," the first from a 17 December 1930 edition of *The Sketch*, the next from the 7 December 1933 *Evening Standard*, and finally one from the 12 January 1935 *Manchester Evening Chronicle*. The endings of the standard English versions of the story, like the standard version of "The Value of Being Seen," modify slightly the biting satire of wealthy privilege achieved by the Basic version. Holden did not paste any Basic translations of her stories in her scrapbooks, only noting that "Death of a Hostess" appeared in English and American editions of Basic Short Stories.

15. Holden did not comment on sexism in the unions or among workers themselves. Her wartime writings represent trade unions as uncomplicated, even idealized, institutions that serve not just the interests of workers, but also management. The surviving typescript pages of a (presumably unpublished) article in her scrapbook of published papers argues that shorter shifts and increased leisure time for workers will solve the problems of absenteeism without impacting production. Strong unions are central to her reformist vision. Her pronouncement, "Unity in a workshop is obviously important, and can introduce self discipline where managerial orders are powerless. This unity can be brought about by a strong Trade Union," sounds more like the prose of a socialist pamphleteer than a *Horizon* highbrow. For a sophisticated analysis of the causes, forms, and effects of discrimination against women in English factories during the years leading up to the war, see Miriam Glucksmann's *Women Assemble*.

16. Date unknown. Clipping preserved in Holden's scrapbook.

17. Orwell's war diary is, by now, more famous, although it began as a failed contribution to what was supposed to be a joint Holden–Orwell project. See Crick 264 for an account of the origins and dissolution of this effort in collaborative authorship.

18. The politics implicit in expanded demands for democratic representation—demands made by writers on behalf of common citizens or by citizens on their own behalf—came in part as a response to the woeful performance of British officialdom. Calder writes that in general, "nothing emerges more forcibly from the blitz than the contrast between laggard councillors, obsessed with their own prestige, and the self-sacrifice of the volunteers who strove indefatigably to remedy the position which bumbledom had created. Most of the 200,000 or 250,000 people who served their fellows in the various post-raid services or in the shelters were volunteers. . . . These were the 'militant citizens' of whom J. B. Priestley wrote. He saw in them the seeds of a new democracy" (193).

19. Calder admits that there was much anger among East Enders at the government's failure to plan for the real nature of the blitz, and he quotes Harold Nicolson's diary entry of 7 September 1940 to support the wider perception of revolutionary danger posed by German attacks against Stepney and West Ham: "Everybody is worried about the feeling in the East End . . . There is much bitterness. It is said that even the King and Queen were booed the other day when they visited the destroyed areas." Calder admits that, "had the East End lost all heart, the chain reaction might have crippled London's morale. This nearly happened, but not quite" (164–65).

20. Haywood's chapter on interwar working-class fictions has a brief section on 1930s Jewish Cockney writers that directs readers toward the novels of Simon Blumenfeld and Willy Goldman, establishing an alternative context for understanding the limits and risks of Holden's stand against anti-Semitism in *There's No Story There*. Lassner's *British Women Writers of World War II* pays close attention to the ways Jews are represented by women writers like Phyllis Bottome and Olivia Manning, both of whom challenge their readers to understand the history and future of Britain through the plight of Jews struggling to survive under Hitler's rule.

21. Historians are as divided as literary critics on the question of the meaning of Labour's victory in 1945. See Arthur Marwick's "People's War and Top People's Peace?" (1976) and Jose Harris's "War and Social History" (1992) for concise summaries and analyses of the positions of earlier historians. Marwick adopts a mediating position between two extremes, claiming that some older writers were wrong to suggest there was revolutionary change after 1945 while others like Angus Calder or Anthony Howard were wrong to "speak of 'a restoration of traditional values'" (162). Writing more than fifteen years later, Harris seems to come to a similar conclusion: that archival study shows British reaction to progressive wartime changes to be both more ambivalent and more contradictory than social histories of the home front once allowed.

CHAPTER 4   GEORGE ORWELL'S
INVENTION: THE LAST MAN IN EUROPE

1. John Atkins goes against the grain of Orwell's self-portraits by emphasizing
   Orwell's sociability at the beginning of his book, *George Orwell*. "It is very easy
   to get a false impression of Orwell from his books. . . . The soured and pessimistic man who speaks to us in the pages of *The Road to Wigan Pier* and *1984*
   was actually sociable and home-loving" (4). Rodden dates Orwell's invention of
   his " 'true rebel' " and " 'outsider' " images to 1927, just after his return from
   Burma (106). Orwell's decision to omit information about his ready access to
   food, housing, and family during his dishwashing and tramping adventures is
   just one example of his attempt to foster the illusion that he experienced what
   his lonely, exiled narrators experienced—that his documentaries were straight
   autobiography. See Crick 112–14. Rodden believes that after Orwell's death,
   Sonia Orwell's refusal over many decades to grant permission for an Orwell
   biography deepened the hold upon the public imagination of Orwell's self-
   portrait as the rebel, "daring to stand alone" (qtd. in Rodden 147).

2. The confusion between Orwell and Winston Smith is just one aspect of the contradictory legacy captured in the word "Orwellian." Rodden's question, "But
   was Orwell, 'the social saint,' 'Orwellian'?" points directly to the problem. On
   the one hand, "Orwellian" means "unimpeachable integrity and plain-spoken
   common sense." On the other hand, its better-known meaning is " 'demonic,'
   'terrifying,' even 'totalitarian.' " In the latter case, "Orwellian" means "diabolical
   deceit and brutal force . . . the very reverse of what the man [Orwell] is supposed to have embodied and championed" (34).

3. See Crick 262 and Appendix A in *George Orwell: A Life*.

4. See Rodden 45–46 for a succinct account of the commercial activity supporting
   the growth of the Orwell myth. He records that *Nineteen Eighty-Four*'s enviable
   success in 1949—selling 22,700 hardback copies in England and rising to #3 on
   the *NYT* bestseller list—was far outdone by its sales in the early 1950s. *Nineteen
   Eighty-Four* sold 1,210,000 copies as a New American Library paperback,
   596,000 copies as a Reader's Digest Condensed Book, and several hundred
   thousand copies in Britain as a Penguin paperback (Rodden 46).

5. Edmund Wilson, in his January 1951 *New Yorker* review of the posthumous
   Shooting an Elephant and Other Essays, is one of several influential critics who
   mythologizes Orwell as a kind of last man: "[Orwell] has recently seemed so
   much to represent a tradition that had few spokesmen in literature—the middle-
   class British liberalism that depended on common sense and plain speaking and
   that believed in the rights of the citizen to earn a decent living, to think and say
   what he pleased, and to enjoy himself unmolested—that one came apprehen-
   sively to feel as if the point of view itself were fading away with Orwell . . . . There
   was no place for him, and he had to die" (Meyers 310). Richard Rovere, in his
   1956 Introduction to *The Orwell Reader* is another: "[H]e stood almost alone in
   his generation as a man of consistent good judgment and as one who never for a
   moment doubted that it was possible to be at once humanistic and tough-
   minded, to make commitments and avoid the perils of commitment" (xvii).

6. That threat obviously works both ways. Orwell's feminist critics, for example, have been greeted with negative responses by members of the largely male club of nonfeminist Orwell critics. Even Christopher Hitchens, an old-style Orwell defender (or claimant, to use Rodden's vocabulary) who goes further than others toward accepting some of the key arguments of feminist critics, shows in *Why Orwell Matters* that he imagines a modern English literature written by and for men. For example, he describes Janet Montefiore as "the most acute feminist" reader of the 1930s literature, but misreads her criticism of Orwell's famous slum girl at the end of *Wigan Pier* and suggests that Montefiore's alternative, "to *be* that woman yourself" (Hitchens 154), is "impossible": "This would be not so much abandoning the subjective as actually becoming the subject—an impossible demand under any circumstances and one that flatly negates the purpose of realistic, first-hand narrative writing" (154). Hitchens's criticism misses the point on two accounts. First, Montefiore is not suggesting that Hitchens (or other male (or female) middle-class readers or writers) need to "become the subject" but rather that they need to read the realistic, first-hand narrative writings of 1930s working-class women whose testimonies point to "different, gendered forms of knowledge" (103). Her point in the chapter from which Hitchens cites rather selectively is that Orwell conforms to the larger pattern evident in the bulk of male-authored, leftist realist writings of the 1930s of representing a radically limited kind of knowledge about class, work, and gender—one that is typically condensed into the image of woman as victim (or alternatively, vamp). Second, Montefiore cites specific texts by working-class women that show it is not so "impossible" as Hitchens suggests to "be the subject" Orwell imagines at the end of *Wigan*. She writes, "the autobiographies of working-class women that I have read do not match these [bourgeois men's] visions of women as passive, trapped victims. On the contrary, one gets an impression of vigour, intelligence and courage against the odds" (102).

7. Aside from Orwell's own writings, sources for this claim include memories of him collected in *Orwell Remembered, The World of George Orwell*, BBC programs, and memoirs by friends and acquaintances like Rayner Heppenstall ("It was perhaps a little odd in itself that he should have wanted to share premises with us rather than with men more precisely of his own generation, among whom, it is true, he did not seem to have any friends, except Sir Richard Rees" (59)), Christopher Hollis ("The Orwellian man, whether we take Orwell's fragments of autobiography or the main characters in any of his novels, is always a solitary—a member of a society which is uncongenial to him—standing out alone in front of it" (1)), and others cited in this chapter. D. J. Taylor interprets Orwell's secretiveness about his social relations in the following way: "Like much of Orwell's life at any time in his existence, this [wartime social life] occupied a variety of compartments: after-work drinks with comparatively humble literary acquaintances at times alternate with somewhat grander surroundings" (298). Gordon Bowker is more judgmental. He criticizes Orwell's method of separating and managing his groups of friends, drawing readers' attention to new materials that suggest "as a man [Orwell] had certain crucial weaknesses," among them "a deceptive streak," which led him to "deliberately [keep] some of his friends apart in order to present them with different faces" (xiii).

8. Orwell's private documents suggest he was often desperately lonely. This is most poignantly illustrated by his pathetic marriage proposals to various women (Celia Kirwan, Sonia Brownell, Anne Popham) after Eileen's death. See Crick 333–36.

9. Davison cites the reviewer's reply to Orwell and identifies the author as most probably Ranjee G. Shahani, a writer who also contributed two essays to *Tribune* when Orwell was its literary editor.

10. Orwell also observes that Anand's entire book is full of "Indian melancholy" and "horribly ugly, degrading scenes." He concedes that it "ends on a comparatively hopeful note" but "does not break the rule that books about India are depressing" (II: 217)—this from the author of *Animal Farm* and *Nineteen Eighty-Four*!

11. There is a curious correspondence between Orwell's attribution of "hate" to the symbolic Indian nationalist he invents in his 1942 review of Anand's novel and his similar attribution of "hate" to the pacifist Roy Walker of the Peach Pledge Union, with whom he exchanged several letters in 1943. Walker had initiated the correspondence with Orwell on 28 September to protest Orwell's "grossly unfair" treatment of Gandhi in his review of Lionel Fielden's argument on behalf of Indian independence in *Beggar My Neighbour*. In his second letter of 25 November Walker writes, "I do not, I assure you, hate you like the devil. . . . May I not hate—if that is the word—the sin (as I see it) without in the least feeling evilly-disposed towards the sinner? And I think it is a little unkind when I send you a copy of my book to reply that I obviously hate you like the devil" (*CW* 15: 340–41).

12. See the introduction for citation of Anand's letter to Darling.

13. In her critique, *Wigan Pier Revisited*, Beatrix Campbell illustrates how Orwell systematically turns workers into passive victims, consumers, not actors. Their historic qualities "of what he calls 'dignity, frugality and stoicism' . . . have been stolen, he says, by our collective subordination to the laws of the market place, and bonds of kinship, good neighbourliness and workplace solidarity [all part of what I mean by 'society'] have been destroyed" (226).

14. The most interesting recent development in the history of readers' conflicted responses to the social work of Orwell's texts took place in the pages of England's and America's popular media in the summer of 2003 upon publication of Orwell's 1949 list, shared with the semi-secret Information Research Department, of writers and artists who he believed were "crypto-communists, fellow-travellers or inclined that way and should not be trusted as propagandists." Ariane Bankes had found the list among the papers of her mother, Celia (Kirwan) Goodman, the employee at the IRD to whom Orwell gave the list. Bankes shared her discovery with writer Timothy Garton Ash, who placed himself at the center of renewed controversy about the meaning of Orwell's collaboration with the IRD by writing the essay "Love, Death and Treachery" that accompanied publication of the list in the 23 June issue of *The Guardian*, (reprinted in America in the *New York Review of Books* of 25 September 2003). The paragraph from Garton Ash's essay that is most germane to this study follows: "One aspect of the notebook that shocks our contemporary sensibility

is his ethnic labeling of people, especially the eight variations of 'Jewish?' (Charlie Chaplin), 'Polish Jew,' 'English Jew,' or 'Jewess.' Orwell's entire life was a struggle to overcome the prejudices of his class and generation; here was one he never fully overcame" (*NYRB* 10).

15. Biographer Michael Shelden describes Orwell's review of Fielden's book as a form of revenge or a "parting shot" at Z. A. Bokhari, his immediate superior in the Indian Service of the BBC and the person to whom Fielden had dedicated his book. The review appeared in the September 1943 issue of *Horizon* and Orwell resigned on the twenty-fourth of that month.

16. Orwell also functions as an important authority on British anti-Semitism and a guide to "a post-Holocaust understanding of European civilization" in several other recent and important studies on Jews and British modernism or modernity (Cheyette, *Constructions* 1). See for example Tony Kushner (his third chapter on Jews in British Society cites Orwell seven times as the voice of the "reasonable man," the trustworthy gentile observer), Bernard Wasserstein (see for example 119), and Bryan Cheyette's *Constructions of "the Jew" in English Literature and Society* (see especially his favorable citation of Orwell as a "startling prescien[t]" observer who anticipated the reasons discussion of anti-Semitism in Britain would be surpressed in public discourse (2). Kushner does finally correct some of Orwell's false claims about anti-Semitism in his fourth chapter. See 131.

    Bauman's unexamined, uninterpreted Orwell epigraph is the most obvious instance of a general pattern of treating Orwell's words as windowpanes through which to view the historical facts of English modernity; Orwell's words appear to transcend analysis, qualification, or historical contextualization. The scholars themselves do not state their reasons for turning Orwell into an unexamined expert witness on Jews in England, anti-Semitism, and the Holocaust.

17. Rodden resists the notion that our intellectual heroes must score "ten out of ten" on every account. He defines the "right side of intellectual hero-worship" in the following way: "It is the generous and discriminating, never self-abasing nor reflexive nor uncritical nor servile, honoring of someone fit to be an intellectual hero" (402). While I admire Rodden's study immensely and second his rejection of a "ten out of ten" standard, I believe it is important to realize that some points count more than others. I assume that Orwell's denigration of disenfranchised people, such as Indians, Jews, homosexuals, and women, deserves harsher criticism—loses him more "points"— than his denigration of, say, fruit juice drinkers and sandal wearers or even Lionel Fielden. My research on Orwell and the Holocaust suggests that the type and quantity of a particular "impurity" in a hero's record cannot be understood or valued apart from "their considerable strengths." The "ethics of admiration" that Rodden cites may require us to focus closely on those "inevitable flaws" that he recommends we acknowledge but then pass over. See Rodden 402.

18. For example, in "Politics and the English Language" (April 1946), the atrocities that Orwell names in order to expose the dangers of political speech are "the continuance of British rule in India, the Russian purges and deportations, the dropping of the atom bombs on Japan" (IV: 136). There are references in

Orwell's works to concentration camps (for example, "London Letter" to *Partisan Review*, 5 June 1945 (III: 382)) and twentieth-century slavery (for example, book review of 21 November 1942 (II: 248)) and more significantly in "Looking Back on the Spanish War": "Who could have imagined twenty years ago that slavery would return to Europe? Well, slavery has been restored under our noses. The forced-labour camps all over Europe and North Africa where Poles, Russians, Jews and political prisoners of every race toil at road-making or swamp-draining for their bare rations, are simple chattel slavery" (II: 259)), but not extended contemplation of the reality or meaning of the Holocaust as such. This view opposes Melvyn New's claim in "Orwell and Antisemitism" that Orwell "came to understand intellectually and, in *1984*, artistically, the full meaning to the future of what has come to be known as the Holocaust" (81–82).

19. My response to Bauman and more specifically my use of the word "development" are influenced by Marshall Berman's *All that is Solid Melts into Air*, the book that has, above all others, shaped my approach to Orwell and the Holocaust. Marshall Berman interprets the experience of modernity through the images and symbols of Marx's writings and what he calls "tragedies of development," best represented by Goethe's *Faust*. For Berman, Faust is the first literary hero of modernity because of his "desire for development," his determination to assimilate all mankind's experience into his self's unending growth (40). Berman writes, "This is the meaning of Faust's relationship with the devil: human powers can be developed only through what Marx called 'the powers of the underworld,' dark and fearful energies that may erupt with a horrible force beyond all human control" (40). If we see "the Jew" in twentieth-century European history and culture as one of Faust's symbolic inheritors, it takes very little imagination to adopt Bauman's perspective and understand the Holocaust as a supremely, devastatingly consistent expression of modernity's forces, rather than regressive deviation from them. It is the logical but by no means inevitable or necessary consequence of modernity's "dark and fearful energies that may erupt with a horrible force beyond all human control."

20. See chapter 1, note 1 in this book, for the definition of anti-Semitism used in this study.

21. Scholars who read Orwell's work with an eye trained specifically on his anti-Semitism tend to disagree with Crick's conclusion that by 1944 Orwell's published comments "show him fully purged of the mild and conventional anti-Semitism" which appeared early in *Down and Out in Paris and London* and lingered in his "War-Time Diaries" (307).

22. Orwell is not unique in his reticence about the Holocaust. Other British writers, including Smith and Anand, ignore it too, but then they have not been adopted by Anglo-Jewish scholars as exemplary spokespersons for gentile resistance to English anti-Semitism. Holden is unusual in her decision to go to Germany after the war as a special correspondent reporting on the Nuremberg trials (Shackelton). I have not been able to locate the journalism that resulted from her travels.

23. To my knowledge, Rodden is the only critic to attempt a fair, careful interpretation of the meaning, for Fyvel, of his conflict with Orwell over Zionism in a world shattered by the Holocaust. See Rodden 303–21.

24. As Rodden and others have shown, much of the inspiration for this series came from the pro-Zionist English intelligence officer, Captain Orde Wingate, who met Fyvel in Jerusalem in the 1930s as he, Wingate, was preparing to lead British and Jewish night squads of soldiers against Arab rebels. Fyvel fell under Wingate's spell, saw him as a prophet, and indirectly communicated Wingate's ideas to the British public through Orwell. Wingate was later to become General Wingate, the famous Chindit Commander who led his forces into Burmese jungles behind Japanese lines (Rodden 316–17). He died in Burma, the country whose loss Orwell was to expound upon in such detail in a BBC internal circulating memo of May 1942 (West 34–35) and in his "As I Please" column of 16 February 1945 (III: 355–57).

25. Orwell's criticism of those (self-righteous) leftists who are indifferent, blinded to, or silent about the injustice of Britain's imperial claim to the lands and peoples of Asia and Africa is more effectively made in his 1939 essay, "Marrakech," which dramatizes the invisibility of peoples subjected to European colonial rule (I: 387–93). This essay also stands out for its unusually sympathetic representations of the oppressive living conditions suffered by Marrakech Jews (see especially I: 390).

26. An 18 May 1944 letter highlights the crude conclusions Orwell derived from comparison of Hitler's aggressive expansion to British imperialism. Here he writes, "All the national movements everywhere, even those that originate in resistance to German domination, seem to take nondemocratic forms, to group themselves round some superhuman fuehrer (Hitler, Stalin, Salazar, Franco, Gandhi, De Valera are all varying examples) and to adopt the theory that the end justifies the means" (III: 149). In an earlier piece, he expressed an opinion he often repeated: "Pacifism is objectively pro-Fascist. [. . .] As an ex-Indian civil servant, it always makes me shout with laughter to hear, for instance, Gandhi named as an example of the success of non-violence" (II: 226–27).

27. Orwell knew firsthand about censorship in India since several of his books had been banned by the Government of India. Orwell's biographers record how in the winter of 1937–1938 A. H. Joyce of the India Office worked to dissuade Desmond Young, editor of the Lucknow *Pioneer*, from hiring Orwell as assistant editor and chief leader writer precisely because he was seen as too likely to turn to nationalist political work. See Crick 239–40 and Shelden 288–89. In September 1941 Orwell had been invited to join the BBC's Indian Section because the educated Indians for whom his program was intended believed him to be an opponent of the Government of India. See Crick 2282–83 for Eric Blair's letter of 15 October 1942 on the propaganda implications raised by his potential broadcasting as George Orwell.

28. Contemporary scholars of Anglo-Jewish history provide a useful context for interpreting Orwell's claims. Bernard Wasserstein records the findings of a January 1942 report of the Home Intelligence Unit of the Ministry of

Information, which determined that there was " 'no indication of any feeling that as a nation we are "Jew-led" on the lines suggested by enemy propaganda.' Rather, it appeared that anti-Semitism was 'latent [. . .] in most districts' " (120). Kushner makes a tentative chronological map of social anti-Semitism in Britain during the war, concluding that it was real, dynamic, unorganized, predominantly private, but never the national threat government bureaucrats liked or pretended to think (98, 101–02). Those public servants who acknowledged anti-Semitism, bringing the subject into "public discourse," often used it to justify policies that exposed Jews to violence abroad in the name of preventing anti-Semitic violence in the safe haven of England.

29. While it is obvious that the risks of unofficial, as well as official, censorship are significant, I am critical of Orwell's position because it does not take into account what life in England would be like for Jews living in England during the Hitler age if individuals were encouraged to express their anti-Semitism in any circumstance for any reason in any way. Orwell's argument is also weakened by his utter lack of reference to Anglo-Jewish history; one need not look too far back to find the free anti-Semitic speech Orwell advocates yet such free speech had never led to greater understanding of the so-called "Jewish problem".

30. Orwell had finished his first major formulation of anti-Soviet, anti-totalitarian fiction/propaganda, *Animal Farm*, in February 1944, and was still waiting for the book to appear in print at the time he was writing his essays on anti-Semitism and nationalism. His journalism of the war years shows how consumed he was at that time with ideas about "totalitarianism," a political system he believed existed under Hitler and especially Stalin and that many leftist intellectuals would have liked to set up in England. On 15 March 1945, when the end of the war was in sight, he dashed off to Germany as a war correspondent (Crick 324). Fyvel remembers that "David Astor told me that Orwell had wanted at all costs to go to Germany for the *Observer* as soon as possible after the surrender to see a totalitarian state before it disappeared, only to find that the Nazi structure of Germany had dissolved overnight as though it had never been. From my Italian experience I could have told Orwell that, I thought" (128–29). Frederic Warburg cites a memo dated 25 June 1945 (not 1946) that suggests Orwell began *Nineteen Eighty-Four* much earlier than anyone supposes and at the same time he was writing "Antisemitism in Britain" and "Notes on Nationalism" (93). In the literary notebook for "The Last Man in Europe," Orwell mentions anti-Semitism twice in his list of major themes, which suggests how important anti-Semitism was to his earliest conceptions of *Nineteen Eighty-Four.*

31. Fyvel made a similar point in his protest against Orwell's representation of a Jewish American officer "getting his own back" on the Nazis by kicking an imprisoned S.S.-man in "Revenge is Sour." Describing their disagreement over this essay as the only real argument of their friendship, Fyvel details his "outburst" and recalls that "Orwell's reaction was one of sheer astonishment: he obviously thought that I was hyper sensitive and overreacting. I don't believe that I had any effect on his views on the responsibilities for the Nazi crimes— in the same article, he wanted Britain to protest against the Soviet expulsion of

Germans from East Prussia as a crime [. . .]." For a full account of Fyvel's argument against the anti-Semitism of "Revenge is Sour," see his memoir, 179–80.

32. Orwell had good reason to be concerned about Stalinist atrocities and I am not arguing that he was wrong in denouncing the repressive policies and practices of the USSR. I am arguing that his means of doing so were not "decent" and "honest," but crude and manipulative.

33. More generously, Orwell published in a 15 November 1946 "As I Please" column the idea that 100,000 Jewish refugees should be invited to England to settle (IV: 238).

34. There is published support for Fyvel's assessment in Orwell's "London Letter" to the *Partisan Review* of [15? August 1945] (*sic*), in which Orwell claims the Palestine issue is "partly a colour issue and that an Indian nationalist, for instance, would probably side with the Arabs" (III: 398). It is unclear what, other than personal experience in Burma in the 1920s, supports this claim about Indian nationalist sympathies. Ironically, V. G. Kiernan compares the role of Indians in Burma to medieval European Jews. Both formed a middle class of retailers and money lenders in an economy dominated by small peasant farmers. Kiernan notes, "Necessary as some of the their [the immigrant Indians'] functions were, like those of Jews in Old Europe, they were heartily disliked by the Burmese and despised by the British" (81). More ironic still, Orwell's resistance to Jewish and especially Zionist claims on the basis of the Jews' "whiteness," contradicts a centuries-long tradition in Europe of discriminating against Jews as "black" or "swarthy." See Sander Gilman 171.

35. Racism has as interesting and complex a history as imperialism itself, and when discussing British notions of race at home and abroad it is important to distinguish between what Van Arkel would call "internal" and "external" racism. Van Arkel argues that "internal European racism had not much to do with colonial racism, although the climate of racist philosophising certainly fostered the latter. [. . .] What they shared were strong nationalist feelings and ego inflation. Both gave meaning to social structures, but these were so different that the particular social situations must be taken into account for purposes of analysis" (31). Van Arkel claims that confusion over the relationship between colonial and non-colonial racism exists in part because "Racism is a social reality even though or [. . .] because the race concept is meaningless. 'Race' is such an unclear concept that biological refutation is of no avail. If it serves a need, people continue to believe in it" (20). In the "interesting case" of England, a country whose history is marked by persecution of Jews but no anti-Semitic mass movements, Empire aroused a need for racism "so racist ideas took the form of the White Man's burden theories" (28).

36. For memorable examples of such racism see 23–24, 31, 118, and 119.

37. While Orwell learned to complicate the color model of imperial oppression evident in the protest of *Burmese Days*, as late as August 1942 he could still describe his Indian colleagues at the BBC in terms that are uncomfortably close to those he used to describe Dr. Veraswami. Upon learning of the Government of India's representation of riots by Indians as "of no consequence" and students' participation in the riots as "boys will be boys" high jinks, Orwell

noted in his diary, "Almost everyone utterly disgusted. Some of the Indians when they hear this kind of stuff turn quite pale, a strange sight" (II: 443). More compromising is Empson's anecdote about Orwell's astonishing address to the Indian writers or intellectuals he was interviewing or vetting at the BBC:

> At first the visitor would do most of the talking, with George increasing his proportion gradually; no doubt he had to lure the visitor into providing an entry for the tremendous remark which one learned to expect towards the end of the interview. "The FACK that you're black," he would say, in a leisurely but somehow exasperated manner, immensely carrying, and all the more officer-class for being souped up into his formalized Cockney, "and that I'm white, has nudding whatever to do wiv it." I never once heard an Indian say, "But I'm not black", though they must all have wanted to. (96)

38. While Orwell's use of "black" to describe Indians might seem strange to North American readers who came of age after the "Black is beautiful" movement and positively associate the term with Africans and their descendants, according to Kiernan, "Englishmen habitually thought of Indians in general as 'black,'" much to the dismay of many Indians. He cites nineteenth-century examples of this bad English habit, including an investigation into the causes of a mutiny in 1844 that recorded the Indian sepoys' resentment of English officers' use of the phrase "black soldiers" (34).

39. Orwell is no different than many well-intentioned and well-read contributors to the twentieth-century leftist press who assume a kind of equivalence between oppression sustained by racial discourse in any given community and oppression sustained by other kinds of discourse (for example, about class, caste, sex, and so on) in the same communities. Frank Furedi argues against "an inflation of the meaning of racism to encompass literally all forms of group conflicts" because factors specific to colonialism, the relation of power and foreign domination, are typically ignored (228).

40. Orwell's vision of a society whose hierarchies of power are based on differences of skin color sits uneasily with his knowledge that race is an abstract construct, defended with biological myths ("bunkum"). His understanding of the ideological structure of race is hinted at in his exposure of the imperialists' belief that Europeans, unlike Burmans or Indians, needed to wear pith helmets at all times to protect their thin, civilized skulls against sunstroke (III: 262–63). Analyzing this anecdote, Douglas Kerr notes, "[T]o reject a biological essentialism is not in itself enough to draw the teeth of the problem of race" (236). In his essay on "Orwell, Animals, and the East," Kerr concludes, "Throughout Orwell's career as a writer, a passionate belief in equality is at war with an ineradicable disbelief in it, so that [Orwell's] most eloquent statements of the right of all people to be treated equally, as human beings, are haunted by the suspicion that some people are more equal than others" (238). See also John Atkins 74–75.

41. Orwell's defense of T. S. Eliot calls for another mention of the January 2003 special issue of *Modernism/Modernity* on T. S. Eliot and anti-Semitism.

42. See especially his "As I Please" column of 11 February 1944 (III: 91) and "Antisemitism in Britain" (III: 338). These are the pieces cited most often to prove Orwell's insights about English anti-Semitism and sympathy for Jews. Cheyette cites the passage where Orwell defends pre-Hitler literary anti-Semitism to show how Orwell, in contrast to most people working in literature and the humanities at the time, engages with the implications of a "post-Holocaust understanding of European civilization" (1).

43. Hitchens points out that in May 1936, nearly six years before Orwell's essay on Kipling was published, Orwell suggested to his agent Leonard Moore that the title "Black Man's Burden" be used for a potential American dramatization of *Burmese Days* (Hitchens 19).

44. The most commonly cited texts on Orwell's years at the BBC, including biographies, memoirs, and relevant documents collected in *CEJL*, do not mention the names of Indians other than Anand, Bokhari, and occasionally Cedric Dover who worked with Orwell. West's *Orwell: The Lost Writings* identifies Indian contributors and assistants, including, Narayana Menon, Princess Indira of Kapurthala, and Venu Chitale (and the Ceylonese poet and editor J. M. Tambimuttu who Empson refers to as "an Indian" in the second program of Orwell's "Voice" magazine), but does not discuss their views on Indian independence or the impact of their views on their relations with Orwell.

45. Anand and Cedric Dover both contributed to Orwell's *Talking to India*. While Anand's contribution, "Letter to a Chinese Guerrilla," is more interesting as anti-Fascist propaganda, Dover's pieces present the clearest challenge to English rule of India. In "Nationalism and Beyond" he declares that "Nationalism means a great deal to me" (127). Given Dover's association with Indian nationalism, it seems more than coincidental that his name comes up in *CEJL* in association with anti-Semitism. In a letter to Roy Fuller, Orwell apologizes for Dover's description of Fuller's story "Fletcher" as anti-Semitic in a *Tribune* review. Orwell writes, "I imagine that what Cedric Dover meant was that the central character was a Jew and also a not very admirable character, and perhaps that counts as antisemitism nowadays. I am sorry about this. [. . .] [By] my own experience it is almost impossible to mention Jews in print, either favourably or unfavourably, without getting into trouble" (III: 104–05).

46. Orwell never betrayed his youthful opposition to official British interests in India. In a diary entry of 10 August 1942, he records with dismay the violent events in India, a "ghastly speech" by Amery, and more generally the "Terrible feeling of depression among Indians and everyone sympathetic to India. [. . .] It is strange, but quite truly the way the British Government is now behaving in India upsets me more than a military defeat" (II: 442–43).

47. Walker's first letter to Orwell of 28 September begins, "So what you've got against Gandhi is that some 'big capitalists' show 'veneration' for him!" (*CW* 15: 222). Walker intelligently challenges every one of Orwell's objections to the Indian leader, expressed in his review of Fielden's book, in the paragraphs that follow. Davison speculates that Walker's letters may have influenced Orwell's more favorable interpretation of Gandhi's character and role in later writings such as "Reflections on Gandhi" (15: 222).

48. Daphne Patai and Andrea Freud Loewenstein demonstrate that Orwell's investment in the code of "Muscular Christianity," a guiding ideology for English middle- and upper-class boys and men of the Edwardian period, prevented him from extending to women, and Loewenstein would add, Jewish men, the respect he extended to English men of any class. Complementing Patai's argument about the transfer of English codes of masculinity to the imperial context, Kiernan writes that behind English color hierarchies

   lay the fundamental [masculine] criterion of strength or courage, of which war was the grand test. [. . .] Generally speaking, the lighter the skin the sharper the sword. [. . .] Nations that remained independent, however precariously, could look down on their fallen neighbors. [. . .] Armenia was partitioned between Turkey and Russia, yet an Armenian in England could boast to George Borrow that his countrymen were less debased and spiritless than the Jews, because they still had a homeland, and sometimes still took up arms. (315)

Bibliography

ABBREVIATIONS

BBCWA British Broadcasting Corporation Written Archives.
CEJL   *The Collected Essays, Journalism, and Letters of George Orwell.* Ed. Sonia
        Orwell and Ian Angus. Volume number is followed by page number.
CP   *Collected Poems* by Stevie Smith.
CW   *The Complete Works of George Orwell.* Ed. Peter Davison. Volume number
        is followed by page number.
MA   *Me Again* by Stevie Smith.

SELECTED WORKS BY MULK RAJ ANAND, INEZ HOLDEN, GEORGE ORWELL, AND STEVIE SMITH

Mulk Raj Anand
Anand, Mulk Raj. *Across the Black Waters.* 1940. New Delhi: Vision Books, 1978.
————. *Anand to Atma. Letters of Mulk Raj Anand.* Ed. Atma Ram. Calcutta:
Writers Workshop, 1994.
————. *Apology for Heroism: A Brief Autobiography of Ideas.* 1946. 3rd ed.
New Delhi: Arnold-Heinemann, 1975.
————. *Author to Critic: The Letters of Mulk Raj Anand.* Ed. and Intro. Saros
Cowasjee. Calcutta: A Writers Workshop Publication, 1973.
————. *The Barbers' Trade Union and Other Stories.* 1946. New Delhi:
Arnold-Heinemann, 1977.
————. *The Big Heart.* 1945. Ed. and intro. Saros Cowasjee. New Delhi:
Arnold-Heinemann, 1980.
————. *Conversations in Bloomsbury.* New Delhi: Arnold-Heinemann, 1981.
————. *Coolie.* 1936. London: Wishart, 1975.
————. *Curries and Other Indian Dishes.* London: Desmond Harmsworth, 1932.
————. *The Golden Breath: Studies in Five Poets of the New India.* London: John
Murray, 1933.

Anand, Mulk Raj. *The Hindu View of Art*. Introductory Essay on Art and Reality by Eric Gill. London: Allen and Unwin, 1933.

———. *The King-Emperor's English; or, the Role of the English Language in the Free India*. Afterward by Maulana Abul Kalam Azad. Bombay: Hind Kitabs, 1948.

———. *Letters on India*. London: Labour Book Service, 1942.

———. *Lines Written to an Indian Air*. Bombay: Nalanda Publishers, 1949.

———. *The Lost Child and Other Stories*. London: J. A. Allen and Co., 1934.

———, ed. *Marg* (Modern Artists and Architects Research Group). Pathway. A Magazine of the Arts. Bombay: 1950– .

———. *On Education*. Bombay: Hind Kutabs, 1947.

———. "On the Genesis of Untouchable." *The Novels of Mulk Raj Anand*. Ed. R. K. Dhawan. New Delhi: Prestige Books, 1992. 9–12.

———, ed. *The Other Side of the Medal*. 1925. Edward Thompson. Afterword Sumit Sarkar. New Delhi: Sterling Publishers, 1989.

———. *Persian Painting*. London: Faber and Faber, 1930.

———. *The Private Life of an Indian Prince*. London: Hutchinson, 1953. Revised ed. London: Bodley Head, 1970.

———, ed. *Sati: A Write Up of Raja Ram Mohan Roy about Burning of Widows Alive*. Delhi: B. R. Publishing, 1989.

———. "The Sources of Protest in my Novels." *Contemporary Indian Fiction in English*. Ed. K. Ayyappa Paniker. Trivandrum: U of Kerala, 1987. 22–31.

———. "The Story of My Experiment with a White Lie." *Critical Essays on Indian Writing in English*. Ed. M. K. Naik, S. K. Desai, and G. S. Amur. Dharwar: Karnatak U; Madras: Macmillan of India, 1972. 6–20.

———. *The Sword and the Sickle*. New Delhi: Arnold-Heinemann, 1942.

———. *The Tractor and the Corn Goddess and Other Stories*. 1947. New Delhi: Arnold-Heinemann, 1987.

———. *Two Leaves and a Bud*. London: Lawrence and Wishart, 1937.

———. *Untouchable*. London: Lawrence and Wishart, 1935.

———. *The Village*. 1939. London: Cape, 1939.

———. "Why I Write." *Indian Writing in English*. Ed. Krishna Nanda Sinha. New Delhi: Heritage Publishers, 1979. 1–9.

———. "Why I Write." *Perspectives on Mulk Raj Anand*. Ed. Kaushal Kishore Sharma. Ghaziabad: Vimal, 1978. 1–7.

——— and Krishna Hutheesing. *The Bride's Book of Beauty*. Bombay: Kutub Publishers, 1947. Rev. ed. *The Book of Indian Beauty*. Rutland, VT: Charles Tuttle, 1981.

Inez Holden

Holden, Inez. "According to the Directive." *Cornhill Magazine* 1947/1949: 384–92.

———. "The Adventuress To-Day." *Daily Mail* 20 July 1932: n.p.

———. "The Art of Ada Leverson." *Cornhill Magazine* 1949/1950: 429–38.

———. "Arolsen." *Nineteenth-Century and After* January/June 1947: 175–85.

———. "Blond Hero." *Harper's Bazaar* February 1934: 30+.

———. *Born Old, Died Young*. London: Duckworth, 1932.

———. "Conversation Tragedy." *Literary Review* January 1937: 31–35.

———. "Country House Bridge." *Harper's Bazaar* September 1934: 67+.

———. *Death in High Society.* London: Kegan Paul, 1934.

———. "Farewell to the Bright Young People." *Evening News* 30 August 1932: n.p.

———. "Fellow Travelers in Factory." *Horizon* January–June 1941: 117–22.

———. "Fox Hunting—Is It Human?" *Harper's Bazaar* November 1935: 94.

———. *Friend of the Family.* London: Arthur Barker, 1933.

———. "The Game of Ghosts." *Harper's Bazaar* March 1942: 50+.

———. "I Could Write a Book . . ." *Harper's Bazaar* July–August 1942: 61–62.

———. "The Importance of Being Seen." *Nash's* August 1933: 68+.

———. *It Was Different at the Time.* London: John Lane, 1943.

———. *Night Shift.* London: John Lane, 1941.

———. "On the Way Home." *Fortnightly* July/December 1938: 337–42.

———. *The Owner.* London: Bodley Head, 1952.

———. "Sir Helter Skelton." *Nash's* September 1933: 70–73.

———. "Some Women Writers." *Nineteenth Century and After* July/December 1949: 130–36.

———. "Summer Journal." *Leaves in the Storm: A Book of Diaries.* Ed. Stefan Schimanski and Henry Treece. London: Lindsay Drummond, 1947. 239–47.

———. *Sweet Charlatan.* London: Duckworth, 1929.

———. *There's No Story There.* London: John Lane, 1944.

———. *To the Boating and Other Stories.* London: John Lane, 1945.

———. "Unaccompanied Children." *Nineteenth Century and After* July/December 1948: 48–52.

George Orwell

Orwell, George. *Animal Farm.* 1945. New York: Harcourt Brace, 1946.

———. *Burmese Days.* 1934. New York: Harcourt Brace, 1962.

———. *A Clergyman's Daughter.* 1935. New York: Harcourt Brace, 1936.

———. *Collected Essays.* London: Secker and Warburg, 1961.

———. *Coming Up for Air.* 1939. New York: Harcourt Brace, 1950.

———. *The Collected Essays, Journalism, and Letters of George Orwell.* Ed. Sonia Orwell and Ian Angus. Vol. 1 *An Age Like This,* 1920–1940. Vol. 2 *My Country Right or Left,* 1940–1943. Vol. 3 *As I Please,* 1943–1945. Vol. 4 *In Front of Your Nose,* 1945–1950. 1968. Boston: David R. Godine, 2000.

———. *The Complete Works of George Orwell.* Ed. Peter Davison. 20 vols. London: Secker and Warburg, 1998.

———. *Down and Out in Paris and London.* New York and London: Harper and Brothers, 1933.

———. *Homage to Catalonia.* 1938. London: Secker and Warburg, 1959.

———. *Inside the Whale and Other Essays.* 1940. London: Penguin, 1957.

———. *Keep the Aspidistra Flying.* 1936. New York: Harcourt Brace, 1956.

———. *The Lion and the Unicorn: Socialism and the English Genius.* London: Secker and Warburg, 1941.

———. *Nineteen Eighty-Four.* New York: Harcourt Brace, 1949.

———. *The Road to Wigan Pier.* Foreword Victor Gollancz. London: Gollancz, 1937.

Orwell, George. *Such, Such Were the Joys.* New York: Harcourt Brace, 1953.

——— ed. and Intro. *Talking to India, by E. M. Forster, Ritchie Calder, Cedric Dorer, Hsiao Chien and Others.* London: G. Allen and Unwin, Ltd., 1943.

———. *The War Broadcasts.* 1985. Ed. W. J. West. London: Penguin, 1987.

———. *The War Commentaries.* Ed. W. J. West. New York: Pantheon, 1985.

Stevie Smith

Smith, Stevie. *The Collected Poems of Stevie Smith.* 1975. Ed. and pref. James MacGibbon. New York: New Directions, 1983.

———. *The Holiday.* 1949. Intro. Janet Watts. London: Virago, 1980.

———. *Me Again: Uncollected Writings of Stevie Smith.* Ed. Jack Barbera and William McBrien. New York: Farrar, Strauss, Giroux, 1981.

———. *Novel on Yellow Paper; or, Work It out for Yourself.* 1936. Intro. Janet Watts. London: Virago, 1980. New York: New Directions, 1994.

———. *Over the Frontier.* 1938. Intro. Janet Watts. London: Virago, 1980.

SELECTED CRITICISM ABOUT MULK RAJ ANAND, INEZ HOLDEN, GEORGE ORWELL, AND STEVIE SMITH

Mulk Raj Anand

Amur, G. S. *Forbidden Fruit: Views on Indo-Anglian Fiction.* Calcutta: Writers Workshop, 1992.

Asnani, Shyam M. "*The Socio-Political Scene of the 1930s: Its Impact on the Indo-English Novel*". *Commonwealth Quarterly* 6.21 (1981): 14–23.

Bamezai, Gita. *Mulk Raj Anand: The Journalist.* New Delhi: Kanishka Publishers, 2000.

Berry, Margaret. *Mulk Raj Anand: The Man and the Novelist.* Amsterdam: Oriental P, 1971.

Chaudhury, Jasbir. "Images of Women in the Novels of Mulk Raj Anand." *Punjab University Research Bulletin (Arts)* 16 (1985): 47–56.

Cowasjee, Saros. *So Many Freedoms: A Study of the Major Fictions of Mulk Raj Anand.* Delhi: Oxford UP, 1977.

———. "Anand's Literary Creed." *The Novels of Mulk Raj Anand.* Ed. R. K. Dhawan. New Delhi: Prestige Books, 1992. 13–18.

Dhawan, R. K. "The Thirties Movement and Coolie." *The Novels of Mulk Raj Anand.* Ed. R. K. Dhawan. New Delhi: Prestige Books, 1992. 54–65.

Dhawan, R. K., ed. *The Novels of Mulk Raj Anand.* New Delhi: Prestige Books, 1992.

Fisher, Marlene. "Apology for Heroism: Autobiography and Mulk Raj Anand." *The Novels of Mulk Raj Anand.* Ed. R. K. Dhawan. New Delhi: Prestige Books, 1992: 193–202.

———. *The Wisdom of the Heart: A Study of the Works of Mulk Raj Anand.* New Delhi: Sterling, 1985.

George, C. J. *Mulk Raj Anand, His Art and Concerns: A Study of His Non-Autobiographical Novels*. New Delhi: Atlantic Publishers, 1994.

Gupta, G. S. Balarama. *Mulk Raj Anand: A Study of His Fiction in Humanist Perspective*. 1974.

Lindsay, Jack. *The Elephant and the Lotus: A Study of the Novels of Mulk Raj Anand*. Bombay: Kutub Popular, 1965.

Mukherjee, Arun P. "The Exclusions of Postcolonial Theory and Mulk Raj Anand's Untouchable: A Case Study." *Ariel: A Review of International English Literature* 22 (1991): 27–48.

Mathur, O. P. "Two Modern Versions of the Sita Myth." *Journal of Commonwealth Literature* 21 (1986): 17–25.

Naik, M. K. *Mulk Raj Anand*. New Delhi: Arnold-Heinemann, 1973.

Niven, Alastair. *The Yoke of Pity: A Study in the Fictional Writings of Mulk Raj Anand*. New Delhi: Arnold-Heinemann, 1978.

Packham, Gillian. "Mulk Raj Anand and the Thirties Movement." *Perspectives on Mulk Raj Anand*. Ed. Kaushal Kishore Sharma et al. Ghaziabad: Vimal, 1978. 52–63.

Parry, Graham. "Anand, Orwell and the War." *The Novels of Mulk Raj Anand*. Ed. R. K. Dhawan. New Delhi: Prestige Books 1992.

Paul, Premila. *The Novels of Mulk Raj Anand: A Thematic Study*. New Delhi: Sterling, 1983.

Rajan, P. K. *Studies in Mulk Raj Anand*. New Delhi: Abhinav Publications, 1986.

Sethi, Vijay Mohan. *Mulk Raj Anand, the Short Story Writer*. New Delhi: Ashish Publishing, 1990.

Sharma, Ambuj Kumar. *The Theme of Exploitation in the Novels of Mulk Raj Anand*. New Delhi: H. K. Publishers, 1990.

Sharma, Kaushal Kishore et al., eds. *Perspectives on Mulk Raj Anand*. Ghaziabad: Vimal, 1978.

Singh, Sutyanarain, ed. *Mulk Raj Anand*. Spec. issue of *Kakatiya Journal of English Studies*. (1977).

Shirwadkar, Meena. *Image of Woman in the Indo-Anglian Novel*. New Delhi: Sterling Publishers, 1979.

Sinha, Krishna Nandan. *Mulk Raj Anand*. New York: Twayne, 1972.

Suryanarayana Murti, K. V. *The Sword and the Sickle: A Study of Mulk Raj Anand's Novels*. Mysore: Gertha Book House, 1983.

Woolf, Leonard. Introduction. *Apology for Heroism: A Brief Autobiography of Ideas*. By Mulk Raj Anand. New Delhi: Arnold-Heinemann, 1975. vii–ix.

Inez Holden

Rev. of *Born Old, Died Young* by Inez Holden. *Times Literary Supplement* 21 April 1932: 293.

Rev. of *Death in High Society* by Inez Holden. *Times Literary Supplement* 6 September 1934: 606.

Rev. of *Friend of the Family* by Inez Holden. *Times Literary Supplement* 19 October 1933: 713.

Goodman, Celia. "Inez Holden: A Memoir." *London Magazine* December/January 1994: 29–38.

Johnson, Pamela Hansford. "Love and Also Munitions." Rev. of *Two Mirrors* by Peter de Polnay, *There's No Story There* by Inez Holden, and *Young Bess* by Margaret Irwin. *John O'London's Weekly* 15 December 1944: n.p.

Muir, Edwin. "New Novels." Rev. of *Delilah* by Marcus Goodrich, *The Skies of Europe* by Frederic Prokosch, and *Night Shift* by Inez Holden. *The Listener* 12 February 1942: 219.

Rev. of *Night Shift* by Inez Holden. *Times Literary Supplement* 7 February 1942: 71.

O'Brien, Kate. "Fiction." Rev. of *There's No Story There* by Inez Holden. *Spectator* 24 November 1944: 488.

Orwell, George. "Rev. of *Edwin and Eleanor* by E. E. Vulliamy; *At Mrs. Lippincote's* by Elizabeth Taylor; *To the Boating* by Inez Holden." *Complete Works*. Ed. Peter Davison. Vol. 17. London: Secker and Warburg, 1998. 306–07.

Powell, Anthony. "Inez Holden: A Memoir." *London Magazine* October/November 1974: 88–94.

Rev. of *Sweet Charlatan* by Inez Holden. *Times Literary Supplement* 25 July 1929: 593.

"Shorter Notice" Rev. of *Night Shift* by Inez Holden. *Spectator* 15 May 1942: 472.

Rev. of *There's No Story There* by Inez Holden. *Times Literary Supplement* 25 November 1944: 569.

Rev. of *To the Boating* by Inez Holden. *Times Literary Supplement* 29 September 1945: 461

West, Rebecca. "The Universal Struggle." Rev. of *Night Shift* by Inez Holden and *Darkness and the Light* by Olaf Stapledon. Source unknown.

George Orwell

Atkins, John. *George Orwell: A Literary and Biographical Study*. New York: Frederick Ungar, 1954.

Beddoe, Deirdre. "Hindrances and Helpmeets: Women in the Writings of George Orwell." *Inside the Myth: Orwell: Views from the Left*. Ed. Christopher Norris. London: Lawrence and Wishart, 1984.

Bowker, Gordon. *Inside George Orwell*. New York: Palgrave Macmillan, 2003.

Calder, Jenni. *Chronicles of Conscience: Study of George Orwell and Arthur Koestler*. London: Secker and Warburg, 1968.

Coppard, Audrey and Bernard Crick, eds. *Orwell Remembered*. London: BBC, 1984.

Crick, Bernard. *George Orwell: A Life*. Boston: Little, Brown, 1980.

Davison, Peter. *George Orwell: A Literary Life*. New York: St. Martin's P, 1996.

Deutscher, Isaac. " '1984'—The Mysticism of Cruelty." *Marxism, Wars, and Revolutions*. London: Verso, 1984. 60–71.

Fenwick, Gillian. *George Orwell: A Bibliography*. New Castle, DE: Oak Knoll P, 1998.

Fink, Howard. "Orwell vs. Koestler: 1984 as Optimistic Satire." *George Orwell*. Ed. Courtney T. Wemyss and Alexej Ugrinsky. Westport: Greenwood P, 1987. 101–09.

Fyvel, T. R. *George Orwell: A Personal Memoir*. London: Weidenfeld and Nicolson, 1982.

————. "Wingate, Orwell and the 'Jewish Question.'" *Commentary* February 1951: 137–44.

Gross, Miriam, ed. *The World of George Orwell.* London: Weidenfeld and Nicolson, 1971.

Hammond, J. R. *A George Orwell Chronology.* New York: Palgrave, 2000.

Hitchens, Christopher. *Why Orwell Matters.* New York: Basic Books, 2002.

————. "Orwell's List." *The New York Review of Books* 26 September 2002. 26+.

Holderness, Graham, Bryan Longhrey and Nahem Yousaf, eds. *George Orwell.* New York: Palgrave, 1999.

Kenner, Hugh. "The Politics of the Plain Style." *Reflections on America, 1984: An Orwell Symposium.* Ed. Robert Mulvihill. Athens: U of Georgia P, 1986.

Kerr, Douglas. "Orwell, Animals, and the East." *Essays in Criticism* 49 (1999): 234–55.

Loewenstein, Andrea Freud. "The Protection of Masculinity: Jews as Projective Pawns in the Texts of William Gerhardi and George Orwell." *Between "Race" and Culture: Representations of "the Jew" in English and American Literature.* Ed. Bryan Cheyette. Stanford: Stanford UP, 1996. 145–64.

Lucas, Scott. *Orwell.* London: Haus Publishing, 2003.

Meyers, Jeffrey. *Orwell: Wintry Conscience of a Generation.* New York: Norton, 2000.

———— ed. *George Orwell: The Critical Heritage.* London: Routledge and Kegan Paul, 1975.

New, Melvin. "Orwell and Anti-Semitism: Toward *1984.*" *Modern Fiction Studies* 21 (1975): 81–105.

Norris, Christopher, ed. *Inside the Myth: Orwell: Views from the Left.* London: Lawrence and Wishart, 1984.

Patai, Daphne. *The Orwell Mystique: A Study in Male Ideology.* Amherst: U Massachusetts P, 1984.

Rai, Alok. *Orwell and the Politics of Despair: A Critical Study of the Writings of George Orwell.* Cambridge: Cambridge UP, 1988.

Rees, Richard. *George Orwell: A Fugitive from the Camp of Victory.* Carbondale: Southern Illinois UP, 1962.

Rodden, John. *The Politics of Literary Reputation: The Making and Unmaking of "St. George Orwell"* New York: Oxford UP, 1989.

Rovere, Richard H. Introduction. *The Orwell Reader: Fiction, Essays, and Reportage.* By George Orwell. New York: Harcourt, 1956.

Rushdie, Salman. "Outside the Whale." *Imaginary Homelands: Essays and Criticism 1981–1991.* New York: Viking, 1991. 87–101.

Seshagiri, Urmila. "Misogyny and Anti-Imperialism in George Orwell's Burmese Days." *The Road from George Orwell: His Achievement and Legacy.* New York: Peter Lang, 2001. 105–19.

Shelden, Michael. *Orwell: The Authorized Biography.* London: Heinemann, 1991.

Stansky, Peter. *From William Morris to Sergeant Pepper: Studies in the Radical Domestic.* Palo Alto: Society for the Promotion of Science and Scholarship, 1999.

Stansky, Peter and William Abrahams. *Orwell: The Transformation.* London: Constable, 1979.

Stansky, Peter. *The Unknown Orwell*. New York: Knopf, 1972.

Steinhoff, William. *George Orwell and the Origins of 1984*. Ann Arbor: U Michigan P, 1975.

Taylor, D. J. *Orwell*. London: Chatto and Windus, 2003.

Thompson, E. P. "Outside the Whale." 1960. *The Poverty of Theory and Other Essays*. New York: Monthly Review P, 1978.

Wadhams, Stephen, ed. *Remembering Orwell*. Ontario: Harmondsworth, Penguin, 1984.

Walton, David. "George Orwell and Antisemitism." *Patterns of Prejudice* 16.1 (1982): 19–34.

Warburg, Fredric. *All Authors Are Equal: The Publishing Life of Fredric Warburg, 1936–1971*. London: Hutchinson, 1973.

Weatherly, Joan. "The Death of Big Sister: Orwell's Tragic Message." *College Literature* 15 (1988): 269–80.

West, W. J. *The Larger Evils: "1984": The Truth behind the Satires*. Edinburgh: Cannongate P, 1992.

Williams, Raymond. *George Orwell: A Collection of Critical Essays*. Engelwood, New Jersey: Prentice Hall, 1974.

———. *George Orwell*. New York: Viking, 1971.

Wilson, Edmund. "Edmund Wilson, *New Yorker*" [Rev. of *Shooting an Elephant* by George Orwell.] *George Orwell: The Critical Heritage*. Ed. Jeffrey Meyers. Boston: Routledge and Kegan Paul, 1975. 309.

Woodcock, George. *The Crystal Spirit: A Study of George Orwell*. 1966. New York: Schocken, 1984.

Zwerdling, Alex. *Orwell and the Left*. New Haven: Yale UP, 1974.

Stevie Smith

Barbera, Jack. "The Relevance of Stevie Smith's Drawings." *Journal of Modern Literature* 12 (1985): 221–36.

Barbera, Jack and William McBrien. *Stevie: A Biography of Stevie Smith*. New York: Oxford UP, 1987.

Bluemel, Kristin. "The Dangers of Eccentricity: Stevie Smith's Doodles and Poetry." *Mosaic* 13 (1998): 111–32.

———. "Not Waving or Drowning: Refusing Critical Options, Rewriting Literary History." *And in Our Time: Vision, Revision, and British Writing of the 1930s*. Ed. Antony Shuttleworth. Lewisburg: Bucknell UP, 2003. 65–94.

Civello, Catherine A. *Patterns of Ambivalence: The Fiction and Poetry of Stevie Smith*. Columbia: Camden House, 1997.

Dentith, Simon. "Thirties Poetry and the Landscape of Suburbia." *Rewriting the Thirties: Modernism and After*. Ed. Keith Williams and Steven Matthews. London: Longmans, 1997. 108–23.

Dick, Kay. *Ivy and Stevie: Ivy Compton-Burnett and Stevie Smith, Conversations and Reflections*. New York: Allison and Busby, 1971.

Gordon, Eleanor Risteen. "Daddy, Mummy and Stevie: The Child-Guise in Stevie Smith's Poetry." *Modern Poetry Studies* 11 (1983): 232–44.

Huk, Romana. "Eccentric Concentrism: Traditional Poetic Forms and Refracted Discourse in Stevie Smith's Poetry." *Contemporary Literature* 34 (1993): 240–65.

———. "Misplacing Stevie Smith." *Contemporary Literature* 40 (1999): 507–23.

MacGibbon, James. Preface. *Collected Poems* by Stevie Smith. New York: New Directions, 1983. 7–12.

Lassner, Phyllis. "A Cry for Life: Storm Jameson, Stevie Smith, and the Fate of Europe's Jews." *Visions of War: World War II in Popular Literature and Culture.* Ed. M. Paul Holsinger and Mary Anne Schofield. Bowling Green: Bowling Green State U Popular P, 1992. 181–90.

———. "The Milk of Our Mother's Kindness Has Ceased to Flow: Virginia Woolf, Stevie Smith, and the Representation of the Jew." *Between "Race" and Culture: Representations of "the Jew" in English and American Literature.* Ed. Bryan Cheyette. Stanford: Stanford UP, 1996. 129–44.

Light, Alison. "Outside History? Stevie Smith, Women Poets and the National Voice." *English* 48 (1994): 237–59.

Pumphrey, Martin. "Play, Fantasy and Strange Laughter: Stevie Smith's Uncomfortable Poetry." *Critical Quarterly* 28 (1986): 85–96.

Severin, Laura. *Stevie Smith's Resistant Antics.* Madison: U of Wisconsin P, 1997.

Spalding, Frances. *Stevie Smith: A Biography.* New York: Norton, 1988.

Sternlicht, Sanford, ed. *In Search of Stevie Smith.* Syracuse: Syracuse UP, 1991.

Stevenson, Sheryl. "Stevie Smith's Voices." *Contemporary Literature* 33 (1992): 24–45.

Steward, Julie Sims. "Ceci n'est pas un Hat: Stevie Smith and the Refashioning of Gender." *South Central Review* 15 (1998): 16–33.

Storey, Mark. "Why Stevie Smith Matters." *In Search of Stevie Smith.* Ed. Sanford Sternlicht. Syracuse: Syracuse UP, 1991. 175–95.

Upton, Lee. "Stevie Smith and the Anxiety of Intimacy." *CEA Critic: An Official Journal of the College English Association* 53 (1991): 22–31.

Watts, Janet. Introduction. *Over the Frontier.* By Stevie Smith. 1938. London: Virago, 1980. 5–8.

SELECTED CONTEMPORARY SOURCES, INCLUDING REPRINTS AND REDISCOVERIES, AND MEMOIRS BY CONTEMPORARIES

Ambedkar, Bhimrao Ramji. *Annihilation of Caste: An Undelivered Speech.* New Delhi: Arnold Publishers, 1990.

Auden, W. H. *The English Auden: Poems, Essays, and Dramatic Writings, 1927–1939.* Ed. Edward Mendelson. London: Faber, 1977.

Auden, W. H. et al. *I Believe.* London: Allen and Unwin, 1942.

Auden, W. H. and Christopher Isherwood. *Journey to a War.* London: Faber and Faber, 1939.

Baker, Denys Val, ed. *Modern British Writing.* New York: Vanguard P, 1947.

Bell, Walter George. *Where London Sleeps: Historical Journeyings into the Suburbs.* London: John Lane, 1926.

Brierley, Walter. *Means Test Man.* London: Methuen, 1935.

Borden, Mary. *The Forbidden Zone.* London: Heinemann, 1929.

Bottome, Phyllis. *The Mortal Storm.* London: Faber and Faber, 1937.

———. *Within the Cup.* London: Faber, 1943.

Brittain, Vera. *Chronicle of Friendship: Diary of the Thirties, 1932–1939.* Ed. Allan Bishop. London: Gollancz, 1986.

———. *England's Hour.* New York: Macmillan, 1947.

———. *Testament of Experience: An Autobiographical Story of the Years 1925–1950.* London: Gollancz, 1957.

———. *Testament of Youth: An Autobiographical Story of the Years 1900–1925.* London: Gollancz, 1933.

Brooks, Collin. *Devil's Decade: Portraits of the Nineteen-Thirties.* London: Macdonald, 1948.

Burdekin, Katharine. *Swastika Night.* 1937. New York: Feminist P, 1990.

Burke, Thomas. *The Outer Circle: Rambles in Remote London.* London: George Allen and Unwin, 1921.

Caudwell, Christopher. *Illusion and Reality: A Study in the Sources of Poetry.* 1937. London: Lawrence and Wishart, 1946.

Chaudhury, Nirad C. *The Autobiography of an Unknown Indian.* 1951. New York: Picador, 1999.

———. *A Passage to England.* New York: St. Martin's, 1959.

Cockburn, Claud. *Crossing the Line: Being the Second Volume of Autobiography.* London: MacGibbon and Kee, 1959.

———. *The Devil's Decade.* London: Sidgwick and Jackson, 1973.

———. *A Discord of Trumpets: An Autobiography.* New York: Simon and Schuster, 1956.

———. *I, Claud: The Autobiography of Claud Cockburn.* London: Hammondsworth, Penguin, 1967.

Common, Jack. *Kiddar's Luck.* London: Turnstile P, 1951.

———, ed. *Seven Shifts.* London: E. P. Dutton, 1938.

Connolly, Cyril. *Enemies of Promise.* 1938. Rev. ed. New York: Macmillan, 1948.

Cowasjee, Saros, ed. *Stories from the Raj: From Kipling to Independence.* London: Bodley Head, 1982.

Cox, Oliver C. *Caste, Class, and Race: A Study in Social Dynamics.* New York: Monthly Review P, 1948.

Crossman, Richard, ed. *The God That Failed: Six Studies in Communism.* London: Hamish Hamilton, 1950.

Day Lewis, Cecil, ed. *The Mind in Chains: Socialism and the Cultural Revolution.* London: F. Muller, 1937.

Decade, 1931–1941, A Commemorative Anthology. London: H. Hamilton, 1941.

Delafield, E. M. *Diary of a Provincial Lady.* 1930. London: Virago, 1984.

Empson, William. *Some Versions of Pastoral.* London: Chatto and Windus, 1935.

Esdaile, Ernest. *Basic English: How to Speak It . . .* Fore. Millicent, Duchess of Sutherland. London: Quality P, 1944.

Fearon, Henry Bridges. *Tramping around London: Forty-One Walks in London's Country*. London: Country Life, 1933.

Fox, Ralph. *The Novel and the People*. London: Lawrence and Wishart, 1937.

Fox-Davies, Moyra. *Eighty Miles around London*. London: T. Nelson, T. C. and E. C. Jack, 1934.

Fyvel, T. R. *No Ease in Zion*. New York: Knopf, 1939.

Goldsmith, Margaret. *Women at War*. London: Drummond, 1943.

Gollancz, Victor, ed. *The Betrayal of the Left: An Examination and Refutation of Communist Policy from October 1939 to January 1941*. London: Gollancz, 1941.

Goodman, Celia, ed. *Living with Koestler: Mamaine Koestler's Letters 1945–1951*. New York: St. Martin's P, 1985.

Graves, Robert and Alan Hodge. *The Long Week End: A Social History of Great Britain, 1918–1939*. London: Faber and Faber, 1941.

Green, Henry. *Living*. London: Hogarth P, 1929.

———. *Loving*. London: Hogarth P, 1945.

———. *Pack My Bag*. London: Hogarth P, 1979.

———. *Party Going*. London: Hogarth P, 1939.

Greene, Graham, ed. *The Old School: Essays by Divers Hands*. 1934. Oxford: Oxford UP, 1985.

Greenwood, Walter. *Love on the Dole: A Tale of Two Cities*. 1933. Garden City: Doubleday, Doran, 1934.

———. *Standing Room Only: Or, A Laugh in Every Line*. London: Cape, 1936.

Grigson, Geoffrey, ed. *New Verse: An Anthology*. London: Faber and Faber, 1939.

Halward, Leslie. *Let Me Tell You*. London: M. Joseph, 1938.

Hanley, James. *Men in Darkness: Five Stories*. Pref. John Cowper Powys. New York: Knopf, 1932.

Harrison, Tom. *Living through the Blitz*. London: Collins, 1976.

Harrison, Tom, ed. *War Factory: A Report by Mass-Observation*. London: Gollancz, 1943.

Harrison, Tom and Charles Madge, eds. *War Begins at Home, by Mass Observation*. London: Chatto and Windus, 1940.

Hawkins, F[rancis]. *The Story of Golders Green and Its Remarkable Development*. Golders Green: Messres. Ernest Owers, Ltd., Auction and Estate Office (facing Tube station), 1923.

Henderson, Philip. *The Novel Today: Studies in Contemporary Attitudes*. London: John Lane, Bodley Head, 1936.

Hendry, J. F. and Henry Treece, eds. *The Crown and Sickle: An Anthology*. 1944.

———. *The White Horseman: Prose and Verse of the New Apocalypse*. London: Routledge, 1941.

Heppenstall, Rayner. *Four Absentees*. London: Barrie and Rockliff, 1960.

Holtby, Winifred. *South Riding*. 1935. London: Fontana/Collins, 1954.

Huxley, Aldous. *Brave New World*. 1932. New York: Harper Perennial, 1969.

———. *Point Counter Point*. 1928. Normal, IL: Dalky Archive, 1996.

Iyengar, K. R. Srinivasa. *The Indian Contribution to English Literature*. Bombay: Karnatak Publishing, 1943.

———. *Indo-Anglian Literature*. Bombay: P.E.N. All-India Centre, 1943.

Jameson, Storm. *Company Parade*. 1934. London: Virago, 1985.

———. *Europe to Let*. New York: Macmillan, 1940.

———. *Journey from the North*. 2 vols. London: Virago, 1969– .

———, ed. *London Calling*. New York and London: Harper and Brothers, 1942.

———. *Love in Winter*. London: Cassell, 1935.

———. *None Turn Back*. 1936. London: Virago, 1984.

Jennings, H. *Broadcasting in Everyday Life: A Survey of the Social Effects of the Coming of Broadcasting*. London: BBC, 1939.

Jennings, Humphrey et al., eds. *May the Twelfth: Mass-Observation Day-Surveys*. London: Faber and Faber, 1937.

Koestler, Arthur. *Darkness at Noon*. London: Macmillan, 1941.

———. *Spanish Testament*. London: Gollancz, 1937.

Lancaster, Osbert. *Pillar to Post: The Pocket Lamp of Architecture*. New York: Transatlantic Arts, 1938.

Leavis, F. R. *Mass Civilization and Minority Culture*. Cambridge: Minority P, 1930.

Leavis, Q. D. *Fiction and the Reading Public*. London: Chatto and Windus, 1932.

Lewis, Wyndham. *Hitler*. London: Chatto and Windus, 1931.

———. *The Hitler Cult*. London: Dent, 1939.

———. *The Jews: Are They Human?* London: G. Allen and Unwin, 1939.

MacNeice, Louis. *The Strings Are False: An Unfinished Biography*. Ed. E. M. Dodds. London: Faber, 1965.

Maxwell, Gordon S. T*he Fringe of London: Being Some Ventures and Adventures in Topography*. London: Cecil Palmer, 1925.

Marriott, Sir John Arthur Ransome. *The English in India: A Problem of Politics*. Oxford: Clarendon P, 1932.

Miller, Betty. *Farewell Leicester Square*. 1941. London: Persephone Books, 2000.

———. *On the Side of the Angels*. 1945. London: Virago, 1985.

Milner, Marion. *A Life of One's Own*. 1934. London: Virago, 1986.

Mitchison, Naomi. *Among You Taking Notes: Wartime Diaries 1939–1945*. Ed. Dorothy Sheridan. London: Gollancz, 1985.

———. *You May Well Ask: A Memoir, 1920–1940*. London: Gollancz, 1979.

Moore, Reginald and Woodrow Wyatt, eds. *Stories of the Forties, Volume I*. London: Nicholson and Watson, 1945.

Moreland, W. H. and Atul Chaudra Chatterjee. *A Short History of India*. London: Longmans, Green, and Co., 1936.

Mosley, Oswald. *The Greater Britain*. London: B.U.F. Publications, 1932.

Muggeridge, Malcolm. *The Thirties, 1930–1940, in Great Britain*. London: H. Hamilton, 1940.

Nixon, Barbara. *Raiders Overhead*. London: L. Drummond, 1943.

Ogden, C. K. *ABCs of Basic English (in Basic) with an Account of the Sounds of Basic English*. London: K. Paul Trench, Trubner, 1939.

———. *Basic English, A General Introduction with Rules and Grammar*. London: K. Paul, Trench, Trubner and Co., 1932.

———. *Basic Step by Step*. London: K. Paul Trench, Trubner, 1939.

———. *Brighter Basic: Examples of Basic English for Young Persons of Taste and Feeling*. London: K. Paul, Trench, Trubner, 1931.

———. Foreword. *Death in High Society*. By Inez Holden. London: Kegan Paul, 1934.

———. *The System of Basic English*. New York: Harcourt, Brace, 1934.

Ogden, C. K. and I. A. Richards. *The Meaning of Meaning: A Study of the Influence of Language upon Thought and of the Science of Symbolism*. London: K. Paul Trench, Trubner, 1923.

Orthological Institute. *Basic English, an International Language*. London: *The Times* Pub. Co., 1935.

Panter-Downes, Mollie. *London War Notes 1939–1945*. Ed. William Shawn. London: Longman, 1972.

Pargiter, Edith. *She Goes to War*. 1942. London: Headline, 1990.

Pathfinder. *The Foot Path Way around London: Field, Path and Woodland Rambles, with Directions and Maps*. London: The Homeland Assn., 1920– .

Piper, Raymond Frank. *Language and World Unity*. New York: International Auxiliary Language Assn., 1937.

Powell, Anthony. *Messengers of the Day*. London: Heinemann, 1978. Vol. 2 of *To Keep the Ball Rolling: The Memoirs of Anthony Powell*. 3 vols. 1976–1978.

———. *What's Become of Waring?* London: Cassell, 1939.

Priestley, J. B. *All England Listened: The Wartime Broadcasts of J. B. Priestley*. New York: Chilmark P, 1967.

———. *British Women Go to War*. London: Collins, 1943.

———. *Daylight on Saturday: A Novel about an Aircraft Factory*. London: Heinemann, 1943.

———. *English Journey*. 1934. Chicago: U Chicago P, 1984.

Pritchett, V. S. *Turnstile One: A Literary Miscellany from the New Statesman and Nation*. London: Turnstile P, 1948.

Raine, Kathleen. *The Land Unknown*. London: Hamilton, 1975.

Rathbone, Eleanor. *Falsehoods and Facts about the Jews*. London: Gollancz, 1945.

———. *Rescue the Perishing*. London: The National Committee for Rescue from Nazi Terror, 1943.

Rhondda, Margaret Haig Thomas Mackworth. *This Was My World*. London: Macmillan, 1933.

Richards, I. A. *Basic English and Its Uses*. New York: Norton, 1943.

Richards, J. M. *The Castles on the Ground: The Anatomy of Suburbia*. 1946. 2nd ed. London: J. Murray, 1973.

Roberts, Michael. *The Modern Mind*. London: Faber and Faber, 1937.

———, ed. *New Country: Prose and Poetry by the Authors of New Signatures*. London: Hogarth P, 1933.

Rotha, Paul. *Documentary Film: The Use of the Film Medium to Interpret Creatively and in Social Terms the Life of the People as It Exists in Reality*. London: Faber and Faber, 1936.

Routh, H. V. *Basic English and the Problem of a World Language*. London: Royal Society of Literature, 1944.

Scott, Peggy. *British Women in War*. London: Hutchinson, 1940.

Smith, Clive R. *Golders Green as It Was*. Greyhound Hill: C. R. Smith, 1974.

Spender, Humphrey. *Britain in the Thirties: Photographs.* Intro. Tom Harrision. London: Lion and Unicorn P, 1975.

Spender, Humphrey. *Worktown: Photographs of Bolton and Blackpool.* Brighton: Gardner Centre Gallery, U of Sussex, 1977.

Sheridan, Dorothy, ed. *Wartime Women: An Anthology of Women's Wartime Writing for Mass Observation 1937–45.* London: Mandarin, 1991.

Spender, Stephen. *The Backward Son.* London: Faber, 1940.

———. *The Destructive Element: A Case Study of Modern Writers and Beliefs.* London: Cape, 1935.

———. *Journals, 1939–1983.* Ed. John Goldsmith. London: Faber, 1985.

———. *World within World: An Autobiography.* 1951. London: Readers Union, 1955.

Symons, Julian. *Notes from Another Country.* London: London Magazine Editions, 1972.

———. *The Thirties: A Dream Revolved.* London: Cresset P, 1960.

———. *The Thirties and the Nineties.* Manchester: Carcanet, 1990.

Thompson, Edward John and G. T. Garratt. *Rise and Fulfilment of British Rule in India.* 1934. 2nd ed. New York: AMS P, 1971.

The Tribute; Tendered by Artists and Advertisers of the Empire on the Anniversary of His Majesty's Recovery. London and Glasgow: John Horn, 1930.

Upward, Edward. *In the Thirties.* 1962. London: Penguin, 1969.

Waugh, Evelyn. *The Diaries of Evelyn Waugh.* Ed. Michael Davie. London: Weidenfeld and Nicholson, 1976.

———. *A Little Learning: The First Volume of an Autobiography.* London: Chapman and Hall, 1964.

———. *Vile Bodies.* 1930. Boston: Little Brown, 1958.

Weber, Conrad G. *Studies in the English Outlook in the Period between the World Wars.* Bern: A. Francke, 1945.

West, Alick. *Crisis and Criticism and Selected Literary Essays.* 1937. London: Lawrence and Wishart, 1975.

White, Antonia. *Frost in May.* Harmondsworth: Penguin, 1939.

Williams-Ellis, Amabel. *Women in War Factories.* London: Gollancz, 1943.

Wilson, Edmund. *The Thirties: From Notebooks and Diaries of the Period.* New York: FSG, 1980.

———. *Europe without Baedeker: Sketches among the Ruins of Italy, Greece, and England.* Garden City: Doubleday, 1947.

Woolf, Leonard. *Barbarians Within and Without.* New York: Harcourt, Brace, 1939.

———. *Downhill All the Way: An Autobiography of the Years 1919–1939.* London: Hogarth P, 1967.

———. *The Journey Not the Arrival Matters: An Autobiography of the Years 1939–1969.* New York: Harcourt Brace, 1969.

Woolf, Virginia. *The Diaries of Virginia Woolf, 1936–1941.* Vol. 5. Ed. Anne Olivier Bell and Andrew McNeille. London: Hogarth P, 1984.

———. "Introductory Letter." *Life as We Have Known It, by Co-Operative Working Women.* Ed. Margaret Llewelyn. London: Hogarth P, 1931.

Yeats, W. B. *The Oxford Book of Modern Verse.* Oxford: Oxford UP, 1936.

Zamyatin, Yevgeny. *We.* 1924. Trans. Clarence Brown. New York: Penguin, 1993.

Selected Anthologies and General Studies
of Postwar Criticism and History

Abrams, M. H. et al., eds. "Stevie Smith." *The Norton Anthology of English Literature.* New York: Norton, 1993. 2221–27.

Alldritt, Keith. *Modernism in the Second World War.* New York: Peter Lang, 1989.

Amur, G. S. *Forbidden Fruit: Views on Indo-Anglian Fiction.* Calcutta: Writers Workshop, 1992.

Anderson, Benedict. *Imagined Communities: Reflections on the Origin and Spread of Nationalism.* London: Verso, 1983.

Arendt, Hannah. *The Origins of Totalitarianism.* 1948. New York: Harvest, 1973.

Armstrong, Isobel. *The Radical Aesthetic.* Cambridge: Blackwell, 2000.

Arnold, Dana, ed. *The Metropolis and Its Image: Constructing Identities for London, 1750–1950.* Oxford: Blackwell, 1999.

Ashcroft, Bill, Gareth Griffiths, and Helen Tiffin, eds. *The Empire Writes Back: Theory and Practice in Post-Colonial Literature.* New York: Routledge, 1989.

Baker, Niamh. *Happily Ever After? Women's Fiction in Postwar Britain, 1945–1960.* New York: St. Martin's P, 1989.

Back, Les and John Solomos, eds. *Theories of Race and Racism: A Reader.* New York: Routledge, 2000.

Bauman, Zygmunt. *Modernity and the Holocaust.* Ithaca: Cornell UP, 1989.

Beachcroft, T. O. *British Broadcasting.* London: Longmans Green for the British Council, 1946.

Berman, Marshall. *All That Is Solid Melts into Air: The Experience of Modernity.* New York: Penguin, 1982.

Barreca, Regina, ed. *New Perspectives on Women and Comedy.* Philadelphia: Gordon and Breach, 1992.

———. *Untamed and Unabashed: Essays on Women and Humor in British Literature.* Detroit: Wayne State UP, 1994.

Bauer, Yahuda. *Rethinking the Holocaust.* New Haven: Yale UP, 2001.

Beauman, Nicola. *A Very Great Profession: The Woman's Novel 1914–39.* London: Virago, 1983.

Beddoe, Deirdre. *Back to Home and Duty: Women between the Wars, 1918–1939.* London: Pandora, 1989.

Bergonzi, Bernard. *Reading the Thirties: Texts and Contexts.* Pittsburgh: U Pittsburgh P, 1978.

———. *Wartime and Aftermath: English Literature and Its Background, 1939–60.* Oxford: Oxford UP, 1993.

Bluemel, Kristin. " 'Civilization is Based upon the Stability of Molars': Dorothy Richardson and Imperialist Dentistry." *Modernism, Gender, and Culture: A Cultural Studies Approach.* Ed. Lisa Rado. New York: Garland, 1997.

———. *Experimenting on the Borders of Modernism: Dorothy Richardson's Pilgrimage.* Athens: University of Georgia P, 1997.

Booth, Howard J. and Rigby Nigel, eds. *Modernism and Empire: Writing and British Coloniality 1890–1940*. New York: Palgrave, 2000.

Bowdler, Roger. "Between the Wars: 1914–1940." *London Suburbs*. Ed. and Intro. by Andrew Saint. London: Merrell Holberton with English Heritage, 1999. 103–29.

Bradbury, Malcolm. *The Modern British Novel*. New York: Penguin, 1994.

Branson, Noreen and Margot Heinemann. *Britain in the Nineteen Thirties*. London: Weidenfeld and Nicolson, 1971.

Braydon, Gail and Penny Summerfield. *Out of the Cage: Women's Experiences in Two World Wars*. London: Pandora P, 1987

Briggs, Asa. *The Golden Age of Wireless: The History of Broadcasting in the United Kingdom*. Oxford: Oxford UP, 1965.

Bryant, Marsha. *Auden and Documentary in the 1930s*. Charlottesville: U Virginia P, 1997.

Cadogan, Mary and Patricia Craig. *Women and Children First: The Fiction of Two World Wars*. London: Gollancz, 1978.

Caesar, Adrian. *Dividing Lines: Poetry, Class, and Ideology in the 1930s*. Manchester: Manchester UP, 1991.

Calder, Angus. *The Myth of the Blitz*. London: Jonathan Cape, 1991.

———. *The People's War: Britain 1939–1945*. New York: Pantheon, 1969.

Carey, John. *The Intellectuals and the Masses: Pride and Prejudice amongst the Intelligentsia, 1880–1939*. London: Faber, 1992.

Cavaliero, Glen. *The Alchemy of Laughter: Comedy in English Fiction*. New York: Palgrave, 2000.

Ceadel, Martin. "Popular Fiction and the Next War, 1918–1939." *Class, Culture and Social Change: A New View of the 1930s*. Ed. Frank Gloversmith. Atlantic Highlands: Humanities P, 1980. 161–84.

Chamberlain, E. R. *Life in Wartime Britain*. London: B. T. Batsford, 1972.

Cheyette, Bryan, ed. *Between "Race" and Culture: Representations of "the Jew" in English and American Literature*. Stanford: Stanford UP, 1996.

Cheyette, Bryan. *Constructions of the "Jew" in English Literature and Society: Racial Representations, 1875–1945*. Cambridge: Cambridge UP, 1993.

Clark, Jon, Margot Heinemann, David Margolis, and Carol Snee. *Culture and Crisis in Britain in the 1930s*. London: Lawrence and Wishart, 1979.

Colletta, Lisa. *Dark Humor and Social Satire in the Modern British Novel: The Triumph of Narcissism*. New York: Palgrave, 2003.

Cooke, Miriam and Angela Woollacott. *Gendering War Talk*. Princeton: Princeton UP, 1993.

Coole, Diana. "Is Class a Difference that Makes a Difference?" *Radical Philosophy* 77 (1996): 17–25.

Cooper, Helen, Adrienne Auslander Munich, and Susan Squier, eds. *Arms and the Woman: War, Gender, and Literary Representation*. Chapel Hill: U of North Carolina P, 1989.

Costello, D. R. " 'Searchlight Books' and the Quest for a 'People's War,' 1941–1942." *Journal of Contemporary History* 24 (1989): 257–76.

Costello, John. *Love, Sex and War: Changing Values 1939–1945*. London: Collins, 1985.

Cowasjee, Saros. *Studies in Indian and Anglo-Indian Fiction.* New Delhi: Indus, 1993.

Creaton, Heather, ed. *A Checklist for the History of London, 1939–1945: A Guide and Bibliography.* London: British Records Assn., 1998.

Croft, Andy. *Red Letter Days: British Fiction in the 1930s.* London: Lawrence and Wishart, 1990.

Crompton, Rosemary. *Class and Stratification: An Introduction to Current Debates.* Cambridge: Polity P, 1993.

Crossick, Geoffrey. "The Emergence of the Lower Middle Class in Britain: A Discussion." *The Lower Middle Class in Britain, 1870–1914.* Ed. Crossick. London: Croom, 1977. 11–60.

Cunningham, Valentine. *British Writers of the Thirties.* New York: Oxford UP, 1988.

Davies, Andrew. "Jack Lindsay and the Radical Culture of the 1940s." *Jack Lindsay: The Thirties and Forties.* London: University of London, Institute of Commonwealth Studies, 1984. 74–80.

———. *Where Did the Forties Go?* London: Pluto P, 1984.

Deane, Patrick, ed. *History in Our Hands: A Critical Anthology of Writings on Literature, Culture and Politics from the 1930s.* New York: Leicester University Press, 1998.

Dear, I. C. B., ed. *The Oxford Companion to the Second World War.* Oxford: Oxford UP, 1995.

Deen, Stella, ed. *Challenging Modernism: New Readings in Literature and Culture, 1914–1945.* Burlington: Ashgate, 2002.

DiBattista, Maria and Lucy McDiarmid. *High and Low Moderns: Literature and Culture, 1889–1939.* New York: Oxford UP, 1996.

Dowson, Jane. *Women, Modernism, and British Poetry 1910–1939: Resisting Femininity.* Burlington: Ashgate, 2002.

———. "Women Poets and the Political Voice." *Women's Writers of the 1930s: Gender, Politics, and History.* Ed. Maroula Joannou. Edinburgh: Edinburgh UP, 1999. 46–62.

———. *Women's Poetry of the 1930s.* London: Routledge, 1995.

Eagleton, Terry. *Exiles and Émigrés: Studies in Modern Literature.* New York: Schocken, 1970.

Eliot and Anti-Semitism: The Ongoing Debate. Spec. issue of *Modernism/Modernity* 10.1 (2003).

Eysteinsson, Astradur. *The Concept of Modernism.* Ithaca: Cornell UP, 1990.

Felski, Rita. "Nothing to Declare; Identity, Shame, and the Lower Middle Class." *PMLA* 115 (January 2000): 33–45.

Fielding, Steven, Peter Thompson, and Nick Tiratsoo. *"England Arise!": The Labour Party and Popular Politics in 1940s Britain.* Manchester: Manchester UP, 1995.

Fox, Pamela. *Class Fictions: Shame and Resistance in the British Working-Class Novel, 1890–1945.* Durham: Duke UP, 1994.

Freud, Sigmund. *Jokes and Their Relation to the Unconscious.* 1905. Trans. James Strachey. New York: Norton, 1960.

Furedi, Frank. *The Silent War: Imperialism and the Changing Perception of Race.* London: Pluto P, 1998.

Fussell, Paul. *Wartime: Understanding and Behavior in the Second World War.* New York: Oxford UP, 1989.

Gallagher, Jean. *The World Wars: Through the Female Gaze.* Carbondale: Southern Illinois UP, 1998.

Gardner, Brian, ed. *The Terrible Rain: The War Poets 1939–45.* London: Methuen, 1966.

Gervais, David. *Literary Englands: Versions of "Englishness" in Modern Writing.* Cambridge: Cambridge UP, 1993.

Gikandi, Simon. *Maps of Englishness: Writing Identity in the Culture of Colonialism.* New York: Columbia UP, 1996.

Giles, Judy and Tim Middleton, eds. *Writing Englishness, 1900–1950: An Introductory Sourcebook on National Identity.* New York: Routledge, 1995.

Gillooly, Eileen. *Smile of Discontent: Humor, Gender, and Nineteenth-Century British Fiction.* Chicago: U Chicago P, 1999.

Gilman, Sander. *The Jew's Body.* New York: Routledge, 1991.

Ginden, James. *British Fiction of the 1930s: The Dispiriting Decade.* New York: St. Martin's P, 1992.

Glucksmann, Miriam. *Women Assemble: Women Workers in the New Industries of Inter-War Britain.* London: Routledge, 1989.

Gray, Frances. *Women and Laughter.* Charlottesville: UP Virginia, 1994.

Green, Martin. *Children of the Sun: A Narrative of "Decadence" in England after 1918.* New York: Basic Books, 1976.

Gubar, Susan. " 'This is My Rifle, This is My Gun': World War II and the Blitz on Women." Ed. Margaret Randolph Higonnet et al. *Behind the Lines: Gender and the Two World Wars.* New Haven: Yale UP, 1987. 227–59.

Gupta, Partha Sarathi. *Imperialism and the British Labour Movement, 1914–1964.* London: Macmillan, 1975.

———. *Power, Politics, and the People: Studies in British Imperialism and Indian Nationalism.* New York: Cambridge UP, 2000.

Hall, Carolyn. *The Thirties in Vogue.* New York: Harmony Books, 1985.

Hall, Stuart. "Out of the People: The Politics of Containment, 1935–45." *Working Papers in Cultural Studies* 9 (1976): 29–50.

Hanley, Lynne. *Writing War: Fiction, Gender, and Memory.* Amherst: U Massachusetts P, 1991.

Hapgood, Lynne and Nancy L. Paxton, eds. *Outside Modernism: In Pursuit of the English Novel, 1900–30.* New York: Palgrave, 2000.

Harris, Jose. "War and Social History: Britain and the Home Front during the Second World War." *Contemporary European History* 1 (1992): 17–35.

Harris, Richard and Peter J. Larkham. "Suburban Foundation, Form and Function." *Changing Suburbs: Foundations, Form and Function.* Ed. Richard Harris and Peter J. Larkham. New York: Routledge, 1999.

Hartley, Jenny, ed. *Hearts Undefeated: Women's Writing of the Second World War.* London: Virago, 1994.

———. *Millions Like Us: British Women's Fiction of the Second World War.* London: Virago, 1997.

Hawthorn, Jeremy, ed. *The British Working-Class Novel in the Twentieth Century.* Baltimore: Edward Arnold, 1984.

Haywood, Ian. *Working-Class Fiction: From Chartism to* Trainspotting. Plymouth: Northcote House, 1997.

Hewison, Robert. *Under Siege: Literary Life in London, 1939–45.* London: Weidenfeld and Nicolson, 1977.

Higonnet, Margaret Randolph et al., eds. *Behind the Lines: Gender and the Two World Wars.* New Haven: Yale UP, 1987.

Hitchcock, Peter. "They Must Be Represented? Problems in Theories of Working-Class Representation." *PMLA* 115 (January 2000): 20–32.

———. *Working-Class Fiction in Theory and Practice: A Reading of Alan Sillitoe.* Ann Arbor: UMI Research P, 1989.

Hobsbawm, Eric. *Industry and Empire.* London: Harmondsworth, 1969.

Hoggart, Richard. *The Uses of Literacy: Changing Patterns in English Mass Culture.* 1957. Boston: Beacon P, 1961.

Holsinger, M. Paul and Mary Anne Scholfield, eds. *Visions of War: World War II in Popular Literature and Culture.* Bowling Green: Bowling Green State University Popular Press, 1992.

Honey, Maureen. *Creating Rosie the Riveter: Class, Gender, and Propaganda during World War II.* Amherst: U Massachusetts P, 1984.

Hunt, Felicity, ed. *Lessons for Life: The Schooling of Girls and Women 1900–1950.* London: Blackwell, 1987.

Hussey, Mark, ed. *Virginia Woolf and War: Fiction, Reality and Myth.* New York: Syracuse UP, 1991.

Huyssen, Andreas. *After the Great Divide: Modernism, Mass Culture, Postmodernism.* Bloomington: Indiana UP, 1986.

Hynes, Samuel. *The Auden Generation: Literature and Politics in England in the 1930s.* Princeton: Princeton UP, 1972.

———. *The Soldiers' Tale: Bearing Witness to Modern War.* New York: Penguin, 1997.

Ingman, Heather. *Women's Fiction Between the Wars: Mothers, Daughters and Writing.* New York: St. Martin's, 1998.

Ingram, Angela and Daphne Patai, eds. *Rediscovering Forgotten Radicals: British Women Writers, 1889–1939.* Chapel Hill: U North Carolina P, 1993.

Iyengar, Srinivasa. *Indian Writing in English.* New York: Asia Publishing House, 1962.

Jackson, Alan A. *Semi-Detached London: Suburban Development, Life, and Transport, 1900–1939.* London: George Allen and Unwin, 1973.

Jameson, Fredric. *The Political Unconscious: Narrative as a Socially Symbolic Act.* Ithaca: Cornell UP, 1981.

———. "Third-World Literature in the Era of Multinational Capitalism." *Social Text* 15 (1986): 65–88.

Jeffreys, Sheila. *The Spinster and Her Enemies: Feminism and Sexuality, 1880–1930.* London: Pandora, 1985.

Joannou, Maroula. *"Ladies, Please Don't Smash These Windows": Women's Writing, Feminist Consciousness, and Social Change, 1914–1938.* Oxford and Providence: Berg P, 1995.

———, ed. *Women Writers of the 1930s: Gender, Politics, and History.* Edinburgh: Edinburgh UP, 1999.

Johnstone, Richard. *The Will to Believe: Novelists of the Nineteen-Thirties*. New York: Oxford, 1982.

Johnson, Roy. "The Proletarian Novel." *Literature and History* 2 (1975): 84–95.

Joshi, Priya. *In Another Country: Colonialism, Culture, and the English Novel in India*. New York: Columbia UP, 2002.

Kenner, Hugh. *The Pound Era*. Berkeley: U California P, 1971.

Kent, Susan Kingsley. *Making Peace: The Reconstruction of Gender in Interwar Britain*. Princeton: Princeton UP, 1993.

Kiernan, V. G. *The Lords of Human Kind: Black Man, Yellow Man, White Man in an Age of Empire*. London: Cresset Library, 1969.

Kirkham, Pat and David Thoms, eds. *War Culture: Social Change and Changing Experience in World War II*. London: Lawrence and Wishart, 1995.

Klaus, H. Gustav, ed. *The Literature of Labour: Two Hundred Years of Working-Class Writing*. Brighton: Harvester, 1985.

Klaus, H. Gustav. *The Socialist Novel in Britain: Towards the Recovery of a Tradition*. Brighton: Harvester, 1982.

Klaus, H. Gustav and Stephen Knight, eds. *British Industrial Fictions*. Cardiff: U of Wales P, 2000.

Knowles, Sebastian D. G. *A Purgatorial Flame: Seven British Writers in the Second World War*. Philadelphia: U Pennsylvania P, 1990.

Kuhn, Thomas. "The Historical Structure of Scientific Discovery." *Science* 1 June 1962: 760–64.

Kushner, Tony. *The Persistence of Prejudice: Antisemitism in British Society during the Second World War*. Manchester: Manchester UP, 1989.

Lassner, Phyllis. *British Women Writers of World War II: Battlegrounds of Their Own*. New York: St. Martin's P, 1998.

———. *Colonial Strangers: Women Writing the End of the British Empire*. New Brunswick: Rutgers UP, 2004.

———. "The Quiet Revolution: World War II and the English Domestic Novel." *Mosaic* 23 (1990): 87–100.

Levenson, Michael H. *A Genealogy of Modernism: A Study of English Literary Doctrine 1908–1922*. New York: Cambridge UP, 1984.

Lewis, Pericles. *Modernism, Nationalism, and the Novel*. New York: Cambridge UP, 2000.

Light, Alison. *Forever England: Femininity, Literature, and Conservatism between the Wars*. New York: Routledge, 1991.

Loewenstein, Andrea Freud. *Loathsome Jews and Engulfing Women: Metaphors of Projection in the Works of Wyndham Lewis, Charles Williams, and Graham Greene*. New York: New York UP, 1993.

Lucas, John, ed. *The 1930s: A Challenge to Orthodoxy*. Brighton: Harvester, 1979.

Madden, David. *Proletarian Writers of the Thirties*. Carbondale: Southern Illinois State UP, 1968.

Marcus, Jane, ed. *New Feminist Essays on Virginia Woolf*. Basingstoke: Macmillan, 1981.

———. *Hearts of Darkness: White Women Writing Race*. New Brunswick: Rutgers UP, 2004.

Marwick, Arthur. *Class: Image and Reality in Britain, France, and the USA Since 1938*. New York: Oxford UP, 1980.

———. *The Home Front: The British and the Second World War*. London: Thames and Hudson, 1976.

———. "People's War and Top People's Peace? British Society and the Second World War." *Crisis and Controversy: Essays in Honour of A. J. P. Taylor*. Ed. Alan Sked and Chris Cook. London: Macmillan, 1976. 148–63.

Marx, Karl. "Communist Manifesto." *The Marx-Engels Reader*. Ed. Robert C. Tucker. New York: Norton, 1972. 331–62.

Maslen, Elizabeth. *Political and Social Issues in British Women's Fiction*. New York: Palgrave, 2001.

McDonald, Robert H. *The Language of Empire: Myths and Metaphors of Popular Imperialism, 1880–1918*. New York: Manchester UP, 1994.

McKibbin, Ross. *Classes and Cultures: England 1918–1951*. Oxford: Oxford UP, 1998.

McLaine, Ian. *Ministry of Morale*. London: Allen and Unwin, 1979.

Mehrotra, Arvind Krishna, ed. *History of Indian Literature in English*. New York: Columbia UP, 2003.

Mengham, Rod and N. H. Reeve. *The Fiction of the Forties: Stories of Survival*. New York: Palgrave, 2001.

Miller, Tyrus. *Late Modernism: Politics, Fiction, and the Arts Between the Wars*. Berkeley: U California P, 1999.

Minns, Raynes. *Bombers and Mash: The Domestic Front 1939–45*. London: Virago, 1980.

Montefiore, Janet. *Men and Women Writers of the 1930s: The Dangerous Flood of History*. New York: Routledge, 1996.

Moore-Gilbert, B. J. *Postcolonial Theory: Contexts, Practices, Politics*. London and New York: Verso, 1997.

———, ed. *Writing India 1757–1990: The Literature of British India*. Manchester: Manchester UP, 1996.

Morgau, David and Mary Evans. *The Battle for Britain: Citizenship and Ideology in the Second World War*. London: Routledge, 1993.

Morley, Dave and Ken Worpole, eds. *The Republic of Letters: Working Class Writing and Local Publishing*. London: Comedia Publishing, 1982.

Mulhern, Francis. *The Moment of Scrutiny*. London: New Left Books, 1979.

Munton, Alan. *English Fiction of the Second World War*. London: Faber and Faber, 1989.

Nabar, Vrinda, and Nilufer E. Bharucha. *Postcolonial Perspectives on the Raj and Its Literature*. Bombay: U of Bombay, 1994.

Neumann, F. *Behemoth: The Structure and Practice of National Socialism 1933–1944*. New York: Harper and Row, 1966.

Ngugi wa Thiong'o. *Decolonising the Mind: The Politics of Language in African Literature*. Portsmouth: Heinemann, 1986.

Nicholson, Linda, ed. *Feminism/Postmodernism*. New York: Routledge, 1990.

———. *The Second Wave*. New York: Routledge, 1997.

Nicholas, Sian. *The Echo of War: Home Front Propaganda and the Wartime BBC, 1939–45*. New York: Manchester UP, 1996.

North, Michael. *Henry Green and the Writings of His Generation.* Charlottesville: U of Virginia P, 1984.

Parry, Benita. *Delusions and Discoveries: India in the British Imagination 1880–1930.* London: Verso, 1998.

Parsons, Deborah L. *Streetwalking the Metropolis: Women, the City and Modernity.* New York: Oxford UP, 2000.

Piette, Adam. *Imagination at War: British Fiction and Poetry 1939–1945.* London: Papermac, 1995.

Plain, Gill. *Women's Fiction of the Second World War.* New York: St. Martin's P, 1996.

Pugh, Martin. *Women and the Women's Movement in Britain, 1914–1959.* London: Macmillan, 1992.

Quinn, Patrick, ed. *Recharting the Thirties.* Selinsgrove: Susquehanna UP, 1996.

Ragussis, Michael J. *Figures of Conversion: "The Jewish Question" and English National Identity.* Durham: Duke UP, 1995.

Rainey, Lawrence. *Institutions of Modernism: Literary Elites and Public Culture.* New Haven: Yale UP, 1998.

Rawlinson, Mark. *British Writing of the Second World War.* Oxford: Clarendon P, 2000.

Reilly, Catherine. *Chaos of the Night: Women's Poetry and Verse of the Second World War.* London: Virago, 1984.

Richards, J. M. *The Age of the Dream Palace: Cinema and Society in Britain, 1930–1939.* London: Routledge and Kegan Paul, 1984.

Rosenberg, Edgar. *From Shylock to Svengali: Jewish Stereotypes in English Fiction.* Stanford: Stanford UP, 1960.

Ross, Robert, ed. *Racism and Colonialism: Essays on Ideology and Social Structure.* Leiden: Martinus Nijhoff, 1982.

Rushdie, Salman. "Outside the Whale." *Imaginary Homelands: Essays and Criticism 1981–1991.* New York: Viking, 1991.

Rushdie, Salman and Elizabeth West, eds. *The Vintage Book of Indian Writing, 1947–1997.* London and New York: Vintage, 1997.

Sabin, Margery. *Dissenters and Mavericks: Writings about India in English, 1765–2000.* New York: Oxford UP, 2002.

Said, Edward W. *Culture and Imperialism.* 1993. New York: Vintage, 1994.

———. *Orientalism.* 1978. New York: Vintage, 1979.

Saler, Michael T. *The Avant-Garde in Interwar England: Medieval Modernism and the London Underground.* New York: Oxford UP, 1999.

Samuels, Raphael. *Patriotism: the Making and Unmaking of British National Identity.* 3 vols. Vol. 1 *History and Politics.* Vol. 2 *Minorities and Outsiders.* Vol. 3 *National Fictions.* London: Routledge, 1989.

Sarkar, Sumit. "Afterward." *The Other Side of the Medal.* Edward Thompson. Ed. Mulk Raj Anand. New Delhi: Sterling Publishers, 1989. 83–126

Scannell, Paddy and David Cardiff. *A Social History of British Broadcasting.* Vol. 1. 1922–1939. Cambridge, MA: B. Blackwell, 1991– .

Scannell, Vernon. *Not Without Glory: Poets of the Second World War.* London: Woburn P, 1976.

Schneider, Karen. *Loving Arms: British Women Writing the Second World War.* Lexington: UP Kentucky, 1997.

Schweik, Susan. "Writing War Poetry Like a Woman." *Critical Inquiry* 13 (1987): 532–56.

Schweikart, Patrocinio. "Reading Ourselves: Toward a Feminist Theory of Reading." *Falling into Theory: Conflicting Views on Reading Theory*. Boston: Bedford Books, 1994. 269–78.

Shelden, Michael. *Friends of Promise: Cyril Connolly and the World of Horizon*. 1989. London: Minerva, 1990.

Shires, Linda M. *British Poetry of the Second World War*. London: Macmilan, 1985.

Shuttleworth, Antony, ed. *And in Our Time: Vision, Revision, and British Writing of the Thirties*. Lewisburg: Bucknell UP, 2003.

Sinclair, Andrew, ed. *The War Decade: An Anthology of the 1940s*. London: Hamilton, 1989.

———. *War Like a Wasp: The Lost Decade of the Forties*. London: Hamish Hamilton, 1989.

Skelton, Robin. *Poetry of the Thirties*. Harmondsworth: Penguin, 1964.

Smith, Clive R. *Golders Green as It Was*. Greyhound Hill, U.K.: C. R. Smith, 1974.

Smith, Harold, ed. *Britain and the Second World War: A Social History*. Manchester: Manchester UP, 1996.

———. *War and Social Change: British Society in the Second World War*. Manchester: Manchester UP, 1986.

Snee, Carole. "Working-Class Literature or Proletarian Writing?" *Culture and Crisis in Britain in the Thirties*. Ed. Jon Clark, Margot Heinemann, David Margolis, Carole Snee, James Klugmann. London: Lawrence and Wishart, 1979. 165–91.

Sonnenberg, Rhonda. *Still We Danced: World War II and the Writer's Life*. London: Brassey's, 1998.

Stallybrass, Peter and Allon White. *The Politics and Poetics of Transgression*. Ithaca: Cornell UP, 1986.

Steedman, Carolyn. *Landscape for a Good Woman*. London: Virago, 1985.

Stetz, Margaret. *British Women's Comic Fiction, 1890–1990: Not Drowning, But Laughing*. London: Ashgate, 2001.

Stevenson, John. "Myth and Reality: Britain in the 1930s." *Crisis and Controversy: Essays in Honour of A. J. P. Taylor*. London: Macmillan, 1976. 90–109.

———. *Social Conditions in Britain between the Wars*. London: Harmondsworth P, 1977.

Summerfield, Penny. *Women Workers in the Second World War*. London: Routledge, 1984.

Symons, Julian. *The Thirties: A Dream Revolved*. London: Cresset P, 1960.

Sypher, Willie, ed. and intro. *Comedy*. 1956. Baltimore: Johns Hopkins UP, 1980.

Taylor, A. J. P. *English History 1914–1945*. New York: Oxford UP, 1965.

Thompson, E. P. *The Poverty of Theory and Other Essays*. New York: Monthly Review P, 1978.

Tolley, A. T. *The Poetry of the Forties*. Manchester: Manchester UP, 1985.

———. *The Poetry of the Thirties*. London: Gollancz, 1975.

Tylee, Claire. *The Great War and Women's Consciousness: Images of Militarism and Womanhood in Women's Writings, 1914–1964*. Iowa City: U of Iowa P, 1990.

Van Arkel, D. "Racism in Europe." *Racism and Colonialism: Essays on Ideology and Social Structure*. Ed. Robert Ross. Leiden: Martinus Nijhoff, 1982. 11–31.

Visram, Rozina. *Asians in Britain: 400 years of History*. Sterling, VA: Pluto P, 2002.

Viswanathan, Gauri. *Masks of Conquest: Literary Study of British Rule in India*. New York: Columbia UP, 1989.

Wallace, Dina. *Sisters and Rivals in British Women's Fiction, 1914–1939*. New York: Palgrave, 2000.

Wallace, Jane and Michael Vaughan-Rees. *Women in Wartime: The Role of Women's Magazines 1939–1987*. London: Macdonald Optima, 1987.

Wasserstein, Bernard. *Britain and the Jews of Europe 1939–1945*. New York: Oxford UP, 1979.

Walker, Nancy. *A Very Serious Thing: Women's Humor and American Culture*. Minneapolis: U of Minnesota P, 1988.

West, W. J. *Truth Betrayed*. London: Duckworth, 1987.

Wheeler, Kathleen. *"Modernist" Women Writers and Narrative Art*. New York: New York UP, 1994.

White, Hayden. "The Value of Narrativity in the Representation of Reality." *Critical Inquiry* 7 (1980): 5–27.

Whitehead, Kate. *The Third Programme: A Literary History*. Oxford: Clarendon P, 1989.

Williams, Keith and Steven Matthews, eds. *Rewriting the Thirties: Modernism and After*. London: Longmans, 1997.

Williams, Raymond. "The Bloomsbury Faction." *Contemporary Marxist Literary Criticism*. Ed. Francis Mulhern. London: Longmans, 1992. 125–45.

———. *The Long Revolution*. London: Chatto and Windus, 1961.

———. *The Politics of Modernism: Against the New Conformists*. Ed. Tony Pinkney. New York: Verso, 1989.

Wolpert, Stanley. *A New History of India*. 5th ed. New York: Oxford UP, 1997.

Wyatt, Woodrow, ed. *The Way We Lived Then: the English Story in the 1940s*. London: Collins, 1989.

Index